FREEDOM OF EXPRESSION

Edited By HERMON OULD

FREEDOM OF EXPRESSION

A SYMPOSIUM

BASED ON THE CONFERENCE CALLED BY THE LONDON
CENTRE OF THE INTERNATIONAL P.E.N. TO COMMEMORATE
THE TERCENTENARY OF THE PUBLICATION OF MILTON'S
AREOPAGITICA: 22-26TH AUGUST, 1944.

KENNIKAT PRESS
Port Washington, N. Y./London

FREEDOM OF EXPRESSION

First published in 1944
Reissued in 1970 by Kennikat Press
Library of Congress Catalog Card No: 73-111309
ISBN 0-8046-0968-3

Manufactured by Taylor Publishing Company   Dallas, Texas

CONTENTS

INTRODUCTION

THIS SYMPOSIUM IS A TRIBUTE NOT ONLY TO A GREAT ENGLISH WRITER, BUT to a great idea—the idea that the human mind, if it is to develop to the full measure of its potentialities, must be free: free to grow, free to express itself, free to blunder, to make mistakes, and try again. There are many ways in which the Tercentenary of Milton's *Areopagitica* might have been celebrated. The way chosen by the London Centre of the International P.E.N. was to provide a platform for the untrammelled expression of views and convictions on perhaps the most important subject that can exercise our minds at the present time—"The Place of Spiritual and Economic Values in the Future of Mankind." We knew that the words "spiritual" and "economic" were ambiguous terms; we knew that the implied antithesis between spiritual and economic would not be generally accepted; but we hoped that from the clash of conflicting opinions some sparks would be struck that would help to illumine our darkness.

The readiness with which leading men of science, letters, religion and philosophy responded to our suggestion that they should give us the freedom of their minds was an indication of the importance which they attached to our theme, and to me it was the most hopeful phenomenon I have witnessed since 11th November, 1918. If the men and women who spoke at the Conference are in any way representative of our intelligentsia— and I do not doubt that they are—and if the eager and combative audiences that attended and debated during the ten two-hour sessions of the Conference may be regarded as a cross-section of the general public, surely between them they can do something to mitigate what is perhaps the most distressing characteristic of the younger generation, a generation which for obvious reasons was inadequately represented at our sessions—its cynicism, its bitterness, its lack of belief, not in this or that creed or philosophy, but in life itself. A similar mood followed the last Great War, with disastrous results. This time the disillusionment has come even before the Armistice. Our task, the task of those who still believe in life, is to restore faith to those whose faith is waning or gone, and to ensure that the post-bellum period shall not become another inter-bellum period.

A few facts should be placed on record. The sessions of the Conference were held twice daily in the lecture hall of the Institut Français du Royaume-Uni in South Kensington, from 22nd to 26th August, 1944. Early on the morning of the 22nd two flying bombs fell behind the Institute, wrecking a number of houses and seriously damaging many more. The Institute itself was not hit, but suffered badly from blasting. Windows and doors which had been patched up after the previous raids were again blown out, and it seemed improbable that our meetings could be held. We were also faced with the moral question, whether we had

7

the right to concentrate in a confined place a number of eminent men
and women and those assembled to hear them, at a time when flying
bombs were dropping at intervals throughout the day and night. After
some discussion we came to the conclusion that the eminent men and
women and those who wished to hear them must be allowed to decide for
themselves; we would make no change in our arrangements which
necessity did not impose. At the opening of each session the audience
was informed that in the event of an air-raid alert, time would be allowed
for those who wished to leave the building to do so; if a flying bomb
were sighted, a special alarm would be sounded, but then it would be
too late to do anything except take cover behind the backs of seats. To
our surprise, we were disturbed only once during the five days.

The vitality and optimism which prevailed throughout the proceedings
were commonly remarked; curiously intensified by the imminence of
danger, the fallen masonry and heaped-up glass, and the hammering of
carpenters botching up the shattered windows and doors. There were
only two interruptions: once, that we might express our sympathy with
the people of Warsaw, then passing through one of the most agonising
phases of the war; the second time, on the 23rd, when we recorded our
joy in the liberation of Paris.

The Conference was held under the Presidency of E. M. Forster, the
chair being taken at the various sessions by (in this order) myself, Peter de
Mendelssohn, Alan Thomas, L. A. G. Strong, Professor W. J. Entwistle,
Arthur Koestler, Rose Macaulay, Desmond MacCarthy, Phyllis Bentley,
and E. M. Forster. It was a great grief that Professor Denis Saurat was
unable to preside at the opening session. His claim to welcome speakers
and audiences was at least threefold: as the Director of the Institut Français,
as a member of the International Presidential Committee of the P.E.N.,
and as a Milton scholar of great originality and subtlety. Alas, a flying
bomb, which had wrecked his house a week or two previously, had
incapacitated him and made it impossible for him to be present at the
Conference.

The following societies collaborated with the P.E.N. in what has been
described as probably the most impressive tribute that has ever been paid
to the power and significance of a single book: The Aquinas Society,
British Association for the Advancement of Science, London Institute of
World Affairs, Institute for Jewish Learning, National Council for Civil
Liberties, Progressive League, Rationalist Press Association, Society for
Cultural Relations with U.S.S.R., Society of Friends, South Place Ethical
Society, Theosophical Society, World Association for Adult Education.

PRESIDENTIAL ADDRESS

By E. M. FORSTER, LL.D.

OUR PRESIDENT STORM JAMESON HAS HAD TO RESIGN THROUGH ILL-HEALTH.
Since she cannot be with us our committee invited me to act as president
for the purposes of this Conference. I accepted at once, and will do my
best, but you will realise with what a handicap we start. Storm Jameson
would have given a lead, a direction, most necessary for our deliberations.
Not only has she a sense of contemporary tragedy (many of us have that),
but she has a vision and inspiration as regards the future. She can see, as
it were, round this nasty corner, and she would have helped us incalculably.
We regret her absence for this, and for other reasons, and we hope for her
speedy return. And now let us do our best.

I won't waste any time in mentioning the distinguished individuals and
organisations who are taking part in our conference. You have a list of
them, and they need no recommendation from me. I will begin instead
by a couple of reminders. The first is that the P.E.N. is an international
body. This cannot be said too often at a moment when internationalism
is unfashionable. The word is not a very good one—supernationalism
would better suit our book—still we have adopted it, we are a world
association of writers, not an association of British or even of Allied writers.
We stand for the creative impulse which existed before nationality was
invented and which will continue to exist when that dubious invention
has been scrapped. We stand for all humanity, apart from the accidents
of government, language, race and colour, and we must recall our position
before we start talking.

This conference is organised by the London branch of the P.E.N.
It is a local conference, and its outlook is likely to be British and in my
own case Cockney. No harm in that so long as we recall our international
implication, and do not imagine that we have a heaven-sent mission to
push British ideas. That is the mission of the British Council, an estimable
body, much of whose work we admire, and all of whose income we envy.
There are, however, disadvantages as well as advantages, in being subsidised
by the Foreign Office, and we do escape the disadvantages. We are poor
but free. We are not bound to consider the spiritual and economic values
of the future as they appear from the windows of Whitehall.

My second reminder may be less congenial. I have to remind you
that the P.E.N. is uninfluential. We are only writers and artists, or at the
toughest, theoretical economists, and these are not the people who will
cut much ice when the work of reconstruction starts. Captains of industry,
managers of Big Business, directors of the Bank of England, heads of
Government departments or of Trade Unions—it is not likely that any of

these are present here, and if they are they have disguised themselves successfully. Yet these are the people who are going to count. I do not suggest that they will be indifferent to economic or spiritual good, but their values will not be ours, and we must be prepared for their contempt. To take an example. Look what seems likely to happen over the rebuilding of the City of London. The artists, the cultivated minority, brought out a plan which was sensitive to tradition and to amenity. The business people have ignored it almost completely. To them the City is an area for offices and in their plan offices rise in every direction to enormous heights with the Cathedral of St. Paul's squatting in the middle like a poached egg. Though our immediate problem isn't here, it is a salutary reminder of our impotence. Nothing we say during the next five days is likely to influence the decision of those who have power.

Why, then, do we meet? Ah, for two reasons. We want to clear up our own ideas about the future if we can because it is a pleasure and a duty to get the mind clear; and, secondly, though we cannot hope to cut any ice we may succeed in melting a little. The influence of the artist, the theorist, the dreamer, upon society is indirect, not direct. It is, from one point of view, insidious. Plato suspected it and the Japanese are well advised to punish dangerous thoughts. As I look back into history, this seems to me the *incidental* triumph of art and thought. Their main triumph has been the creation of works of art, the elaboration of theories for their own sake, the disinterested dreaming of dreams, but we are here concerned with the incidental triumph, our insidious influence on society, our success in melting a little ice. We have not done what we would like, but we have achieved more than might have been expected, and we must not lose heart. Perhaps if the Royal Academy and others hadn't made their plan for the rebuilding of the City of London the business men, when they came to make their plan, would have scrapped St. Paul's altogether and built offices, offices, offices on its site. After all, why not? God can be worshipped anywhere, whereas some areas have a higher rateable value than others. I discern no flaw in this manly argument, but in his muddled way the artist dislikes it, whatever his religious opinions, and protests against it through the ages. Beside performing his specific job, he melts a little ice.

Our subject is large and complicated. I have been wondering not so much about our conclusions as about the apparatus which we are likely to employ in reaching them, and (to interest myself rather than to guide you) I have made a sort of map. I have divided potential speakers into two classes to whom I will give the names of the "oughts" and the "musts" in accordance with the bent of their minds. All, or almost all, of us are interested both in economic and spiritual values, and desire improvement in either, but we shall differ not merely in the remedies we propose but in our apparatus, and it is this that I have in mind in my division.

To begin with the "musts." They appeal to history. They think they understand the past, not of course in its details, but as a process, they think they understand the present, and they foretell with more or less confidence what is bound to happen in the future, as the result of historical laws. They do not agree upon what will happen, for history is an accommodating mistress, and responds to each man according to the quality of his embraces, but each of them holds that something, and something now discoverable, is bound to happen. Let us take a couple of pure-bred musts and turn them loose on the subject-matter of our conference. They will come galloping back at once with contradictory answers in their mouths. One will report, "Economic changes must inevitably precede spiritual change. Let us therefore—so far as we are free agents—concentrate on material problems: better housing, food, clothing, etc.—for ourselves and our fellows: and perhaps when these problems are solved we shall have become better men. Anyhow, we can't behave decently until we are comfortable; to put spiritual change first is to contradict the process of history." That's one report. The other report reveals the same mentality working in the reverse direction. The second "must" will say, "Spiritual changes must inevitably precede any economic change: such is the verdict of history. Let us therefore—so far as we are free agents—practise first things first. Let us improve our psychology, and practise and preach honesty, sympathy, unselfishness, awareness. When we are better men, we may find our economic conditions are becoming better. Anyhow a community of brutes and thieves can't improve itself materially, however much it wants to. We can't expect to be comfortable until we behave decently; history shows it."

I speak of "pure-bred musts," but a really pure-bred would scarcely bother to be here. He would foresee the inevitability of developments and do nothing. The majority of "musts" are not pure-bred, and they believe in hurrying up events. They observe which way history is going, and give the old girl a shove, so that she arrives sooner than she expected. Several distinguished hurriers-up will be speaking. Some of them, to judge from their names, will be accelerating the spiritual process destined for humanity, others the economic process. They will differ violently. Let us leave them and turn to the "oughts."

The "oughts" bring to our problem a completely different set of instruments. They have in the first place no opinion on the subject of history, and do not appeal to it. They would agree with a distinguished historian, H. A. L. Fisher, who could discern no rhythm, pattern or plot in the past, and who could predict for the future nothing except the play of the contingent and the unseen. The problem to them is immediate, here and now. *What ought I to do now?* And they attack it by appealing to something within—to conscience, to a sense of social duty, or to supernatural promptings. They, too, differ among themselves. Some of them feel called to attack the economic trouble first and to work for better housing, but in the hope—it is only a hope—that better houses will result in better men.   Others want to make men better right away, even when they are homeless; the houses can rip provided the soul improves; we have done what we ought, and can do no more.

That is my little map.   It is an amateur's attempt to classify us not by the conclusions we may reach but by the apparatus we shall use.   The "musts" and the "oughts" may often be voting for the same spiritual or economic item, but they will arrive by different routes—one of them following his interpretation of history, the other relying on his inward promptings.   Where do I place myself on my map?   I am an impure "ought," which tentative answer suggests that other speakers may not stay hard and fast in their categories either.   I am certainly an "ought" and not a "must," for I can discern no inevitable process at work in society, whereas I can see something at work in myself—call it taste, call it conscience. It tells me—this inner voice or inner mumble—that the immediate need for humanity is spiritual, and the better men are more likely to produce better houses than *vice versa*.   I want the better houses.   The pure "ought," who says, "Let's be good and damn the consequences," is too bleak for me, and it's probable that the pure "ought" will pair off with his opposite number, the pure "must," and abstain from the deliberations of the P.E.N.

Our conference falls upon the tercentenary of the *Areopagitica*.   Several Miltonian scholars will be speaking, though a leading one, our host, Denis Saurat, has been prevented from coming, to our deep regret.   The *Areopagitica* and its relation to our own difficulties will be thoroughly covered and one of our sessions will be specially devoted to the subject of freedom.   So I will keep off that aspect of the conference, except as regards one point, which I want to put before you.   Don't you think that when the war ends or eases off the first thing we must do is to work for the minimum of secrecy in public affairs?   We should demand that information as to the state of this country and the world be more accessible.   How can we try to improve the world when we do not know what the world is like?   It is like trying to arrange things in a room where all the lights have been extinguished.   You do not know where the things are, you may break them, and incidentally, you may hurt yourself.   The world has become a darkened room, with more and more proceedings in camera, secret committees, national and local, banned books, withheld lists of banned books, censorships, prohibited areas, and officials so esoteric that they can scarcely be mentioned even in cipher.   It must be tiresome enough for a Nazi to live in such a world, and, after all, he asked for it. We are supposed to be democrats.   Peace, when it comes, is going to be more like war than we can bear to think—indeed I have a secret fear that peace and war represent a vanished and Victorian antithesis.   But there are two rough tests by which we can still continue to distinguish them: the amount of bloodshed in the world and the amount of hush-hush.   Secrecy is bad for the husher's soul, but that is not the aspect of the evil now in my mind.   I'm concerned with the withholding of information which is bound, incidentally, to enfeeble our conference. Whether you want to discuss the economic or the spiritual future of mankind, whether you are a "must" or an "ought"—how can you discuss usefully when you are so ignorant of what is happening now? You know almost nothing and you may travel scarcely anywhere. These limitations are necessary in war-time, but when peace or the shadow of it arrives they must stop. The lights must be turned up a little so that the contents of the room may be seen. When we can see we can arrange. At present we are muddling about in the dark.

I remember a significant little incident after the last war. The London Library, a learned and reputable institution, wanted to bring its German books up to date. It had been forbidden to import during hostilities, but when the war to end war had been won it applied for a permit. This was refused. After steady pressure for fifteen months the permit was granted, with the proviso that all newly purchased German books must be kept under lock and key and only shown to seasoned officials. (A history of Austria, published in 1860, fell into this category.) The Government responsible for this ban had also locked up its own German books in a cellar where it could not get at them, and then it wanted to write a series of handbooks based on the unobtainable material. It could only do its work by borrowing from the Library which it had persecuted. The Librarian, Hagberg Wright, has given in his pamphlet, *The Soul's Dispensary*, an account of this comedy and he remarks on the contempt for the knowledge derived from the printed word shown by the majority of those invested with temporary authoritative powers. What happened on a small scale then will happen on a large scale now. It will be many, many years before we shall be allowed to read books published by our present enemies. The Ministry of Information will tell us what they contain instead. And until we are allowed to read, to hold them in our own hands, I shan't myself feel that peace is peace, or that I am equipped to envisage the future.

Secrecy, then, is our immediate enemy. That is the lesson I draw from the *Areopagitica*. I am not so soft as to suppose that we can abolish secrecy, for it has seeped into every cranny of modern civilisation. But we can decrease it, we can melt a little ice. It's good that anxiety about this is spreading. I was pleased the other day, and also rather amused, when Mr. Herbert Morrison rebuked certain municipal organisations in the north for conducting their proceedings in camera. There must not be so much hush-hush in low circles, is the Home Secretary's opinion.

The name of Milton is not the only one to be commemorated at this conference. It happens that this month (29th August) is the centenary of the birth of Edward Carpenter, and one of his friends will be paying a short tribute to him. Carpenter is rather forgotten to-day, partly because he was a pioneer, whose work has passed into our heritage. He was a poet and a prose writer, and a reformer and a mystic and socialist and a manual worker who preferred the working classes to his own. He won't be easy to sum up. There is one remark of his which I would like to quote because it might almost serve as a motto for our coming deliberations. He was asked how he combined his socialism with his mysticism. He replied in his quaint, gay way, "I like to hang out my red flag from the ground floor and then go up above to see how it looks." Put "economic values" for socialism and "spiritual values" for mysticism and isn't that what we are doing ourselves? We want to arrange the world on the material level and then look at it from above.

I must end now. I have never given a presidential address before, and am not sure of the rules of the game or gambit. But it is certainly my duty, as it is my pleasure, to welcome you and to wish you success in your deliberations. I should like to give a special welcome to those members and visitors who come from other lands. Their presence at a conference organised by the London branch is very valuable. They will help to recall us to our true, our wider function. The P.E.N. is international.

A DREAMER PLEADS

By HSIAO CH'IEN

ON THE TOP LAYER OF THIS PARADOXICAL WORLD OF OURS STAND THREE fellows: the thinker, the dreamer and the doer. Of the three, the doer runs most of the show. He was christened by our president thirty years ago as Mr. Wilcox. Mr. Wilcox is contemptuous of the other two. The dreamer (is she Margaret Schelegel?) is the most lyrical but also the most impractical and at times pathetically futile of the three. Once or twice the dreamer, annoyed with his own helpless position, seeks to combine the power of the thinker, or even the doer, as Chinese writers have tried in the last three decades. In most cases he has to surrender most of his dreamy qualities without achieving the same result as the doer. That dreamy quality, incidentally, is the one asset the miserable dreamer can't afford to lose.

Each time I watch a formation of four-engined bombers flying in the blue sky on one of the sunny afternoons here, I feel puzzled. Undeniably the symmetrical pattern formed by those silvery wings is more than thrilling to watch; you can imagine all sorts of things: fireflies in a jungle, or swordfish gliding at the bottom of a glass bowl. But to me there are two distinctly different ways of looking at this marvel of symmetry. One exalts the delightful pattern, the other deplores the death it will cause. Both sides have the right to accuse the other of insensitiveness, for they are both sensitive in a different direction. Of course only the Italian futurists have literally written lyrics on machine-guns and dive-bombers, but haven't we sometimes also shown a love for that pure pattern which annoys the other chaps?

The truth is that it is just as difficult to be detached as undetached. Just lately I met an Arabian friend. When he talked about the unpleasant relations between the Jewish and the Arabian population in the Near East, of which I knew nothing, he mentioned an aesthetic aspect of the question. Apparently the farmers in Iraq, still cultivating their land with primitive methods as we do in China, were leading a happy and contented existence. The Jews, he said, being much more enterprising, introduced mechanised farming. As a result the Arabs proved no competitors and consequently had to sacrifice their taste and accept the motorised tractor. I don't know how authentic all this is, but I mention it just to point out a sharp paradox of our contemporary life as has already been demonstrated here first by the electric power plant on the Scottish Loch and now the threat to the view of Durham Cathedral. Two months ago the shelling of Cassino presented us with another paradox. I ask myself, do I wish to see more corn in the barns of my Near East friends or do I wish to preserve their countryside? Frankly, I do not know where I stand at all; for in some ways spiritual and economic values are relative and the sooner we admit this the nearer to the ground we shall be.

In 1940, whenever I went to an English home, I was usually shown the goldfish pond or the rose garden. But during the last three years, owing to the successful "digging for victory" campaign, it is not uncommon for a visitor to be shown the vegetable garden soon after his arrival. No host, however reserved, can hide his pride in the size of his cabbages or the heavy clusters of his tomatoes. Roses to-day are often to be seen only in odd corners, though one must add that however crowded an English garden may be, some roses are still to be found. Admittedly the prominence of roses is dwindling as the war lengthens. If we take the rose for spiritual value and the cabbage for economic value, which I hope you will think appropriate, then the amount of accommodation given to each has to be fought out in a tug-of-war. In one house I did find plenty of roses: I was told that a vegetable van called there every afternoon. That vegetable van somehow symbolises to me your many though distant colonies all over the world where cabbages can be conveniently grown.

Our forefathers, I mean yours and ours, were fortunate enough to be able to combine the rose with the cabbage. They made non-utility pottery which was good both for utensils and as works of art. But our spiritual and economic life to-day has been disintegrated beyond repair. A maker of machine-guns may go to the National Gallery at lunch time to listen to a seventeenth-century fugue but she can't very well combine her machine-gun making with Bach. So it is not sufficient for us all to shout to the future mankind, "Plant more roses!" We have to make that possible.

No one, not even a staunch materialist, doubts that spiritual value is infinitely more permanent, but it is also more delicate and therefore more vulnerable. Let us this time substitute the metaphor of the rose for that of a walnut. If spiritual value is the delicious fruit inside, the sad truth is that the walnut requires a hard shell outside. Each time I pass the National Gallery, I cannot help asking myself, would there be a National Gallery without a victory at Trafalgar? The tapestry at Bayeux and the leaning tower of Pisa are both objects of eternal delight, while a gunshell once fired is gone for ever. But those objects of eternal delight are so helpless under the blind gunshells. "It is inconceivable that a holy thing like culture should be defended" was the dictum of some Peking professors in 1936, arguing against the fortification of that city; but there are too many inconceivable things in this absurd world of ours.

To my mind we could do one of three things:

(1) Build a hard shell round each cultural unit in terms of battleships, panzer divisions which means returning to the good old days before war—each guard his own door.

(2) The second best thing we can do is to build a huge and hard shell to protect the spiritual values of all countries, a stronger League of Nations as statesmen are planning this moment at Dumbarton Oaks.

(3) But how much more economical if the necessity of a hard shell can be altogether removed so that we can devote our energy to creative work.

I know both the animal instinct and the eternal historical truth of power politics deny this, but then, like many of you, I am also a dreamer.

WHAT *ARE* "SPIRITUAL" VALUES?

By OLAF STAPLEDON

WHAT *ARE* THESE SPIRITUAL VALUES THAT WE ARE ASKED TO CONSIDER IN relation to economic values and the future of man? It seems important to form a clear idea of them at the outset of this conference, lest we should be talking at cross purposes.

Let me begin by describing a little experience of my own, and asking whether in its humble degree it deserves to be called a "spiritual" experience, concerned with "spiritual values."

In the field next my house there are two colts, inseparable companions. They like standing head to tail, so that each one's face may have the benefit of the other's fly-whisk. One of them is a bit queer. He has a Roman nose, a serpent's eye, a mop of a mane that would seem more appropriate on a toy horse, and legs that are almost too sturdy for his still rather slim adolescent body. He often stands quite still for a long time with his head held fantastically high, like a cavalry charger standing at attention. The other day I saw him eating my young and struggling hedge; not for the first time. I rushed at him with fierce noises. He moved a yard or two away, and regarded me with cold resentment, sidelong, out of his serpent eye. I stood watching him watching me. Presently, whether because of his Roman nose (reminiscent of I know not what prehistoric beast) or because of my own prehistoric hullaballoo, the past seemed to flood upon me. I saw the two of us as brothers in evolution. Behind us trailed our ancestries, our long separate ancestries and our longer common ancestry. Primitive mammals, reptiles, fishes, worms, the warm primeval ocean, the fluid jet which was to become the planets, but had first to be plucked from the fiery flesh of the sun—all this, and more, crowded upon my imagination. The experience moved me deeply, not violently, but deeply; with a sense first of the reality of that colt as a conscious though alien being. Like Martin Buber, I inwardly said to him, "Thou!" And compassion seized me, for him and for the two of us, as products of mighty forces and the sport of obscure powers, which neither of us, not even my humanly superior self, could understand or control. But laughter also moved me, laughter at the two of us, each so annoyed at the other over that hedge. And though, of course, I did not forget that my equine brother was in many ways quite a bit more stupid than myself (which is saying a lot, if I am to accept the verdict of some reviewers), yet I was stirred with a strange sense of our kinship, each with the other, but also with the flies that were teasing both of us, and with the unfortunate hedge, and the wind, and the sun himself, and the unseen stars and galaxies. And over and above this sense of the kinship of what theists would call all "creatures," all "created things," I was struck mentally dumb for a moment with a feeling of something else, something alien to all creatures. Something dark-bright, terrible and beautiful. Something "other." For all I know, that something was just the prodigious bulk and power of the universe itself, confronting one of its tiny members through the medium of his imagination. Anyhow, the upshot for me was that something seemed to have "come at me" through the appearance of that colt, something to which I had to respond with greeting, but also with obeisance.

Of course there was nothing specially mysterious or mystical or in any way inexplicable in this odd little experience. Modern psychology could give a very reasonable account of it; up to a point at any rate. But I am inclined to say that it was a "spiritual" experience and concerned with "spiritual values." It was "spiritual," I should say, because it was a case of behaviour on a relatively high level of psychological development; high for me, anyway. It involved a kind of apprehension or sensitivity which discovers values not revealed on lower planes of development, values connected with self-awareness and awareness of other selves. In another sense also, I should say, it was spiritual. It was a reaction of this most developed and awake level of my personality to the universe *as a whole*, or rather to *my* experienced universe as a whole. I am suggesting that the word "spiritual" should be reserved for experience on the distinctively human level of development. Such experience discovers values that cannot be fully described in terms of lower levels. It issues in action ("spiritual" action) which is a response of the awakened personality as a whole to its world as a whole. If it does not thus issue in action, its frustration inevitably causes some degree of spiritual ill-health. The action, however, may be no single act but rather, as in my experience with the colt, a general fortifying for future action.

Of course, the word "spiritual" may be used simply in contrast with "material"; but I cannot believe that this is the significant use of it to-day. That the universe is made up of two distinct stuffs or substances, matter and spirit, is at any rate very debatable. On the other hand, the distinction between "economic values" and "spiritual values" is in the last resort equivalent to the distinction between the lower-level and the higher-level needs of men, and is significant. Of course, the two kinds of values are often inextricably tied up together, and both are necessary to fullness of life. For instance, no really satisfactory human living is possible without both good food and art. In certain circumstances each of these may be rightly pursued simply for its own sake. But, given enough good food, art is a more deeply and comprehensively satisfying activity than eating. In the last analysis it is more true to say that the spiritual activities are the "right" goal of living than that the economic activities are so. On the other hand, there are many occasions when the truly spiritual act is to sacrifice some obvious spiritual value for the sake of some economic value without which the spirit cannot flourish. There may well be moments in world-history when it is more truly spiritual to strive for an economic revolution than to enjoy art for its own sake.

But why, it may be objected, call these upper-level activities "spiritual"? "Spirit" and "spiritual" are very ambiguous and emotive words. Some sticklers for clear thinking urge us to abandon them altogether. Yet it is difficult to do so. Often when talking to materialists I feel bound to use them, not merely to shock but to emphasize that the spiritual values are not reducible to primitive values. Yet, frankly, when theists and other spiritists use these words, I myself am often shocked.

To-day it is peculiarly important that we should find a clear meaning for "spirit" and "spiritual values." Recently it was fashionable, and in some quarters it is still fashionable, to say that, after all, the so-called "spiritual values" were only sophisticated forms of primitive values, or that spiritual motives were only disguised expressions of primitive instinctive motives, such as self-regard, sex and gregariousness. There is to-day a widespread emotional revulsion against this view, which is beginning to seem too clever by half. In blood and tears we are learning that there really are some values which are in some important sense sacred, some ways of experiencing and behaving which are better than others in some fundamental manner, and other ways of behaving which are utterly wrong.

This painful rediscovery and restatement of "spiritual values" I believe to be the most important feature of our time. But it brings with it a great danger. Many who have found that, after all, pure materialism is not enough are tempted simply to accept uncritically the teaching of some religion, generally the Christian religion, or at any rate, some kind of theism. But the spiritual problem of our day is not to be solved as easily as that. While we have indeed to outgrow simple materialism and ethical nihilism, we must not forget all that we have learnt from the great movement of scepticism. And while we have, I believe, to re-learn a great deal from Christianity, we must continue to regard all its doctrines about the nature of the universe and the destiny of human individuals with profound scepticism. What we have to re-learn from Christianity is not metaphysical doctrines but an emotional attitude, namely, the longing to dedicate oneself wholeheartedly to the "spiritual values." Indeed I will dare even to go so far as to say to dedicate oneself to "the spirit." But in saying this I must guard myself by emphasizing that by "the spirit" I do not mean a deity, personal or "super-personal" (whatever that is); I mean a way of life and an attitude of mind. I mean the most integrated and conscious sort of human behaviour. Sometimes I mean "that in us" which behaves in this way, without specifying whether "that in us" is simply the individual personality in its most fully developed form or something which extends far beyond the individual personality. We have no assurance whatever about the status of "the spirit" in the universe. We know "the spirit" only in ourselves and in our relations with one another. It *may* be also a mighty power in the universe at large; it *may* be in some obscure sense a personal or super-personal God. But we cannot know this—not yet, at any rate. Human intellect is not yet sufficiently developed to form trustworthy concepts in such high spheres. The chances are thousands to one that all our most carefully conceived ideas on these subjects are more false than true. To say that there is a personal God, or that there is not, to say that human individuals have eternal life, or that they have not, are probably almost as naïve statements as to say that the earth is carried on the back of an elephant which stands on a tortoise. If our spiritual values need the support of such beliefs, or indeed of any beliefs, their position is indeed precarious. But they don't; any more than the earth needs the support of the elephant and the tortoise. The earth does not even "stand on its own feet." It needs no feet, and no standing. It is itself the ground of all *our* standing. Similarly with "spiritual values." The Churches thought it was necessary to support them with doctrines about God and immortality. When the support began to seem very insecure, many good people supposed that the spiritual values must crash, that they *had* crashed, that they were illusory. But to-day, just because spiritual values have been so violently discarded, and we have been flung into hell on earth, we begin to realise their authority far better than we did in the time of our comfortable beliefs.

At this point someone may protest that, even if it is excusable to use the phrase "spiritual values," it is misleading to speak about "the spirit," unless one means by the word a substance, contrasted with "matter." I sympathize with this contention; but, after all, we speak of "the spirit of the meeting" and "the spirit of the game" without implying that the meeting or the game are infused or possessed by a spirit-substance. And further, even though it is impossible to give any clear intellectual content to "the spirit," it seems important to retain the word so as to emphasize that we *feel* emotionally bound in loyalty to "something" *in* ourselves yet more than ourselves, and indeed more than mankind; "more," at least in the sense in which an ideal is more than any particular approximation to it.

It may be said that to take a position between the materialists, who recognize no spiritual values, and the theists, who ground the spiritual values in their belief in God, is to go between the devil and the deep sea. And so perhaps it is. But there is a strait and narrow way between the devil and the deep sea, and it is the only way of life in our day.

Traditionally, the spiritual values, I suppose, are goodness, truth and beauty. Traditionally, spiritual experience and action are the experience and action distinctive of "spirits." Traditionally, human individuals are "spirits" capable of spiritual and of unspiritual or positively wicked behaviour; and their salvation lies in behaving in a manner true to their essential nature as spirits.

Even if we are sceptical about the idea that we are "spirits," metaphysical substances having eternal life, we can significantly make use of the old terminology, since we do distinguish between the upper and lower levels of our nature. There is a very real difference between them, both biologically and psychologically. Julian Huxley has recently made a strong plea for the objectivity of the concept of development. Human experience and behaviour are objectively more developed than an ape's. Some kinds of human experience and behaviour are more developed than other kinds; though within the human sphere it is often immensely difficult to judge between different kinds of behaviour in respect of development. Who shall judge whether Shakespeare or Plato was, on the whole, the more developed human being? Nevertheless we cannot but *try* to apply this standard in judging one another and ourselves.

By saying that some human behaviour is more developed than others the biologist and the psychologist mean simply that it is more sensitive, more comprehensively and more finely graded in relation to the environment, more integrated, more accurately related to the environment as a whole.

But what has this to do with spiritual values? Is developed behaviour ethically *better* than less developed behaviour? It is. But ethical judgments can be made only at a relatively high level of development, and about behaviour on relatively high levels. Even so, ethical judgments are apt to be confused by incursions from lower levels. At a certain level of development new kinds of experience become possible; new values, values of a new order come into view, and in relation to them, new kinds of behaviour are demanded.

Roughly we may say that the spiritual experiences and values and behaviour are those which are distinctive of a certain high degree of self-awareness and other-awareness, and intellectual abstraction, and aesthetic sensibility. They are concerned with personality, community, intellectual integrity, the aesthetic aspect of all experience, and (so to say) the need to establish some sort of adjustment to, or accord with, the whole of one's experienced universe. The spiritual attitude includes a tendency to regard particular events as in one way or another symbols with very far-reaching significance. My incident with the colt became a symbol of the whole drama of life in this universe.

In this last connection consider the difference between the spiritual attitude to existence and the unspiritual. The unspiritual is said to be "addicted" to lower-level ends, such as self-interest, sex, the group. The fully spiritual attitude, though it does not necessarily reject these ends, pursues them with detachment because it is addicted wholly to the spiritual end, which is the fulfilling of the spiritual capacities of selves (whether of myself or other selves is in the *last* resort irrelevant), and of the human race as a whole, and equally of any other potentially spiritual beings, if there are any, anywhere in the universe.

The goal or rather direction of spiritual development, so far as I can see, is very roughly this: precise and comprehensive awareness of the world, including oneself and other selves; precise feeling about all this; and coherent and creative action to open up ever new possibilities of the life of the spirit. This goal is essentially a communal, not an individualistic or private, goal. The self-centred individual can never even begin to seek it. It is the way of life for individuals, but only for those who feel themselves to be "members one of another."

Both strict humanists and theists might, I think, be persuaded to agree on some such terms. What they would certainly disagree about is the status of spiritual values. Humanists might indeed quite well call the values of the developed consciousness "spiritual," and might even speak of "the spirit of man" or the "human spirit"; but without implying that a metaphysical substance of spiritual nature resided in or possessed all human individuals. The human spirit, they might say, is simply the form of behaviour or way of life which is distinctive of the human species, even though no human beings succeed in living permanently on that high level. The spiritual values are the values recognized by man on that highest plane of his development.

True! But I think strict humanists do not always realize the full implications of this kind of statement. They fail to realize that to say this is to accept a standard other than sheer humanity.

Theists and other religious believers protest, rightly, I think, that to make man the criterion of the "spiritual" is to deprive the word of its most significant meaning. Spiritual values, they say, are spiritual not merely because they are human; they are spiritual in their own right, so to speak. And for man the way of life is to approximate to them. Man's true nature is indeed spiritual; but there is also much in him which is not spiritual. He can fulfil his spiritual nature only in so far as he allows himself to be possessed by "*the* spirit," which they regard as superhuman and universal.

I shall not enter into this controversy. Probably as with so many hoary controversies, the issue is wrongly posed, like the time-honoured question as to whether the hen came first or the egg. Tentatively I suggest some such compromise as the following. The humanists are right in saying that we know nothing of the spirit save in ourselves and our relations with one another; but the religious people are right in insisting that the spirit confronts us as *something* more than our ordinary selves, something claiming, and rightly claiming, absolute authority over our ordinary selves, something to which our ordinary selves, when they are sufficiently awake and not perverted by irrelevant cravings of lower order, cannot but will absolute loyalty.

It comes to this. In this great problem the heart, sufficiently purged and fortified, is a more trustworthy guide than the intellect in its present fledgling state. And the heart feels with profound conviction, especially in these days of blood and hate and folly and barbarian values, that human individuals and the race as a whole must be judged according to a criterion independent of the actual extant nature of man. The fundamental spiritual values are, after all authoritative, even though our intellects cannot yet satisfactorily explain their authority. Whatever the truth about God and immortality and the nature of the universe, we know in our hearts absolutely that we ought to regard ourselves as instruments though imperfect instruments of the spirit. Even on the plane of pure intellect it is more true to affirm this than to deny it. If we have not this conviction, there is no health in us. We are damned. We are non-interventionists, Munichites. We make intellectual scepticism and detachment an excuse for moral detachment.

But though loyalty to spiritual values should, I feel, lead us to go thus far with the theists, farther we must not go. For intellectual integrity also is a spiritual duty. We must not persuade ourselves into belief in doctrines which go beyond the proper range of extant human intellect. The only piety that we can permit ourselves is an agnostic piety.

So much for the status of "the spirit" and of "spiritual values." Let us now consider some of the kinds of experience and action which may reasonably be said to be concerned with spiritual values. I shall dwell mainly on the kind which I believe to be most significant for us to-day, neglecting others equally important in the long run, such as the intellectual and aesthetic values. Of these I would merely insist that they really are spiritual values. But I would add that the spiritual attitude to them involves a realization of their limitations. Though within its proper sphere intellect is paramount, there are regions of human experience where, for the present, at any rate, it cannot go far; and, when it falsely claims to have gone far, it becomes dangerously misleading. The chief of these regions is, of course, the whole vast sphere of the status of the spirit and of spiritual values. Similarly with art. Within its proper sphere aesthetic sensibility is paramount; but to care *only* for the aesthetic aspect of life is to betray, not serve, the spirit.

In order to complete the picture one point should be briefly added. in its more awakened mood the mind may find a "spiritual value" even in the simplest and most commonplace experiences. Sense-perceptions and simple muscular activities, and indeed all kinds of events, may seem to yield up their inner nature, may become arresting simply through their vividness and precision of form, so that we feel ourselves confronted with the features of a living reality other than ourselves. Or they may come to us rich in symbolization. We drink cold water on a hot day. How many millions of beings, human and sub-human, have delighted in that penetrating coldness! Thus the sensations become at once an exquisite confrontation with reality and a ritual act of worship, an act done "for the glory of God." Even if one is no theist, one may recognize the emotional truth of the phrase.

The spiritual values which I want to discuss in more detail, are those connected with personality and community. Let us begin with compassion. Many people would say that compassion has always a spiritual aspect. But surely we must distinguish between two kinds of compassion, one spiritual, the other not. The unspiritual, or only rudimentarily spiritual, kind of compassion is that which is common to men and beasts. The other is distinctively personal, and may be called "compassion with insight." The bitch is compassionate towards her pups, in that she is distressed by their distress, and so on; but she lacks insight into them as conscious beings. Jealous possessiveness may actually drive her to eat them. Even human mothers may fail through insufficient imaginative insight into their children's peculiar needs and capacities. In truly personal compassion on the other hand, there is a much higher degree of insight into the other's actual nature as a conscious being *other* than oneself. And this insight may lead to a different kind of behaviour, in fact to behaviour in accord with a true personal relationship. Such compassion and such behaviour are spiritual in that they are concerned with a spiritual value, namely, personality. They are also sometimes spiritual in another sense. In compassion with insight and in every truly personal relationship there is often a sense of universal significance, of insight *through* the particular symbol into the universal plight of personalities in this formidable universe.

Compassion with insight is something different in kind from sheer anima affection, and not reducible to it; though of course, it includes it. Compassion with insight is an activity distinctive of the self-conscious and other-conscious level of development; and therefore "spiritual."

As with compassion, so with all fellow-feeling. Animal gregariousness is fellow-feeling without insight, or with a minimum of it. The sick sheep may be persecuted by the flock. The eccentric human being may be persecuted by the mob. On the other hand, human comradeship, love, and all the kinds of true community are fellowship with insight into the other, or others, as conscious beings with peculiar character, needs, powers. The values which this relationship generates are spiritual values.

Take the case of sex-relationship. In the most developed form of it other-consciousness dominates the whole relationship. There is a passionate coming together of two diverse personalities through the exquisite physical medium. Because of the diversity there is inevitably conflict, overt or suppressed; but if there is sufficient self-awareness and other-awareness, and sufficient mutual valuing, the very conflict may become a source of enlargement to both parties. The essence of personal love is delighted awareness of the other as different, though of course fundamentally akin. There is mutual acceptance, mutual responsibility and cherishing, with consequent self-discipline for the other's sake, and emergence into a richer self, which is felt to be organic to the precious community of the two lovers.

Genuine personal love of every kind, sexual and non-sexual, is spiritual in that it is concerned with personality and community. It may also be spiritual in that it includes a sense of universal significance. In love's young dream, or calf-love, there is a sense of the "divinity" of the beloved. In an obscure way he or she becomes a symbol of something universal. A gesture, a look, a tone of voice, may seem to be intimations of something superhuman. They promise something not yet experienced, not yet conceivable, but felt to be of immense significance. On the other hand, consider mature love, by which I mean love between two (or more) persons who have known one another for a long time, and who, in spite of inevitable conflicts, have grown together into an indissoluble symbiosis, in which each is necessary to the other and shaped by the other. Here the promise has been up to a point fulfilled; and the gift is precisely this symbiosis, this participation in a common life, this creation of a spiritual value which is impossible for either in isolation. In mature love there come moments in which one has a quite indubitable conviction that this little communion of diverse personalities is a symbol, an epitome of *something* very far-reaching and important in the universe. Cherish this conviction, by all means; but do not suppose that therefore there must be a God who is the almighty lover, and that human individuals must be immortal. One may feel imaginatively the presence, as it were, of the whole past biography of this most precious little community of two persons, and of the whole past of humanity, as essentially a precarious groping towards something spiritually far more developed, awakened. One may even feel, or seem to feel, possessed by that supreme something itself, by a very God of Love. But beware, beware! *Any* intellectual formulation of such experience is certain to be mainly false. Nevertheless the feeling itself is a source of strength and light. And this kind of living, one feels, is what human beings are for. In *some* obscure sense, far too difficult for our intellect to clarify, we are all instruments for this music, for the fulfilling of this spirit.

Personal love cannot be healthy if it is simply an end in itself. In one way or another the community of the lovers must include active partnership or comradeship in a common task, which may be the rearing of a family, or some external work common to both, or separate social undertakings which both value. This sense of partnership in a common task, conceived as more important than any private satisfaction, is the only sentiment which can effectively unite a large group of human beings. The common task may be good or bad, spiritual or non-spiritual. The unifying passion may be nothing more than the will for the group's dominance over other groups, for instance in prestige or war or trade or economic imperialism or racial supremacy. One kind of group sentiment alone is genuinely spiritual, namely the will that the group shall be an effective instrument of the spirit, that its whole life shall be organized so as to make the most of all its members, that all its members may be as fully developed human persons as possible, consciously united in service of the spirit. Examples of associations of human beings dominated by this will in one form or another are the early Christian Church, the early French Revolution, the early Labour Movement in England, the early revolutionary Communist Party in Russia. All these I regard as cases of the widespread grasping of a spiritual value, in fact, of *the* supreme spiritual value, namely the rightness of true human fellowship or community.

The Russian case is most striking because owing to special circumstances the experience was combined with a wholesale rejection of metaphysical doctrines about the fundamentally "spiritual" nature of the universe. I should say that the Russian Revolution has proved that an essentially spiritual will, namely the passion for comradeship and right human relations, may effectively inspire large numbers of men without their fully realizing that their motive is spiritual, and without their believing in any metaphysical doctrines. It *may* be that since the early days of the Revolution the original revolutionary will has been to some extent confused by impulses which are not consistent with the spiritual goal, that there has been a good deal of violation of the spiritual goal in some respects; but this makes no difference to the fact that Lenin and his followers were inspired by the will to found a society in which the necessary conditions should be secured for the fulfilling of personality in every individual in free participation in the common life. The Communists may have had an imperfect view of what, in its loftier reaches, the life of the spirit really involves; but they disciplined themselves heroically for an ideal which was essentially spiritual. And whatever their faults and their failures, I at least believe that they achieved a necessary economic revolution and founded a new kind of society in which the spirit may in time find fuller expression than has before been possible. The spirit is not served by our merely praising it. We have to live and if necessary die for it.   There's the rub!   Further, I should guess that in many cases the social revolutionary's passion is spiritual not only in that it is concerned with the spiritual value of comradeship but also that it is accompanied by at least some sense of universal significance; which, of course, may or may not be consciously recognized as such. In striving to create a world-society in which every individual shall have the fullest possible opportunity of development in personality and in community with his fellows, the revolutionary is trying to release the frustrated spiritual potency of our species.   He works for a future in which the spirit shall triumph on this planet.   In the past, economic forces inevitably played the major part in determining the course of history; but in the future, near or far, men may succeed in founding a world in which, the spiritual will is the main controlling power.

MILTON AND THE MODERN PRESS

By B. IFOR EVANS

I AM DELIGHTED TO SPEAK AT THIS CONFERENCE WHICH IS BRINGING MILTON'S name into more general public attention. There has been among certain younger critics an attempt to obscure the merits of his poetry, an attempt which has been as impertinent as it has been uninformed. Here we celebrate the tercentenary of the best-known of his prose works, and one closely associated with the British tradition of liberty and of freedom of speech.

I sometimes think that we take both the merits of the prose style of the *Areopagitica* and the eternal validity of its argument too much for granted. The *Areopagitica* does contain some of the most magnificent passages of Milton's prose. They are bound to be quoted many times during this conference:

"Truth indeed came once into the world with her divine Master, and was a perfect shape most glorious to look on; but when he ascended, and his apostles after him were laid asleep, then straight arose a wicked race of deceivers, who, as that story goes of the Egyptian Typhon with his conspirators, how they dealt with the good Osiris, took the virgin Truth, hewed her lovely form into a thousand pieces, and scattered them to the four winds. From that time ever since, the sad friends of Truth, such as durst appear, imitating the careful search that Isis made for the mangled body of Osiris, went up and down gathering up limb by limb still as they could find them.. We have not yet found them all, Lords and Commons, nor ever shall do, till her Master's second coming; he shall bring together every joint and member, and shall mould them into an immortal feature of loveliness and perfection."

Or that other passage so frequently quoted:

"I cannot praise a fugitive and cloistered virtue, unexercised and unbreathed, that never sallies out and sees her adversary, but slinks out of the race, where that immortal garland is to be run for not without dust and heat."

The main body of the prose of the *Areopagitica* does not live up to that standard. Milton's mind was so complex that he found grammatical structure at times an embarrassment, and the inflected Latin sentence did not help him to keep straight in the looser structures of English. I have always found that parts of the Divorce Tracts are more straightforward in their style than is the *Areopagitica* taken as a whole. It is, however, not with the style, but rather with the thought that I would deal.

Milton is making a plea for unlicensed printing. He defends that plea on the grounds that men and women will be able to protect themselves against what may be corrupting in evil books. It is not that Milton denies that some restraint is necessary, but that he believes that the control should be rather an inner one, inside the personality itself, than an external one, dictated by some outside authority.

It seems at first sight that such a conclusion is opposed to the doctrine of *Paradise Lost*, where Adam and Eve fall because they do not obey a regulation which has been externally imposed upon them. To examine the full relationship of the thought of *Areopagitica* and *Paradise Lost* would take me outside my main argument here. It may well be that we can accept with Professor Saurat (who, I am glad to see, celebrates at once the republication of his book on Milton and his escape from enemy action in London at almost the same time) the view that the prohibition which Adam and Eve disobeyed was connected mainly with a sexual theme and belonged to a different part of Milton's thinking from that involved in the printing of unlicensed books. I think it can be further maintained that whatever Milton may have to say in *Paradise Lost* on obedience to a law outside oneself, he does reassert before the close his faith in a way of life where the only control is that exercised by an internal judgment. I have always myself attached particular importance to that final speech which Michael makes to Adam in the 12th Book of *Paradise Lost*:

> "To whom thus also th' Angel last repli'd:
> This having learnt, thou hast attained the sum
> Of wisdom; hope no higher, though all the stars
> Thou knewst by name, and all th' ethereal Powers,
> All secrets of the deep, all Nature's works,
> Or works of God in Heaven, Air, Earth, or Sea,
> And all the riches of this World enjoydst,
> And all the rule, one empire; only add
> Deeds to thy knowledge answerable, add faith,
> Add virtue, patience, temperance, add love,
> By name to come call'd charity, the soul
> Of all the rest; then wilt thou not be loth
> To leave this Paradise, but shalt possess
> A Paradise within thee, happier far."

Given this, the problem which occurs to me is whether Milton would have still preached his doctrine at the present day, and whether we have not accepted what we believe to be Milton's doctrine too easily and with effects which have not been desirable on the nation as a whole. Milton could not have foreseen a situation in which an individual, or a small group of individuals, could, by financial power, obtain control of the press of the country. He could not have foreseen a condition in which those individuals, without any recognised channels of responsibility to the nation as a whole, put forward views which may be infecting the mind of the nation and, indeed, destroying its capacity for consecutive thought.

I need not be more specific, for you must all realise well what I have in mind. It is true that my first version of a title for this talk was "What Milton would have said to Lord Beaverbrook," but I was using Lord Beaverbrook rather as a symbol than as an individual. We have, it seems to me, been so content with merely repeating our praises of Milton's conceptions of liberty as not to face the practical problem of how we manage organs like the modern Press within a State which has a high mechanical organisation behind it.

The whole problem of propaganda, the dissemination of opinion, the distribution of printed matter, has changed entirely since Milton's day. Milton's conception of the circulation of ideas was that which might have prevailed in Greece—a small audience, all of whom are capable of forming their own judgments, with discussion to correct false emphasis. He has in mind the formulation of an adequate judgment by a Socratic method. Even the England of his own day did not fit into that picture altogether, and the world of our day does not fit into it at all. One man, or one group of men, can, by subtle, psychological methods, and by use of the newspaper and the radio, effect a secret tyranny over the minds of millions. We in England seem content to allow that sort of thing to continue and to soothe ourselves mentally by repeating our praises for arguments such as those Milton has put forward, or, if this is unjust to Milton, to make Milton an excuse for not trying to discover what should be the appropriate action.

I have always been interested to see that Dr. Johnson was not taken in entirely by the simplicity of Milton's plea as it has been popularly interpreted.

"About the same time Milton published his *Areopagitica*, a speech for the liberty of unlicensed printing. The danger of such unbounded liberty, and the danger of bounding it, have produced a problem in the science of government, which human understanding seems hitherto unable to solve."

Milton himself, it must be remembered, did clearly distinguish the difference between liberty and licence.

I am not attempting to-day to suggest the solution of this problem, but I think it would be a very appropriate practical conclusion to this conference if instead of all going away praising the liberty of speech, we did attempt to formulate what should be the proper regulation of the Press and radio after this war. Whatever may be the evils of the irresponsibilities of the Press, I am personally of the view that they are less than the evils of censorship. I think though that we could come to a more healthy condition by certain other steps. In the first place, journalism should be built up into a profession with regulations of its own and standards of discipline of its own, such as the medical and legal professions possess. Further, although I profess I do not know how this is to be done, the journalist should be protected from his employer to a far greater extent than he is at present.

I would go even further than this myself, and would suggest that all display advertisement should disappear from newspapers after the war. This would, of course, render them commercially impossible on their present scale, but that, I think, would be desirable. I am of the view that any newspaper with a 3,000,000 circulation is an unhealthy phenomenon in a State with a 40,000,000 population. We should have smaller newspapers, smaller circulation, but a greater variety of papers, and under those conditions I think we would come back to a state where Milton's views would be valid.

We in the Democracies must confess that our standards of public morality have been low and the artist has been to my mind far too tolerant of them. When he has opposed them at all it has usually been with satire or abuse. I think the time has come when those who belong to the profession of writing should try and approach these questions in a more constructive manner and this tercentenary of Milton's pamphlet might be a good occasion for the P.E.N. Club to institute such an inquiry.

MAN'S SUPERIORITY TO THE BEASTS

LIBERTY VERSUS SECURITY IN THE MODERN STATE

By C. E. M. JOAD, M.A., D.Lit.

I WOULD HAVE LIKED TO HAVE FOLLOWED PROFESSOR EVANS IN SPEAKING about Milton, but really I do not know enough about him and must be excused by my poetic illiteracy.

I did notice that there were some other topics down for discussion on the programme and I looked through them, wondered which was the one least likely to be chosen by other speakers, and plumped for "Man's Superiority to the Beasts," conjoined with "Liberty *versus* Security in the Modern State." I propose to speak on those two apparently unrelated topics.

In what, then, I want to know, do men differ from and excel the beasts? In swiftness and ferocity the deer and the lion have us beaten every time; in size and strength we must give way to the elephant and the whale; sheep are more gentle; nightingales more melodious; beavers more diligent; and I suppose the ants run the Corporate State much better than any Fascist. Our bodies are ill-adapted to survival, the prey of innumerable diseases, and it is only by covering them with the skins of other animals that we are able to protect ourselves against the vagaries of the climate. Therefore, if we value ourselves on the score of strength, ferocity, uniformity, herd spirit, loyalty, speed, toughness, endurance, we value ourselves in respect of qualities in regard to which the animals have us beaten every time.

In what, then, does our superiority consist? Wherein are our distinctive excellences to be found? I venture to suggest in three qualities: (1) in our reason; (2) in our sense of beauty; (3) in our sense of right and wrong. In regard to each one of these three, I take it that we are distinctive. I think it is also fairly clear, though obviously one cannot pursue this fascinating topic, that if any claim can be made in respect of human freedom it would have to be located in two, if not in all three of these characteristics. That is to say, so far as our bodies are concerned, so far as our passions, so far even as our emotions, there is, I think, no answer to be found to the case of the Determinists. If an answer is to be found to Determinism at all, if any claim is to be made for human freedom, it is in the free exercise of our reason, our freedom to choose the right and eschew the wrong, and the freedom with which our sense of beauty flowers into art, music and literature.

Now it is one of the most distinctive characteristics of our age, as it is also one of the most humiliating, that we have grown up to pride ourselves not upon excellence in respect of these distinctive characteristics of mankind, but upon those characteristics which I enumerated a moment ago in which the animals are our superiors. We have grown up into a world in which toughness, endurance, ferocity, herd loyalty, uniformity, are regarded as the most desirable virtues in the citizen, and it is partly because of this misplacement of values that the star of freedom has in our lifetime been in some countries completely, in all countries partially, eclipsed.

One asks oneself why that should be so. I think there are two main reasons, with regard to only one of which do I propose now to say a few words.

Let me first specify the one in regard to which I have *not* time to speak. It is that the man who follows the life of reason, the man who wishes to live according to the spirit, even the man who strives to live according to Christian virtue, is a bad consumer. I mean a bad consumer in the sense that he makes fewer demands upon the productive resources of the community, for gramophones, for radio sets, for refrigerators, for motor-cars, for Fun Fair at Blackpool, for dirt-track racing, for dog-racing and all the rest of the commercialised amusements of society, than the ordinary, Philistine, low-brow chap. The man who wants to be free, and independent, and to live his life according to reason, is the supreme example of what has come to be known as a sales-register, and all the forces of modern advertisement are accordingly devoted to a subtle denigration of the life of the mind and the spirit. Consider the highbrow—that word of shame; consider the intellectual, regarded in this country, as our visitors will have seen, with almost universal disrespect, which deepens at times into suspicion, hardens into hatred. Why? Partly because he is not doing his bit in the matter of consumption. Is he rushing about over the surface of the earth in a vehicle propelled by petrol? No, he is not. He is probably walking over the fields or hiking along the road. Is he at the cinema? Not very often. Is he listening to the radio? I hope not. Is he rushing down water-chutes at Blackpool, or watching motor-cycle races, or even dancing? No, he is doing none of these things. He is content with "a green thought in a green shade" costing nothing at all, or a Pelican costing ninepence. What a bad consumer! And, therefore, what a bad citizen! Consequently, in a world which under our existing economic system is constantly at a loss how to get rid of its surplus products, the highbrow, the intellectual, the man who excels in respect of those qualities in which freedom is to be found, is a target for almost universal opprobrium.

That would be one theme for discussion and, indeed, I have a talk on it which I hope to give at some later time. I now come to the talk which I propose to give here.

This consists of an examination of the other reason why the qualities we share with the animals are encouraged and why our distinctive qualities are in this age discouraged and palpably diminishing. I think that other reason is to be found in the power of the modern State. The modern State does not want its citizens to reason, it does not want them to create works of art; I am not sure that it wants them to know the difference between right and wrong. What it does want is that they shall all obey its orders and toe the line it has drawn, so that it can count on them to kill and to be killed whenever it, the State, deems the mass slaughter of the citizens of some other State to be desirable. Hence, it encourages the qualities we share with animals, and discourages the qualities in which human beings exhibit their distinctive excellences. Now it may be said that States and their characteristics have always been with us. Wherein, then, is to be found the distinctive danger of the State in our own time?

The distinctive danger resides in two aspects of the modern State. First, in the multiplication of its officials. The business of a modern State is enormously complex; officials breed and are bred like the sands of the shore in order to cope with that business. Now you know how it is with officials. Once put a man into an elected or appointed position, and almost immediately he gets too big for his boots and starts throwing his weight about. How well one knows that curious change that somehow comes over us all when we are elected or appointed to some official job under the State, the change whereby, instead of thinking that we are there for the public's benefit and advantage, to do the things it wants us to do, to serve its convenience, to minister to its welfare, to make life easier for our fellow citizens, we somehow get things the other way round and think that they are there for our own advantage, to make things easier for us, to redound to the glory of the particular department which we happen to represent: in other words, to sign their forms quickly and get out of the office and not be a damned nuisance. It is against this curious change that I should have thought all free men must always protest, regarding officials as the enemy, precisely because it is in this encroachment of officials upon the freedom of the individual's life that one of the greatest enemies of freedom is to be found.

Here is a story which is true and apt, a story which illustrates the right attitude of a man who cares for freedom in face of the growing encroachment of the army of officials. My mind goes back to the General Strike of 1926. All foreign observers thought the strike was going to lead to revolution until one day the strikers were found to be playing football with the police, and there was no revolution. You remember that during the strike all forms of transport were monopolised either by the State or by the Trades Unions. Cars and lorries in particular seemed to have been taken over entirely by the T.U.C. and used to drive about bearing a notice: "Driven by permission of the T.U.C." I was walking along the street in the middle of the strike, when an even larger lorry than usual thundered past, driven by an obvious Cockney, a wiry little chap, bearing on its front the notice: "Driven by my own bloody permission." That seems to me to be the right attitude of the free man confronted with the throwing about of official weight.

I would like to suggest remedies for the plague of officials, but I still have to come to the main part of my address, so I must give that a miss and come to what I consider the more important of the two reasons for the encroaching menace of the State upon freedom, and its increasing encouragement of these un-free, animal-like qualities which I began by specifying.

The nation State is on its defensive, is, in fact, on its last legs. And because it *is* on its defensive and on its last legs, because it knows itself to be hard-pressed, it becomes doubly bellicose, arrogant, aggressive, acquisitive, and extends its hold increasingly over the lives, the time, the energies, the loyalties and the thoughts of its unfortunate members.

The reasons for this development take us very far afield. They are due to the familiar fact that the world is becoming increasingly a single economic whole. It is a world which, owing to the diminution of distance, is becoming, from the economic and technical points of view, increasingly a unity. It is like a whispering gallery in a mine; anything done in any part of it reverberates all over it. But what should be the single, unified surface of this economically unitary world is, in fact, divided into sections, bounded by the frontiers of the separate sovereign nation States, many dating from the remote past, even the most recent knowing an origin not much later than the eighteenth century. As the world contracts and contracts, these States are thrust ever more uncomfortably one upon another. Think of a dozen sleepers in a vast bed; the bed contracts and the sleepers are jostled ever more uncomfortably one on top of the other until presently there is a row and someone is thrown out. In other words, there is a modern war. States in this predicament adopt every conceivable artificial device to build up barriers against one another in order to preserve their integrity in the face of the increasing world-drive towards unity. There, I think, you see the reason for the policy of Economic Nationalism which we deplored before the war, the Customs duties, the passports, the tariffs, the favoured-nation clauses, the quotas, the currency restrictions. What were they but artificial barriers to keep States apart in face of the world-pressure driving them towards unity?

It seems to me clear that part of the trouble of our time arises from the fact that our world is in travail with the birth of a new political form, the Federal or International State. Against the emergence of that form the existing sovereign national States are fighting with all the resources at their command. To me, one of the most sinister things about the plans for the post-war world is that they all still envisage alliances between independent sovereign national States no one of which is to be asked to surrender an iota of its independent sovereignty.

Now, if you look back through history, you can see how the course of evolution has consisted not in an enlargement of the creatures successively evolved but in an enlargement of the area over which organisation has prevailed. The earliest form of creatures, the amœba and so on were uni-cellular. Then you get your first advance, one single-cell creature joining with another, to make a multi-cellular organism; the next advance, one multi-cellular organism joining with another to make a family; next, family joining with family to make the tribe; next, tribe joining with tribe to make the canton, county, province. Remember Shaw's play, *Saint Joan*, and the difficulty Joan had to get her armies to think of France: Burgundy, yes; Picardy, yes; Artois, yes. But France—what was that? Something which had not yet been born. And in our own country, isn't it just the same? You can go back to the days of the Heptarchy, Wessex fighting against Northumberland, then England fighting against Wales or England against Scotland, then the British Isles against France, then the British Empire against the Axis Powers. The area of organisation grows and grows, and I can see no logical end to that enlargement until State is merged with State to make some kind of federal union.

It seems to me that the particular danger of our time arises from the fact that the nation State is on the defensive, that it is being made gradually to yield its position before the coming of a new world-order. And because it is on its defensive, fighting hard to retain its independent sovereignty, trying hard to bolster up its integrity, it threatens so terribly the freedom of its citizens. The greatest menace of our time is the power of the national State. There can be no freedom in the world until that menace has been overcome. I have lived through two wars and seen the power of the State grow throughout the period between the wars, until I have come to hate the whole conception of the national State with its foreign office, it war office, its army with its special national tradition and code of honour, its special national history books each with its special national lie about history, its special dictionary of national biography claiming all discoveries for its own nationals, its peasant costumes and folklore, its flag with its bars going this way or that way or crossways for variety, and its army of young men disciplined and trained behind its frontiers to defend it against another army of young men, equivalently trained behind an opposite frontier, whenever it wishes to extend its dominion or power on the pretext of self-defence.

Isn't it time that we transcended a conception of national greatness which can only be secured by inflicting the maximum injury on the citizens of another State at the cost of terrible suffering to our own? And isn't it time that we saw, as Wells has seen, that the power of the national State is the greatest menace to the individuality and freedom of its citizens, precisely because the national State encourages and promotes herd-like animal qualities to assist in its own defence, and correspondingly distrusts and fears those qualities of individuality and freedom which we meet here to celebrate? Wasn't it Wells who said that the whole mind of mankind is now in revolt against this obsolescent, murderous nuisance, the power of the national State? He should have said that the mind of mankind *ought* to have been in revolt. But you know, as well as I do, that nine-tenths of us are far too good citizens ever to question the power of the State which threatens our freedom, and by so questioning to make of this conference one of the most important and necessary which has been held in the whole period of war.

SOVIET WRITERS AND THE WAR

By the Hon. IVOR MONTAGU

I WANT TO APPROACH THIS SUBJECT ON THE BASIS OF VALUES. ON THE BASIS of the values that are inherent in the Soviet State and community and which therefore shape and determine the writer's relation to Soviet society and his role in it.

As I see it the Soviet Union is heir to the humanistic tradition. It is not a question of how adequately or inadequately so far Soviet literature continues the line of the great humanistic achievements of the past, it is a matter of the direction, the path on which the whole Soviet "experiment" and life is oriented.

There never was a greater error—a more Himalayan error to use Mr. Gandhi's graphic phrase—than that of the Western intellectuals who visited the Soviet Union after the last war and came back horrified at what they conceived the "materialistic" bias of Soviet society. I remember

Bertrand Russell after a world tour coming back from the U.S.S.R. and roundly condemning the purblindness of what he called making labour an end in itself, he even burbled of bees and hives.

I think such intellectuals were completely deceived by surface appearances. They came from a society in which mental activity had become so divorced from physical that the glorification of toil and the toiler that they found in U.S.S.R. scared them out of their wits and certainly out of their judgment and sense of proportion. The sweat of fear started out upon their foreheads so much more readily than the sweat of hard physical work. I remember in this connection the Film Society, when it showed one of the first Soviet sound-films—Dziga-Vertov's *Enthusiasm—the Symphony of the Donbas*. The picture was, in fact, almost a cacophony rather than a symphony of the noises of heavy industry. Dziga-Vertov himself was disappointed to find that at the Tivoli the sound-reproducing apparatus possessed safety-stops that prevented the volume of sound from rising above a certain definite maximum. At the *première* in Moscow, he said, with a disappointed sigh, the walls of the theatre had actually shaken.

Well, our film art-student heroes of the Society, who had cheerfully bled in sympathy with the arduous struggle for liberty in the great revolutionary films of the years before, for the most part sat simply sweating in fear, indignation and horror at the glorification of hard work shown in the Donbas Symphony. They did not feel any sympathy at all. They could not perceive the primary and basic truth that the hard work was a means to an end—the economic value underlying the spiritual value, so to speak.

Neither the labourer nor labour is glorified in the Soviet Union as an end in itself, but the one is heroised as the representative of the class destined by history to restore humanism to mankind, and the other as the indispensable means.

Liberty is not won by romance alone, if there is romance in the struggle for liberty. Toil, arduous toil built the industries that decided in 1941-44 whether the spiritual gains of the revolution were to be a permanent gain of mankind or just a dream flashing by. Toil, arduous toil, builds the material background, enables the leisure, on which cultural life rests and in which it flourishes.

Those who have taken the trouble to delve beneath the surface of Soviet society, to study the works of the founding fathers, of Lenin, Stalin and, before them, of Marx and Engels, will have found that the end conceived is completely humanistic, it is the conception of the 100 per cent., even 200 per cent. release of human powers.

Lenin's vision of the complete man, the many-sided or even all-sided person, is a fascinating one. It is entirely in the tradition of the Renaissance ideal, the image of the Admirable Crichton. It is, in fact, the Renaissance ideal on a higher plane of social production, which enables its realisation not by single individuals but by all individuals.

The specialist, in this view, is a man with all sides but one of him atrophied. The life of the new, Socialist, society, and the opportunities it gives, are to enable the development on the contrary of all-round man. Everyman shall have many interests. His hours of labour shall not be such that when the day's work is done he drops exhausted into mere relaxation. He shall be alive all the time he is awake. He shall enjoy the world and all his potentialities. He may have simultaneously many interests, and many skills. It will be a world—so far as the artist is concerned—of a myriad amateurs, and in which—much to the indignation possibly of the M.C.C.—the line between amateur and professional is altogether blurred.

I give this picture because I think that only when it is grasped can we place in perspective the peculiarities of the contribution of the artist and intellectual—it is, of course, the writer who specially concerns us—in the Soviet framework.

Firstly, that contribution has a chance of being immensely big. In a society based upon this sense of values, there is an immense eagerness to absorb every intellectual contribution. The immense material rewards for writers, based upon a royalty index, reflect directly the honour they are paid and the influence they exert. The pre-war reduction of hours of labour in the U.S.S.R. to seven per day (six in certain heavy categories) created an objective background in which man could exert talents, and taste the talents of others, on a widened scale. Figures of fantastically large editions, not only of fictional literature but of literature of the most erudite and esoteric kinds, testified to the degree to which this background was developing a response. Art in general, including literature, became a necessity of life in U.S.S.R.

I will cite merely one item that expresses this: the printing to-day of 30 million books as a necessity of first priority for the devastated and liberated areas of the Soviet Union. Three hundred books, in editions of 100,000 each, to replace the libraries deliberately massacred by the German occupationists, rank tops beside food, shelter, drainage and seeds. They are, of course, the seeds of intellectual life. And I cannot refrain here from a digression, noting in illustration of the catholicism of Soviet humanism, eager to embrace all that is of value in the culture of the past and of other lands, that we find represented in this first batch the following English writers: Dickens, Chaucer, Shakespeare, Kipling, Wells, Conan Doyle and Shaw.

Next, the nature of the contribution made in this circumstance of brilliant opportunities.

This is best expressed by a phrase of Stalin which has captured the imagination of the whole Soviet writing world. Stalin called the writer "the engineer of the soul." By this he draws attention to the relation between writer and audience, to the "something godlike" attribute of the writer, in that he contributes to the creation of the soul of his readers. The reader is not the same before and after reading, and that difference is the deed of the writer, a creation by him—not an independent creation certainly, but a creation effected by the values the writer has gathered from the life around him before transmuting with his personality.

It is a great responsibility. And I think that, understanding its magnitude and the awareness of it by Soviet writers, writers abroad will find it easier to understand the devotion of Soviet literature to what is called there "Socialist Realism." Socialist Realism is not a genre, it can include an infinite multiplicity of genres. There is not the slightest reason why it should not—and, in fact, it does—include fairy stories, so long as the characters and circumstances in these spring from the realities of human relationships, character and tradition. "Realism" in this sense has nothing in common with Naturalism. It is opposed especially to Formalism, as a fleeing from his responsibilities by the artist, a diversion of his attention away from life and the problems of life to intricacies that at the best are exercises of specialist interest only. The only demand of Realism is that it must be rooted in truth, close enough to actuality to reflect, and reflect upon, living people. As Zhdanov, the leader of Leningrad during the siege of the city, has expressed it: "To be an engineer of the soul means to stand with both feet planted in the realities of life."

As for the adjective "Socialist," that simply indicates the extension of the humanistic tradition of Realism into the epoch of Socialism. In an epoch in which human relationships point toward Socialism, reason Soviet writers, the true reflection of reality must be a Socialist Realism and help toward building the new Socialist Society, the new Socialist man. It cannot escape so being, so long as it is true.

As for varying interpretations in more detail of what Socialist Realism is, ought to be or may not be, there is room—as anyone who has ever attended any of those violent and voluminous literary discussions in the Soviet world will most certainly have been convinced—for a real infinitude of opinion. Indeed such discussions would exactly delight and be applauded by Milton himself. Milton would have hated fascism, and roundly condemned that miscalled Liberalism that paved the way for it by the pernicious doctrine that freedom means liberty for freedom's enemies to destroy freedom. Indeed, he wrote, in the *Areopagitica* which we are celebrating, of the wrongness of tolerating that "which as it extirpates all religious and civil supremacies, so should itself be extirpate . . . that also which is impious or evil absolutely either against faith or manners, no law can possibly permit which intends not to outlaw itself," while at the same time he contrasted these impermissibles with the allowable and to-be-encouraged "neighbouring differences, or rather indifferences, whether in some point of doctrine or of discipline, which, though they may be many, yet need not interrupt the unity of spirit. . . ." This precisely is the spirit of Soviet freedom and free cultural life.

After all this preliminary, then, we can get down to characterising in its context the role of the Soviet writer in war-time.

Milton, who was fully aware of the necessity of practical battle for his humanism, would have himself felt thoroughly at home fulfilling this role. The writer, the "engineer of the soul," in the great emergency of his people and the entire world, fights, with his own weapon, the pen. Wh.   e need of the world is for heroes, it is for him to create the heroic.   vn literature we know the influence that writing can have in   id fastening in real life a type that may not have existed so   before the writer wrote. The British soldier of a certain   d to owe a good deal to Kipling's Mulvaney, Ortheris and   , u, to say nothing of Edgar Wallace's Smithy and Nobby. The task of the Soviet writer in war-time was to help create a warrior, civil as well as military, who should be steadfast, dutiful, enterprising, individual, unconquerable and conquering. Of course the writer cannot achieve such magic out of nothing, but only if the potentialities that he brings to life are real and latent in his subject. If they are there to be written, so to speak, and if the writer goes to reality to find them and then achieves them realistically. The Soviet writer contributes to the creation of his nation of heroes, but only by himself plunging into and sharing its heroism. It is not in the least surprising, but an incidental part and parcel of the nature of Realism as a style, that the leading Soviet creative writers of the day should for the most part be men working in the front line, sharing the experiences of every front, and that poets, even long relatively silent ones of past pre-revolutionary days such as Vera Inber, should have been woken to eloquence by the experiences of a siege.

It is impossible to doubt the efficiency of the work of these Realists taken as a whole. I will not analyse its effect, future historians may do so. I will merely note as one of the glories of human intellectual creation the influence in inspiring as well as recording the achievements of the Soviet people that has been exerted by the contribution of the Soviet writers.

There are direct, obvious results. For example, a young Leningrad writer wrote a tale of an artillery officer who, happening to pass a playground where children had been killed by German shells, and ascertaining their names, noted them in his diary and thereafter gave orders to his battery, "Revenge for so-and-so—Fire," individualising each salvo. The story was read everywhere and started a furore of imitation, and one may imagine with what augmented care and accuracy gunners fired as they wrought vengeance for the personalised victims of the enemy. Sometimes these results are so obvious that they can even be put into figures, as with the contest of Kazakh bards—or "akyn"—which inspired farmers, workers, engineers in Kazakhstan to rise to unprecedented heights in order that the "akyn" of each locality might have giant achievements to extol and thus a favourable chance to win the contest. One oil derrick gang that was behind its schedule rose to top place after a visit from the bards.

But, of course, of more significance is the all-persuasive subtle influence that inspires indirectly. Tikhonov, the Leningrad writer and poet, tells a remarkable circumstance of one army group where Nikolai Ostrovsky's *The Making of a Hero*—you can see a film based on it to-day in the Charing

Cross Road—"became a sort of evangel." I know no literature-army relationship comparable except perhaps that narrated in Kipling's conspiracy of the "Janeites," but that was a much gentler influence.

Well, Tikhonov writes: "How it began nobody knows. But the novel was read and re-read in every company and battalion. There was once almost a fight between the units on the question of whose turn it was to read the book. One claimed priority because it had killed so many Germans. 'But we killed more than you did,' protested the other. 'So you should, there are more of you,' replied the first, refusing to give way. The commanders even started referring to the new recruits as 'Korchagins'" —the name of the book's hero—"But the title had to be earned. The book took such a hold on the men's imaginations that once, when a company was almost surrounded and had succeeded in fighting its way out, one Red Army man said after the battle: "Phew, that was hot, I don't think I would have managed to stick it if I hadn't felt that old Nikolai Ostrovsky was lying behind that machine-gun on our right flank, helping us out."

And has there ever been a greater compliment paid to a writer than the guerrilla Order of the Day which ran: "Any piece of newspaper may be used as cigarette paper, with the exception of pieces containing Ehrenburg's articles"?

It is with a brief quotation from Ehrenburg that I should like to finish, because I think that it perfectly expresses the pride with which Soviet literature is there, in the front line, fighting, three hundred years after 1644.

"Fascists are killed by metal, it is true, but it is not an abstract wind of history that fans anger in the heart of the soldier who wields the metal. It is weak human breath.

"When he writes of purity and valour, even the most helpless journalist becomes a prophet who burns hearts.

"In these days of super-powerful tanks and many-ton bombs, I still believe in you, the pen, the piece of wood with the metal point, and in you, the human word."

EDWARD CARPENTER

By LEONARD GREEN, M.A. (OXON)

"Truth is compared in Scripture to a streaming fountain; if her waters flow not in a perpetual progression, they sicken into a muddy pool of conformity and tradition. A man may be a heretic in the truth; and if he believe things only because his Pastor says so, or the Assembly so determines, without knowing other reason, though his belief be true, yet the very truth he holds becomes his heresy."—*Areopagitica*.

AT AN AREOPAGITICA CONFERENCE, WHOSE THEME IS: "THE PLACE OF SPIRITUAL and economic values in the future of mankind," a few words on Edward

Carpenter's contribution to freedom of thought and courage of expression will not be out of place.

Carpenter was born at Brighton on the 29th of August, 1844. He died at Guildford on the 28th of June, 1929, and few members of the present generation have ever heard of him. It is odd that one should be celebrating the centenary of someone whom one has known intimately, and loved. It is even more odd that a pioneer, thinker and poet, who has so recently left us, should be so completely forgotten except by those who came into contact with him.

Perhaps it is because the causes for which he stood have been so largely won. The free relationship of the sexes; the recognition of the equality of women in industry and politics; the power and influence of the Labour Party.

I am not sure that he would have regarded the present position of the Labour Party as a fulfilment of his ideals. He never had much use for organisation, or for committees, or for dialectic. His heart was always stronger than his head. That, indeed, is what you would expect of a dreamer and of a poet, but if he had done nothing else except write, as he wrote, the words and music of "England Arise," a battle hymn which used to be sung at every Labour gathering, he would have made his mark on a movement which has developed away from emotion, and become a systematised procedure. It is the inevitable progress from religion to theology.

Like so many others of his educated generation, he took Orders in the Anglican Church. He became a Fellow of Trinity Hall. But his gradual disillusionment with the circumstances of his own comfortable upbringing, (for he belonged to the upper-middle-class with a distinguished naval record amongst his forebears), combined with a growing impatience with mental shackles of all kind, caused him to throw up his Orders and his Fellowship and to go in for university extension lecturing in Sheffield.

He was overwhelmingly drawn to the working classes, and, like his friends, William Morris, Walter Crane, and other stalwarts of that period, he perhaps idealised the dignity of manual labour excessively. On the other hand, it is no bad thing for an intellectualised person to have, at least, to do some household chores, though perhaps most of us, at the present time, are suffering from a surfeit of these domestic dignities.

Carpenter's success with his working-class friends was, however, not due solely to the interest of his lectures but mainly to the ardent love of mankind, and the sense of comradeship, which made him not only a great teacher but a great friend.

The escape from mental anguish and from dissatisfaction with his surroundings, and with himself, was expressed in that bundle of poems: *Towards Democracy*, the theme of which is the immortality of life; the immortality of love; the insignificance of death, except as a natural partner in that great trinity. There is for him no difference of class, of race, of colour, because all life is one, and all men are his brothers.

It is a cheap sneer to say that *Towards Democracy* is "Whitman and

Water." Carpenter, himself, acknowledges the influence of Whitman. He says:

"I met with William Rossetti's little selection from 'Leaves of Grass' in 1868 or 1869, and read that and the original editions continuously for ten years. I never met with any other book (with the exception perhaps of Beethoven's sonatas) which I could read and re-read as I could this one. I find it difficult to imagine what my life would have been without it. 'Leaves of Grass' 'filtered and fibred' my blood: but I do not think I ever tried to imitate it or its style. . . . Whatever resemblance there may be between the rhythm, style, thoughts, constructions, etc., of the two books, must I think be set down to a deeper similarity of emotional atmosphere and intention in the two authors—even though that similarity may have sprung and no doubt largely did spring out of the personal influence of one upon the other."

Some prophets have no sense of humour. Carpenter's sense of humour was keen and pungent. He relates this incident in his autobiography: "A friend suggested that I should put up at the gate a board bearing the legend, 'To the Asylum,' then the real lunatics would avoid the neighbourhood!"

I have referred to his two outstanding qualities being courage and vision. Another instance of his courage (and also of his publishers' courage) was in issuing the two books: *The Intermediate Sex* and *Love's Coming of Age*. In these books Carpenter shed a clear, sane light upon the hidden places of the human heart. I think that perhaps his greatest service to his generation was to explain in simple intelligible language the complexity of the emotions, and, in particular, the complexity of those emotional natures in whom the masculine and the feminine elements are mixed unequally, with all manner of possibility of aberration and even of disaster.

The advance of medical and psychological science tends to reduce man's emotional nature to a matter of endocrinal adjustment, but when all the conditioning and the mechanism is explained away, there still remains the fundamental stuff of one's emotional outlook. It is, of course, a matter of individual preference, but I own I would rather be a poet and a lover than a specialist in the endocrine glands.

Carpenter's understanding and penetrating sympathy made him the recipient of many confidences from people all over the world, and innumerable were the lives that he helped to make orderly and staved from disaster.

It was, I think, largely because he was also a mystic. He had cleared his mind of debris, just as he rejoiced to rid himself of possessions and property, and he was always conscious of that other land—"Where the great voices sound and the visions dwell." To a faith so rooted there is nothing common or unclean in love, and there is nothing terrifying in death.

Of his books, which were many, I think some will live, and I would like to see a three-volume edition issued of which the first volume would be: *My Days and Dreams*; the second would be *Towards Democracy*; and the third would contain excerpts from *Love's Coming of Age*, the *Intermediate Sex*, *The Art of Creation* and the *Drama of Life and Death*.

It is difficult in a few minutes to sum up the life and work of so many-sided a man.

I will finish by reading to you the poem out of *Towards Democracy* that seems to me the most moving, and that expresses most pithily Carpenter's point of view. I read it at Carpenter's funeral.

"INTO THE REGIONS OF THE SUN"

So at last passing (the great sea stilled, the raging ocean)—passing away,
All sorrow left behind, the great intolerable burdens which men vainly try to
carry,
All all abandoned, left there lying—
Suddenly lightened, like a bird that shakes itself free from the limed twigs,
Soaring, soaring, into joy supernal passing,
Lo! the dead we leave behind and pass to the realms of the living.

And not we alone.
By our love poured out, by the manifold threads and strands of attachment to
others—which cannot now be severed;
By not one inwardly refused or disowned whom we have ever met;
By the dear arms of lovers circling each other all night long, by their kisses
and mingled breath,
And love by night and day—thinking of each other when absent, rejoicing so
to be near;
By tramps over the hills, and days spent together in the woods and by watersides;
By our life-long faithful love—(ah! what more beautiful, what in all this world
more precious!)
By the life-long faithful comradeship now springing on all sides, the Theban
band henceforth to overcome the world—its heroisms and deaths—
And him who gave the calamus-token first;
By all these—
Not alone, no longer alone—

But drawing an innumerable multitude with us,
Into the regions of the sun, into the supernal aether,
With love perfected, bodies changed, and joy—ah! joy on earth unutterable—
Lo! the dead we leave behind, and pass to the realms of the living.

A PLEA FOR RATIONALISM

By C. BRADLAUGH BONNER

I COME AS REPRESENTING THE RATIONALIST PRESS ASSOCIATION TO ASK YOU to consider a method, a scientific method, in the study of our present madness. When my Society was asked to support this conference and send a delegate, I confessed that I knew very little about Milton and that I did not understand the subject set for discussion at the conference. It was unanimously decided that I therefore ought to go and learn something; and here I am. Ever since that day I have been turning over in my mind what questions I was going to ask you, and my fate was the common one these days; that, after the buzz-bomb burst I left that blasted place, my home, and sought a tranquil spot far from London. When I got there, I thought for the moment that I had found peace. But the tanks and the bulldozer and the guns came and gave me a foretaste of what Milton would have called Pandemonium, and made my mind turn with considerable longing to the future, the near future, I hope, when there would be a place for other values than those; when the Yank tanks would cease from rumbling, and the poor atheist be at rest. Evidently not a case of detached, but of wishful thinking. So I came here, returned to the place of reception of fly-bombs, in the search of satisfaction, both intellectual and quiet.

I came here yesterday and listened with immense interest to the speeches made, and admired the touch of wizardry that was evident, in that they went widdershins through the order of Holy Writ, beginning with some kind of Revelation and working towards some Genesis. So I am in the line of this incantation that I, too, have started with a revelation. Whether it is worth while remains to be seen.

I said that I knew very little about Milton and one of my colleagues did not see why a Rationalist should support a celebration in favour of Milton, so I turned to my Milton and, if you will permit me a quotation or two, I found these lines:

> What though the field be lost?
> All is not lost—the unconquerable will,
> And study of revenge, immortal hate,
> And courage never to submit or yield;
> And what is else not to be overcome
> That glory never shall his wrath or might
> Extort from me. To bow and sue for grace
> With suppliant knee, and deify his power
> Who from the terror of this arm so late
> Doubted his empire; that were low indeed,
> That were an ignominy, and shame beneath
> This downfall; since, by fate, the strength of gods,
> And this empyreal substance, cannot fail:
> Since, through experience of this great event,
> In arms not worse, in foresight much advanced,
> We may with more successful hope resolve
> To wage by force or guile eternal war,
> Irreconcilable war to our grand foe,
> Who now triumphs, and, in the excess of joy
> Sole reigning, holds the tyranny of heaven.

What words express more powerfully the rejection of authority for which I stand? As you will see, Milton expresses himself elsewhere on much the same lines, and further on I found:

> The mind is its own place, and in itself
> Can make a Heaven of Hell, a Hell of Heaven.

And when I see the sort of Fools' Paradise into which many people these days can withdraw themselves, I am certainly of that Devil's Party which would make them think, endeavour to turn their Heaven into what they probably regard as a kind of Hell.

If I may make a further quotation I would this time give you a definition of Rationalism which was put forward just about forty years ago at an International Congress of Freethinkers in Rome. I will just take a few lines from it:

> "It is not a corpus of doctrine, but a method, which includes the meaning of terms and the reference to previous experience. It cannot allow the right of any Authority to oppose, or impose itself on, reason; nor can it take into account speculations which go beyond the compass of human understanding. The test of reason is applicable not only to current dogmas, but can be employed in the formulation of new ideals. The Freethinker refrains from yielding to the temptation to formulate cut and dried systems, but offers to mankind the unceasing investigation of the truth."

Or, if I may make another quotation, in which Milton made an appeal:

> So much the rather thou, Celestial Light
> Shine inward and the mind through all her powers
> Irradiate; there plant eyes; all mist from thence
> Purge and disperse that I may see and tell
> Of things invisible to mortal sight.

The dispersal of the mists of the obscure by the celestial light of reason.

Milton, then, I claim as a Freethinker and in a book which has recently appeared by Mr. Denis Saurat, *Milton, the Man and Thinker*, which was reviewed in the *Observer* last Sunday, he says:

> Milton's creed, it seems, was a kind of Deism, or pantheism, definitely heretical even by Puritan standards. He did not believe in the duality of body and soul, and therefore only doubtfully believed in individual immortality. As he saw it, the Fall and the Atonement were a struggle that took place in every human being, and it was the struggle between Reason and Passion rather than between good and evil.

So that my first difficulty was solved. As a Rationalist, I could certainly join in the celebration of Milton's work.

My second difficulty was the meaning of the subject set, and I was glad to notice yesterday that a similar difficulty had seemed to beset other speakers. Mr. Stapledon dedicated himself to the elucidation of the meaning of the word "spiritual." He said that all in this hall knew what "spiritual" meant but those outside did not. As I was sitting near the door, I felt that I probably belonged to those outside, and I think he was probably right from the appearance of Harrington Road! When I got home, I therefore looked up the word "spiritual" in two dictionaries which were handy and I found that there were a very large number of definitions. Most of them were connected with "spirit" or defined "spirit" from the ecclesiastical or devotional points of view, or as being concerned with supernatural beings, but I found that the word could mean mental, intellectual, pertaining to the moral feelings, concerning the higher moral qualities, and being characterised by a high degree of thought or feeling. I also heard someone say here yesterday that the word "spirit" came from a word meaning "to breathe." But I imagine from what Mr. Stapledon said that for him "spiritual" meant the action of emotions of which he approved. I hope that is correct. And I suggest that the use of the word "spiritual" in the subject given to us is somewhat misleading. One of those who spoke in the course of the discussion yesterday linked it up with religion and I found a large number of definitions of religion in my dictionaries, only one of which was not connected with some kind of belief in a supernatural Being, and that was: "devotion to some principle; conscientiousness." Well, if it means that in this case, if the word "spiritual" has such a connection, I say it would be simple to use "conscientious" or some other word than the word "spiritual."

I suggest to you that the changes in meaning that have been adopted for words like "spiritual" and "religious" are due in part to a very common mental inertia, to a desire to be like other people, to the fact that so many of us have been brought up to believe that we ought to have some kind of religion and it is a bad thing not to have that religion, and therefore, whatever we think on certain subjects we must adopt the word "religious" or "spiritual" to describe it, and that such people are something like those referred to in the *Areopagitica*, when Milton said a man could be a heretic in the truth and if he believed things only because his pastor said so, or the Assembly, without having any other reason for his belief to be true, yet the very truth he held became his heresy.

A young friend of mine told me that for a thing like religion I must not reason; all that was required was to believe, an act of faith, and I asked whether that would not apply to any kind of belief, to a belief in fetishism, anything whatever—only want to believe, and then you are happy and can go on. Another told me that there were meanings which were worldly and could be tested by reason and others that were divine, which would be revealed at some later date. Now what I am asking you to-day in the assessment of the subject before you is to advise yourselves of things like that. I should like to know what you do think this subject means, that is to say, the place in the near future of economic values and spiritual values, and I suggest, in order to get light, that it may mean the manner in the near future in which man's lot will be moulded by the action, on the one hand, of the supply and demand for things which satisfy man's first needs for living, and on the other hand, the play of his aspirations towards some state of life which he has been taught to consider ideal, praiseworthy. And, if that is so, will the power of the first forces, the economic values, be so great, immediately after the war, as to nullify the latter? Must the economic appetite be satisfied to some degree before our aspirations to something higher can operate at all? And are we so dissatisfied with the possibilities of liberty under the present social system that we prefer some other form of society, possibly some authoritarian or totalitarian form? Or do we consider a step desirable in the direction of the freedom such as is promised by anarchists? That, I hope, we shall hear later in the week. In fact, which is to be the stronger, the urge which we find in us which allows us to live in flocks, to subordinate our own personal considerations to the demands of the majority, or our individual desire for freedom of action? Or can they be combined? I ask you, in trying to arrive at some conclusion, that you should divest yourselves of all conventional notions, if you can, for in the words of the *Areopagitica*, "I fear lest this iron yoke of outward conformity hath left a slavish print upon our necks; the ghost of a linen decency yet haunts us."

FREEDOM OF CONSCIENCE

By ROBERT S. W. POLLARD

I AM SCHEDULED IN THE CONFERENCE PROGRAMME TO PROVIDE SOME REMARKS on "Freedom of Conscience." On looking over my notes last night, I decided that they might equally well be intituled "A Resistance Movement in England."

In an assertion of liberty against a claim of the state, there may be a moral element involved which can be properly regarded as a manifestation of conscience. A defender of some particular civil liberty asserts explicitly or by implication that it would be morally wrong for the authority he is resisting to use its power in some specified way. This stand for freedom of conscience—for the right freely to pass moral judgments on the actions of authority has, from Socrates to the present day, continually challenged the claim, whether of church, king or the modern state, to decide that it knows best, and that if necessary it will coerce the individual.

Each century sees the struggle for liberty continuing on all fronts, but with changing circumstances emphasis is transferred from one to another of them. In the midst of the seventeenth century struggle for religious supremacy, a group arose denying the state's right to exact conformity to any established form of religion. It was Milton who saw that religious freedom involved freedom of expression. In the eighteenth century the conflict became more an attempt to secure this, and with it, the liberty of the Press. This struggle continued well into the nineteenth century, and indeed still goes on, but the main emphasis of the nineteenth century was on freedom of association and meeting, and, in particular, on the right to form trade unions and to hold public meetings. None of these liberties is perfected, and, while up to 1914 they were being extended, the effect of war on liberty was to contract it. I refer to Acts such as the Trade Unions and Trade Disputes Act, 1927, and the Incitement to Disaffection Act, 1934, together with a number of decisions of the law courts.

The growing knowledge in the nineteenth century of the laws of health gave a new point for both individuals and for local communities to the text, "We are members one of another." State intervention to enforce current medical ideas has now achieved so much acceptance that it may surprise many to-day to be reminded that the vaccination law was long and ardently opposed on moral grounds. It was an opposition that enjoyed, moreover, considerable success. By an Act of 1854, vaccination of every child was required before it was three months old, under penalty of 20s. fine, and by an Act of 1867, the defaulting parent was made liable to repeated prosecutions until the child attained the age of fourteen. Whether rightly or wrongly from a medical point of view, the Acts provoked intense opposition which grew until it was successful in getting the law changed. Between 1869 and 1881, Charles Nye was imprisoned nine times for refusing to pay fines, while in Ashford, 1885-1889, Charles Haywood was imprisoned fifty times for fines imposed in respect of four children. The length of imprisonment varied, but was in one case for five weeks. In those days prisons were not what they are now, and there was no classification of offenders. Some of these "criminals" were given oakum to pick and made to walk on the treadmill. During the ten years ending August, 1889, 11,408 persons were fined for breach of the vaccination laws. In 1876, the Keighley Board of Guardians refused to enforce the vaccination laws despite a mandamus from the High Court, and were committed to prison for contempt of Court. And thousands of children remained unvaccinated. It was found impossible to enforce the law, and, after appointing a Royal Commission in 1889, the Government passed the Vaccination Act of 1898, allowing exemption from vaccination if the parents satisfied two lay magistrates or a stipendiary magistrate that they conscientiously believed that it would be prejudicial to the child's health. This did not prove satisfactory, since it left magistrates free, if they had no wish to be impartial, to declare themselves unsatisfied. The later Act of 1907, still in force, allows exemption if a statutory declaration to the same effect is made within four months of the child's birth, with the result that now more parents sign the declaration than have their children vaccinated.

No one now knows the names of these obscure objectors. But here we have what was supposed to be a major sanitary measure defeated by the common people of England. The genuine anti-vaccinator, in fact, said to the state: "I do not believe that vaccination is a protection, and I deny your right to compel my child to suffer it."[1] Of the same kind, though less effective, was resistance to the payment of an education rate, imposed

---

[1] See Joseph P. Swann: *The Vaccination Problem.* C. W. Daniel. 1936.

under the Education Act, 1902, which enabled the State to give financial assistance to Anglican schools. The furniture of objectors was distrained upon and sold. Since friends often brought it back, neither State nor objectors were always much the worse for the transaction. The latter were not, on the whole, quite so tough as the anti-vaccinators, though probably much more self-conscious. Yet both, I think, were in the true line of succession.

The typical twentieth-century contributor to this curious principle of social development is the conscientious objector to military service. He is, I am convinced, performing the same service for the cause of liberty as did those who have struggled for other liberties, and I submit that his record by and large stands up well to the comparison. The origin of the demand for this particular personal freedom may be found in the Society of Friends, who, from their formation in the seventeenth century, not only demanded and helped to win religious freedom and established, by the famous trial of Penn and Meade, the right of a jury to give its verdict without dictation from the Bench, but also denied the right of the State to force men to kill. Quakers who were seamen were from time to time in the seventeenth and eighteenth centuries seized by the press gang and persecuted when they refused to serve. In 1694, Thomas Chalkley, as a boy of nineteen, was "seized near his Southwark home, brought on board ship and thrown into the hold, where his physical discomfort was overshadowed by his moral shrinking from the 'dark and hellish' conversation of his fellow prisoners. When the longed-for morning came and they were brought on deck, the lieutenant asked him whether he would serve the King. 'I answered that I was willing to serve him in my business, and according to my conscience; but as for war or fighting Christ forbid it in His excellent Sermon on the Mount: and for that reason I could not bear arms, nor be instrumental to destroy or kill man.' Then the Lieutenant looked on me and on the people and said, 'Gentlemen, what shall we do with this fellow? He swears he will not fight.' The commander of the vessel made answer, 'No, no, he will neither swear nor fight.' Upon which they turned me on shore." During the two Jacobite rebellions, Quakers refused to serve in the Militia. Special provision was made by the Militia Acts for the goods of refusing Quakers to be distrained or to provide a substitute.

Meanwhile in Pennsylvania, the Quaker State granted freedom to all who "confessed and acknowledged the One Almighty and Eternal God to be the Creator, Upholder and Ruler of the world, and held themselves obliged in conscience to live justly and peaceably in civil society." The provisions in Charles II's charter giving William Penn power to train men in arms for use against savages and robbers were omitted from the founder's own constitution, "A Frame of Government." The Quaker Assembly constantly refused to vote money for military purposes, gave general grants on condition they were not "dipt in blood" and were, I fear, in continual opposition to the Governor. Perhaps to us it is strange that until 1756, when Quaker control of the colony ceased, Pennsylvania was able to live in peace with the Indians, while bloody wars raged in other parts of America.[1]

With the first world war, the problem of compulsory military service returned in a much heightened form. The State recognised the claim for freedom conscientiously to object by the Military Service Act of 1916 and tribunals were set up, before which objectors to compulsory military service might appear. These tribunals were profoundly unsatisfactory, and frequently disregarded the law both in spirit and in letter. An example of the type of tribunal member appointed is a chairman who said to a young man explaining the meaning of a certain passage of the Bible in the Greek, "You don't mean to tell me that Jesus Christ spoke Greek—he was British to the backbone." A military representative asserted that Jesus said, "an eye for an eye and a tooth for a tooth." Some 5,970 conscientious objectors were rejected by the tribunals, but were able to show their sincerity by enduring repeated court martials and imprisonment and some physical ill-treatment while in the army,[2] in which they were "deemed to have duly enlisted."

At the same time, the conscientious objectors of 1914-1918 strove for other liberties.[3] They or their organisations were frequently prosecuted for publishing or distributing pamphlets and other literature. Their paper was confiscated, and remarkably efficient underground arrangements were made for its publication.

This struggle for freedom of conscience began again with the passing of the Military Training Act, 1939, and the later National Service Acts, which again set up tribunals, but this time in a much more equitable form. Some 60,000 conscientious objectors have been dealt with by tribunals, and, apart from the natural disadvantages of a body of persons trying in a limited time to judge a stranger's conscience, their decisions have been more acceptable to the conscientious objectors appearing before them than were those of tribunals during the last war. More than in 1916, the tribunals have maintained their independence from the state apparatus of coercion, but they have, nevertheless, perhaps inevitably, tended to sympathise with authority, and to take action to ensure that, if a conscientious objector will not join the army, he shall at any rate do something which, in fact, is helping the nation's effort. However, since modern war is totalitarian, it would probably be impossible, whatever action he took, for an objector to escape indirect participation in some form. Despite these provisions, fairer and better as they are than in any dominion or allied country, 2,424 objectors up to the 30th June, 1944, have been prosecuted for refusing medical examination, 772 in the army have been court-martialled (86 of them three times or more), 1,287 have appeared before magistrates

[1] See Margaret E. Hirst. "*The Quakers in Peace & War.*" Allen & Unwin 1923.

[2] J. W. Graham: *Conscription and Conscience.* Allen and Unwin. 1922.

[3] See my *Conscience and Liberty.* Allen and Unwin. 1940.

for refusing industrial conscription, Home Guard or Civil Defence, and 372 women have been prosecuted for refusing to take part in some national activity.[1]

The state now recognizes that opposition to its views on war is based on grounds wider than the rather narrowly religious ones of the seventeenth and eighteenth centuries, and in this country the recognition of conscientious objection to military service neither in 1916 nor in 1939 has been limited to religious objectors, as is the case in the U.S.A. A conscientious objection may have all kinds of origins, although the final decision will be the same. The Appellate Tribunal recently registered a man as a C.O. whose objection was to fighting in this war only, and was derived from his Indian Nationalist views. He was a member of Congress. In other words, the moral element is now often realised to be the essential factor in this sort of situation.

Where will the struggle for freedom of conscience next take shape? If, as is threatened by the militarists, military conscription continues after the war, conscientious objection to it will continue. But the modern state, apart from war, is increasing its control of economic and social life, and this inevitably carries with it more control over individuals. The vaccination question was merely an early example of the sort of difficulty likely to arise. Before the war the Unemployment Insurance Acts authorised the stoppage of benefit if the claimant refused work in a new occupation. Under Defence (General) Regulation 58A, made under the Emergency Powers (Defence) Acts, there is already complete industrial conscription during the war, since the Minister of Labour can direct any person of whatever age, sex or nationality to do any work at wages and under conditions decided by the Minister. There is no conscience clause, but there is a right of appeal against such a direction of a National Service Officer of the Ministry of Labour to a Local Appeal Board. This right, however, is not worth much, since the officer need not implement the Board's findings. Moreover, at the appeal, appellants are denied skilled assistance in presenting their cases. Under this power, accountants and teachers have been put on land work, and there has been little or no protection against arbitrary administration. Four hundred and fifty-six men and 250 women have been prosecuted for refusing directions on grounds of conscience. A planned economy, whether socialist or capitalist, would find some such power very useful. Can this claim of the state be accepted?

The present situation is very different from that existing in Bensalem, described by Viscount Samuel in his *An Unknown Land*[2], where compulsory work known as "duties" amounted to only nine hours each week. There, "duties" involving unpleasant work were often less than nine hours a week, and were distributed among a larger number of workers. People spent

---

[1] Figures supplied by The Central Board for Conscientious Objectors.

[2] Allen and Unwin. 1942.

the rest of the time upon "secondary" occupations entirely free from intervention. Citizens were not even bound to their compulsory occupations for their lifetime, but could often change them. We have not, however, reached that happy condition, and are not likely to attain it for many years. Even if hours of labour were reduced to forty or under, the earning of a livelihood would still occupy the major portion of a man's time and energy. Is the artist, the writer, the person with a sense of vocation, whether religious, political or social, to permit the state to decide his life work for him, overriding what he believes it should be? Will not conscientious objection arise in industry, denying the state its right to decide against a man's better judgment how he shall spend the greater part of his time? Will at least a few men and women not believe and say that it is morally wrong for the state to interfere in such cases by exercising compulsion, and that if the state wants to interfere with the labour market it must do it by other means, such as careful adjustment of economic rewards and other inducements, the provision of public recognition and honours, propaganda (and not too much of that), the inculcation of a sense of public responsibility and duty in citizens through education and the home? And even there we shall have to be on our guard against a blind "conditioning" of the child. On the other hand, the state may say that, in administering schemes of social insurance, it must establish conditions and standards of conduct which the socially irresponsible must observe. It is obvious that such people exist. Can a plea of conscience be legally permitted behind which slackers may shelter? Is the solution to be found on the lines of conscientious objectors' tribunals?

I have asked a number of questions which are very difficult to answer. This, and the problem of liberty of expression in a planned economy with collective control of theatres, cinemas, publishing, the press and radio, seem to me two of the main problems which believers in liberty will have to face in the future, and it is urgent that groups such as this of creative workers, who will be most sensitive to such interference, should give thought to it now.

I hope I should be the last to echo the dishonestly expressed fears of the reactionary press that this may become at long last "the century of the common man." I have shown that the common man centuries ago found other means than war to express his conviction that there is a moral justification for the liberty of the individual. He also, therefore, as well as you yourselves may find Milton's *Second Defence of the People of England* not without its current application: "If after being released from the toils of war you neglect the arts of peace—if war be your only virtue, the summit of your praise, you will soon find peace the most adverse to your interests. Your peace will only be a more distressing war: and that which you imagined liberty will prove the worst of slavery . . . you will find that you have cherished a more stubborn and intractable despot at home than you ever encountered in the field."

SOME INTERNATIONAL ASPECTS OF ADULT EDUCATION

By G. W. KEETON, M.A., LL.D.

I HAVE RECENTLY BEEN READING A GOOD DEAL OF LITERATURE WRITTEN AT the close of the first world war upon the general theme of adult education, and I have been struck with the fact that, although the writers approach the problem from widely-differing viewpoints, nevertheless certain closely associated ideas recur in all their writings. These ideas have a close connection with the occasion for this conference, for they are the ideas which generally underlie Milton's *Areopagitica*. First and foremost, there is the idea of freedom of thought, without which serious writing and adult education are alike valueless. The second general idea is that of democracy, which was seen essentially as a political problem in 1919, but which we realise to-day has economic and social implications also. The third idea is that of world peace and the maintenance of the spirit of co-operation for the general good, as much in international as in national affairs. Each of the writers was convinced that these three ideas, which I have imperfectly expressed, were among the main objectives for which we had been fighting, and every writer also was clear that all three had been threatened by German militarism. With German militarism apparently finally destroyed, the way was clear for the fuller realisation of all three ideas in human affairs. Finally, each of the writers emphasised that this could only be achieved if adult education were developed to an extent not contemplated before 1914, and furthermore, that adult education must not be undertaken in a spirit of national exclusiveness or from a purely partisan viewpoint. It must be broad in outlook and content, and it implied a capacity among the wide classes in all nations to give prolonged consideration to the main problems affecting social and international concord.

It is a salutary corrective against over-optimism to-day to remember that in the inter-war period a ruthless and successful assault was made upon all three ideas in the major nations of the Continent of Europe, as well as in Japan, where "dangerous thoughts" (which obviously could mean anything displeasing to the controlling clique) became a punishable offence, for which some of Japan's progressive thinkers and writers have already lost their lives. Never was a movement for the improvement of humanity, and its liberation from intellectual chains undertaken with so much enthusiasm by so many ardent spirits—not even during the Renaissance in the sixteenth century—and never has such an endeavour so completely collapsed before the irresistible power and all-embracing demands of the totalitarian State. It is a position which would have been unimaginable to Milton, three hundred years ago, chafing at the restraints reimposed by Presbyterians, when the censorship of the Prelates had been destroyed, and it gives renewed significance to the often-quoted statement that the victories of freedom are never finally won. Each age must assert the rights of humanity afresh against newer and sometimes more subtle challenges than those with which preceding ages were faced.

To-day, as we look at the wreckage and desolation which Hitler has substituted for civilisation in Continental Europe, we realise that adult education completely failed to achieve its purpose in the inter-war period, and that it failed most conspicuously in Germany where, on paper, at least, it reached its maximum European development during the existence of the Weimar Republic. But exactly as Germany was unable to derive strength from any inner spiritual conviction to resist the onset of Nazi-ism, and the progressive liquidation of all rival bodies, so in the cultural sphere, the adult education movement of Germany collapsed when the elaborate support afforded to it by the State was either withdrawn or turned to avowedly Nazi purposes after 1933. The German adult education movement, that is to say, lacked that spiritual fire which would have aided it to maintain its integrity in face of Nazi pressure; and this, in spite of the fact that the ordinary citizens of Germany were as well-informed upon current problems as any in the world before 1933. It is possible, therefore, to trace a close connection between a sound adult education movement, based upon a free Press and vital voluntary organisations, and a healthy political democracy. It is no accident that the strongest adult education movements in the world have long been those of Great Britain, the British Dominions, Norway and Sweden; and it is also only natural that in these countries, the State has contented itself in the main with aiding the efforts of the universities and the voluntary bodies, and has refrained from prescribing either the form or the content of the education which its adult citizens will receive.

The present war has seen enormous changes in prevailing ideas upon adult education, and once again there is a demand for more comprehensive provision at the end of the struggle, and for the same reasons as those which were advanced at the end of the first world war. This time, however, there is a note of greater urgency in the demand, for in the occupied countries, those who would naturally take the lead in the development of the national culture have been singled out for torture and death, so that several of them will be building afresh and with difficulty from the foundations to a degree that was not apparent before, whilst it is universally recognised that Germany presents a problem in adult education of bewildering complexity and size. Yet, if that problem is not solved, the outlook for world peace is bleak. It is a problem upon which writers and teachers will have to concentrate for the next fifteen or twenty years, for the peaceful development of Europe depends upon the restoration of that consciousness of a common civilisation which Stephan Zweig described so sensitively in *The World of Yesterday*. Whilst it is obvious that in so far as Germany is concerned, the part played by adult education (in the stricter sense) will be a limited one, as compared with the parts played by the

cinema, literature, and art; and also, whilst it is also clear that the
re-education of the German people is essentially a German task, nevertheless
the part of adult education will be an important one, and it is worth while
examining what it can do, and how it might do it. It will be essential that
this time Germany's adult education activities should be firmly based upon
a democratic and peace-loving tradition. It may, perhaps, be asserted that
this was exactly what it was hoped was done last time, but the facts of the
last ten years abundantly prove how thin that veneer was. It covered an
unrepentent nationalism which, if less virulent than Hitler's, was as deep-
rooted, and offered little or no effective resistance to the onrush of Nazi-ism.
In saying this, I am aware that there were some fine exceptions, mainly
outside Prussia, but their numbers and influence were small in comparison
with the total of effort.

However we look at it, the next fifteen or twenty years will see a bitter
struggle for the soul of Germany, waged under the most difficult conditions. The result of that struggle will determine whether Germany can
become a peaceful and valuable element in European civilisation, or whether
she must remain outlawed, with the hand of every European nation
potentially raised against her. In that struggle, which is, in the broadest
sense, a struggle towards the re-education of the entire German people, we
shall need to enlist the aid of every constructive force inside Germany,
whether it be that of a religious community, or of a trade union; and we
shall need the aid of every modern vehicle for the interchange of ideas,
and especially we shall need the aid of the Press, the radio and the cinema.
For more than twelve years, Germany has been a closed room. We must
open it to the stimulating currents of unregimented thought, in the hope
that the intellectual vigour of the German people will react in the way in
which alone Europe can enjoy a peaceful and prosperous future. Education,
therefore, in the broad sense, and more particularly adult education, is a
vitally important element in a durable peace, but it must be emphasised
that the contribution which it can make is a limited one, and that there
will be little value in developing intellectual attitudes of reconciliation
and development unless the political and economic policies of victors have
a similar objective. This, I need hardly stress, is a problem quite distinct
from that of the war-guilt of the German people, or that of the proper
treatment of German war criminals.

An almost equally great responsibility attaches to the leaders of thought
in the countries of occupied Europe, and also in Great Britain, the United
States and the U.S.S.R. There can be little surprise that after the horrors,
destruction, and intolerance of this war, the creed of retaliation should
attract a wide allegiance; nor will it be a matter of surprise if there are
instances of excesses, as distinct from acts of retribution, in the hour of
victory. We shall deceive ourselves if we expect that at the end of this
war we shall forthwith step into an ordered and peaceful world. Nevertheless, I consider it to be the primary function of all those who have some
share in the formation of public opinion and national policies to emphasise,

as never before, enduring values in social relations. What we are seeing at the present stage of the world's history is nothing more or less than a world revolution, as Mr. Sumner Welles, in his recently published book, *The Time for Decision*, has indicated, and the responsibility for the direction which that revolution eventually takes will depend primarily upon those who mould the opinion in those communities in whom the power to reshape the world will rest at the end of the war. It can be developed in one of two ways—in a spirit of narrow nationalism or in a spirit of world organisation. In other words, the link between education, purposive literature and international peace has never been so close as it is at the present moment. A second failure to solve the major problems of our time would produce consequences too calamitous to contemplate with equanimity, and to-day there is no part of the population of the entire globe which can afford to look upon these problems with any kind of detachment at all. There is no community anywhere which has not been profoundly shaken-up by the impact of this all-embracing war; and whole continents have been opened up in a few years to a degree which would have taken generations of peace-time development. The effects of this upon policy may be studied as far as British colonies in Africa are concerned, in the excellent report prepared by a committee of the Colonial Office, entitled *Mass Education in Africa*, which contemplates a comprehensive scheme of adult education, including not only the achievement of literacy, but also of social responsibility and political development, intimately linked with far-reaching changes in material environment, such as no Government department within the British Empire has ever considered previously. This is the direct consequence of new conceptions of colonial empire which have developed during the war in response to frank, and sometimes not over-friendly, criticism from the United States, but this changed attitude opens up a whole continent to cultural development, the future consequences of which are at present unpredictable. Who, for example, would have believed, eighty years ago, that the impact of the West upon Japan, would have led ultimately to a major war in the Pacific, or on the other hand, that the collapse of the Tsarist Empire in 1917 would have been succeeded, a quarter of a century later, by the most prodigious exertion of military strength that the world has yet seen, engineered by the unconquerable spirit of the Soviet Union, firmly based as it is upon the spiritual awakening of the united peoples of that great federation? Developments so tremendous in the past foreshadow the momentous changes which are now taking place, and call for a revision of our existing conceptions of what is possible in world organisation. They also emphasise survival of an anachronistic narrow parochialism in a world in which, without undue effort, you can breakfast in Washington, and dine in Piccadilly, or in which natives of the interior of Africa fight in Burmese jungles in the same military operations as Chinese from the recesses of Shensi.

I have mentioned the great project of mass education which the Colonial Office has prepared for the African colonies when the war ends. This, however, is merely one of several tremendous tasks of this kind which cannot be postponed. There are even bigger ones to be undertaken in India and China, whilst throughout those countries of the Far East which are now in Japanese occupation, the Japanese are making tremendous efforts to eradicate all traces of Western influence, and to substitute the ascendancy of Japanese culture, so that Japanese influence may persist, even when Japan is defeated. Very little attention is at present being paid to this very serious problem. For that reason, I may perhaps be forgiven if I quote the opening paragraph of an article which I contributed in December last to *The Journal of Education*:

"A recent article in *The Times* has drawn attention to the earnest and far-reaching efforts which the Japanese are making in the vast areas now under their control to spread and perpetuate their cultural influence. The article is extremely timely. We have with difficulty freed our minds from the fallacy that the Japanese are inferior in the craft of war to the greatest or Western nations—a fallacy which brought in its train defeats more humiliating than British arms have been called upon to suffer for over a century and a half, and which will not be without influence upon the relations of the West with the Far East, even when the present war is won. To-day, however, we are in danger of falling victims to a second, and equally serious, fallacy—that after the Japanese have been expelled from the areas they occupy, we can somehow return in fundamentals to the old relationship between East and West which existed before December 7th, 1941. Coupled with this is the delusion that Japanese cultural efforts are primitive, contemptible, and even semi-humorous, so that they can on that account be ignored. Nothing could be further from the truth, and it is known that the Chinese Nationalist Government is very seriously concerned at the headway which the Japanese are now making amongst the Chinese populations in the occupied areas. The Japanese have one immensely powerful weapon of propaganda—their appeal to Eastern peoples to free themselves from the exploitation of the white race. That this may be no more than an exchange of comparatively tolerant masters, political and economic, for a ruthless machine of exploitation, operating in the interests of a fanatical racial superiority, may be apparent to one or two of the more thoughtful readers of Far Eastern peoples, but it is completely unknown to the millions of peasants to whom all Government has in the past been a synonym for exploitation, and it would probably take upwards of half a century for them to find out. Moreover, the Japanese have the immense advantage of being an Asiatic race, which has assiduously devoted itself for half a century to the task of informing itself of the mentality, aspirations, prejudices and defects of those peoples with whose assistance it hoped to achieve world domination. Many of the Japanese fifth columnists with whom the Philippines, Netherlands-India, and Malaya abounded even before the outbreak of war were as much interested in the social and cultural possibilities of these areas as they were with politics, economics and military intelligence. The Japanese have made lengthy and complete preparations for the present war, which they expect to be a very long one. They also anticipate that before it is ended they will have so permeated the life of the peoples under their control that they will have eradicated all Western influences, and replaced them with Japanese cultural notions. They are making a determined effort to replace English as a second language, and as the universal language of commerce, with that most improbable of all commercial media—Japanese. It is possible they think that if the war should have any other termination than their own unconditional surrender (which no Japanese regards as a serious possibility) the headway they have made during the years of occupation will permit them to continue the struggle during the years of instability which would follow a negotiated peace. Finally, it should be noticed that the Japanese are learning from the Nazis' mistakes. They are making a determined attempt to win the confidence of the peoples of the occupied areas.

They are also paying attention to groups whom no Western community, with the possible exception of the missionaries, have regarded as worthy of prolonged attention. For that reason, accounts such as those which appeared in *The Times* recently, of an influx of Japanese educators into the Philippines and Malaya, of Greater East Asia Medical and Literary Conferences in Tokyo, of East Asiatic students being given grants to study in Japan, and of new universities and technical schools being founded in occupied areas, should be weighed very carefully indeed by the United Nations. Here is a problem of the very first magnitude. It will continue to exist even after Japan has been defeated."

In the article from which that is an extract, I was dealing exclusively with the problem presented by Japanese occupation of wide areas of the Far East. There is, however, an equally serious one presented by Japan herself. It is quite evident that whilst Japan to-day has acquired all the technical proficiency which the West can teach her, spiritually she remains fundamentally as antagonistic to the West as she was a century ago. Most persons with knowledge of the Far East agree that the defeat of Japan will be followed by a revolution which will dig right down to the foundations of her social structure. What the upshot of that revolution will be, no one as yet can foretell with any degree of certainty, but it is quite obvious that unless Japan is to present us with a similar problem in the Pacific to that which Germany has presented in the West during the past three-quarters of a century, one of the results of that revolution must be a closer spiritual accord with Europe and America than Japan has hitherto achieved.

I have mentioned only one or two of the major tasks which must be undertaken by adult education in the period of reconstruction which will follow this war. They are so important that they would merit a special section of the United Nations organisation to deal with cultural development and relations. I do not want to be misunderstood in this, however. I do not want a United Nations' Ministry of Information. I firmly believe that our way of life requires no such official participation in what are essentially tasks to be discharged in other ways. But I can conceive that a United Nations' counterpart of the British Council might supply a widely felt need. To it might be entrusted the encouragement in the broad sphere of culture, of those ideas for which we have been fighting, and which we must now realise on the world scale, if we are to realise them at all. To such an organisation, organisations such as those we represent to-day might properly turn for support in the tasks which I have mentioned very briefly.

There are two organisations with which I am connected which have a special interest in the things which I have been discussing, and I would like to crave your indulgence for mentioning them briefly this afternoon. The World Association for Adult Education was founded immediately after the last war, under the inspiration of Dr. Albert Mansbridge, to whom British adult education owes so much. In the address which led to its foundation, Dr. Mansbridge said:

"A League of Nations has been conceived and constructed under the stress of war and a realisation of the destructive powers generated by men. The British Empire has been gathered together during the last centuries by the energy, persistence, and wisdom of our peoples, and can only be held together by the development of common understandings set in common friendship. If this be true of the British Empire, how much more true it is of the League of Nations. The demand of the time is that men living in different countries, who are eager and active in the performance of any specific necessary work, shall seek to make friends with one another and to share the results of their experience and investigations. This, quite simply, is the aim of the World Association, so far as adult education is concerned. The League of Nations is, as it were, a rope made up of many strands—Adult education is one of those strands, and by no means the least important."

In the inter-war years, the World Association had to its credit an extremely impressive record of work successfully accomplished all over the world, and it was the only body which fostered international contacts between adult education movements for the promotion of a stronger sense of our common intellectual inheritance. But the rabid nationalism of the period immediately preceding the outbreak of the present war limited its sphere of usefulness, and curtailed the support which it should have received. In the post-war world, the World Association ought to play a great part, but in order to do so, it needs a greater measure of support than it enjoys to-day.

The second organisation which I represent is the London Institute of World Affairs, which will be holding an Autumn School upon Some Main Problems of the Peace Settlement and Afterwards at University College, London, in the first two weeks of September. The Institute is now in the eleventh year of its existence. It was founded as an international institute for the study of problems of international order, democracy, and social justice, and it is attempting, as far as its means permit, to realise the ideals which I set out in a pamphlet entitled *The Case for an International University*. It is hoping in the post-war period to develop the characteristics of an international club and educational centre, and it has agreed to work in closest association with the World Association. Once again, however, we need a substantial increase in membership if we are to realise our aims, which, in the case of both organisations, are to play our proper part in the vast programme of adult education which must be undertaken if the human mind is to be deflected from the work of world-wide destruction which modern war necessarily implies to world-wide co-operation which Mr. Wells, one of the former Presidents of this Association, has so trenchantly and so frequently pointed out, must be established, and quickly, if the human race is to escape final calamity.

LIBERTY IN SOCIETY

By Salvador de Madariaga, M.A.

THE TIME AT OUR DISPOSAL IS SHORT AND THE THEME IS VAST, BUT I THINK I must devote a few minutes, since I am in this house, first to remember our friend Saurat, away convalescing from a wound and shock received in conditions you all know, and send him our best greetings. Then to celebrate the liberation of Paris by the Parisians themselves. If I were to indulge in all I feel and you feel about this, no time would be left for the rest of what I have to say, so I shall pass on.

First, a few words about Milton and the *Areopagitica*, since, after all, that is supposed to be the occasion, maybe the pretext, of our meeting. As I see it, there are at least two reasons which would fully justify our celebration of Milton and the *Areopagitica* as great achievements in the history of freedom of thought and of expression of thought. The first is that at no time that I know of was that noble cause expressed more nobly in greater words and with finer music, and, after all, though I know some hold other opinions, the P.E.N. Club is supposed to be composed of artists, and it is to artistry that our first allegiance should go. As an artist Milton stands supreme and as the artist battling with artistry for freedom in expression of thought, he stands more supreme than anyone else. Then again, he would also deserve to be remembered as a man who never put his personal convenience in the foreground, who never deflected under the attraction of authority or the even more insidious attraction of popularity the plain and direct expressing his thought. From that point of view I am sure you would all agree that Milton also deserves to be here celebrated. I should add, and I hope I shall not be misunderstood, that so far as I can see, there the merits of Milton as an apostle of freedom end. For, by other criteria, I think he failed to live up to our standards of what an apostle of freedom of thought should be. Firstly, I do not think that his thought was vigorous enough, strong enough, in fundamentals. One generation after Bacon, and one century after my countryman, Vives, who formulated Baconian principles as clearly as Bacon in 1526, Milton in 1673 was still putting forward authority, and not merely authority but Bible authority, as the standard of truth. And although you may say: "What matters the quality of thought, on condition that the freedom of its expression is assured?" and although there is something in that, I believe that it is dangerous to listen to one who claims freedom of thought in the name of an orthodoxy, for, on the moment when that orthodoxy gets hold of authority, freedom of thought will disappear again. Measured by that standard it does not seem to me that Milton is an apostle of freedom of thought.

There is another standard, the willingness to grant to others that freedom of thought that you want for yourself; and from that point of view I am not certain that Milton satisfies us. Indeed, I am tempted to think he did not. For again, while in 1644 he fought in the *Areopagitica*, as you all know he did, for freedom of thought and of its expression, in the pamphlet on *Religion, Heresy and How to stop Popery in England*, in 1673, he definitely declared against tolerating what he calls Popery; and, while there might be some temptation to agree on the basis of the principle of the French philosopher, Renouvier, that you cannot be tolerant towards the intolerant, it is a dangerous road in which to engage; Milton took it and it made him intolerant towards a form of opinion with which he was not in sympathy.

Finally, there is a third aspect under which I am not quite sure that Milton was as good an apostle of freedom of thought as he might have been: he did not quite keep his thought clean enough from his passions. You are all familiar with the fact that he bethought himself of the importance of divorce when he found it necessary to divorce his wife. That line of criticism that Milton's thought is the sublimation of his passions, can be consistently established. Indeed our friend Saurat has gone a good way to establishing it in his book. But there is another aspect of the influence and deflection of the passions on Milton's thought which is even more unpleasant; I mean his tendency to attack his adversaries in terms and on a level unworthy of the great, the majestic poet of *Paradise Lost* and *Lycidas*. In his polemic with Saumaise he demeans himself—no matter how his adversary demeans himself—into arguing with insults; a practice which is one of the most dangerous enemies of freedom of thought and freedom of expression of thought that could be imagined. For, of course, the worst enemies of freedom are always inside and not outside.

So much for the figure and the book that are the occasion of our gathering. But before I leave him I should wish to observe that Milton found it necessary, indeed how necessary, to defend freedom of thought and freedom of the Press in 1644, taking up work done by a Greek 300 years before Christ in the same direction, and that here we are in 1944, 300 years later, and can we say that freedom of thought is assured in our world? Here, in one of the countries with the cleaner, perhaps the cleanest record in the matter, here you may be or feel about safe. If there were any doubts about it it would not be for me to raise them, since I came here in search of freedom, and in my own country my own books are banned from circulation and import. But I do feel that these facts, that we are now, in most countries, and we may be in fewer countries in a few months, but perhaps in more countries in a few years, in more or less the state in which England was in Milton's days, show the pre-eminence of the problem; as they prove also that freedom of thought is not a conquest of human nature that remains once it has been won and goes on to better itself; but that, on the contrary, freedom of thought is a form of living, a form of collective living, which can only be ensured by constant watching, and even then often falls short of itself and has to be fought over again. So the problem arises, is it normal, is it natural, is it good? May it not be that we, all of us who are in favour of it, are mistaken and that freedom of thought and, in general, liberty, is a will-of-the-wisp, is a phantasy, something that neither individual man nor the collective life called society can ever hope to achieve on a permanent basis because there is no reality in it? That is why the problem of liberty in society must be before us and must be re-examined by us every time in the light of the general run of the principles, trends, modes of thinking, prejudices indeed, which at any moment may circulate.

So far as I am concerned, I feel that the problem has been obscured far too often by the tendency to imagine that collective life can be explained by simple principles and particularly can be reduced to one simple school of thought, let it be Liberalism or Communism, Socialism or Authority or Anarchism; and perhaps by an insufficient realisation of the fact that in the life of man the demands of these two forms, man as an individual, and the society of men, which, as a matter of fact, cannot be imagined separately, have each an ultimate value which thought cannot reconcile under a general idea or principle, and can only be gotten together empirically as we jumble along in life. If you would allow me a simile, I should say that the position is very similar—not identical—with the position of physics between the atom and the wave. There is the wave theory to explain things in physical matter and there is the atomic theory. The atomic theory presents events as the movements of individual agents called atoms, and the wave theory presents events as motions in wave form. The one cannot explain the whole of physical life; the other one cannot, either. But by a combination of the two we can get a pretty good view of what matter is and, what is of more import, a certain amount of prevision. Man knows as much as he can do, says Francis Bacon; therefore if we can foresee events, thanks to all this system, it is good enough for us. The number of persons that go from one town to another in a year obeys certain wave-rules, even if every one of those who go, goes according to his free volition. The approach of our mind must be twofold: psychology on the one hand, statistics on the other; the first, corresponding to the individual atom; the second to the mass-wave.

When dealing with the problem of liberty, as I fancy it, we are in this advantageous position, that we can justify liberty equally from the point of view of the individual and from the point of view of collective life. From the point of view of the individual liberty justifies itself very simply, starting from the fact that the individual is the ultimate, or at any rate, one of the two ultimates. As I am now dealing with it I call it the ultimate. It is so much the ultimate that even society can only express itself through individuals. Whatever you may call a Committee or State or Parliament or Assembly, there is always some Tom, Dick or Harry who speaks for that thing. Moreover, apart from collective life expressed through individuals, there is in each individual something which is not interchangeable, something which is unique, never to be reproduced exactly, something which makes some of us suspect, others know (if they have the faith) that there is an eternal existence in the individual; even if the idea of survival is not one that convinces us, we do not know enough about the nature of man, we do not know enough about the essential or non-essential value of the individual life that we possess in this world to pronounce ourselves as to eternity. And in that case we can, with Pascal, choose the brighter side of doubt and say, "Anyway, no one can prove that we are not essential and eternal, even if there is no survival for this very life here may be eternal in some way we are not aware of." Therefore the meanest man that lives is sacred and this is one of the great principles which we have retained in our modern life possibly strengthened after the three great Revolutions, the English, the American and the French, but which was first planted in the Western consciousness by Christianity. From that point of view, from that basis, flows the necessity of liberty, from that sacred element which exists in the humblest man. And not perhaps so much, as the fashion goes to-day, so that he can express himself and rise and succeed, but so that he can search and possibly err and maybe fall, but succeed inwards and realise himself; a far more important point of view than that which would see the key to the realisation of the personality in external success, in climbing the ladder of society.

While personally, then, I should put the value and the foundation of liberty for the individual on the worth of the meanest man, I should be tempted to put the value of liberty for society on the unworthiness of the greatest man. Society cannot fully know itself. Indeed, this is obvious, since even man cannot fully know himself. Society cannot know itself and the only approach to knowledge which may enable a society to live not quite as a lunatic asylum is through study of collective life. Now the complexity, the subtlety, the vastness of collective life around us is so monstrously out of proportion with the powers of even the cleverest of us that nothing but the free exchange of trials and errors of all the men of good will in society can bring that knowledge of itself, or at least that attempt at knowledge of itself which is indispensable for society to live in a sane way. So that a free exchange of thought, through printing, radio and the rest, and a free association and a free discussion are elements which are co-substantial with the life of a society. No society that is put under an orthodoxy can prosper, because no orthodoxy, however clever, can ever hope to express the complexities of a society which, being life, is bound to escape the squares and triangles of the net of thought. These two opposing principles, the worth of man and the unworthiness of man, seem to me to be the fundamental principles that nothing can change on which to establish liberty.

It follows that in life, in collective life, liberty need not be justified at any point. The only point that has to be justified at every stage is the limitation of liberty. The process therefore should not be, as it was for historical reasons in the old days, that the central authority delegates liberties to individuals, but that the individuals delegate to the central authority any liberties they may think it possible to do without for the sake of other liberties, always taking great care not to go beyond what is absolutely indispensable and, in doubt, falling back on liberty. Liberty must be the rule, and limitation of liberty the exception.

May I give an example: if we grant (in thought, not in politics: because in politics, as I have just expressed it, we have not got to grant liberty; we have to take it for granted) if we grant liberty to a society, that liberty, owing to the different qualities and vigour and class of man, will produce inequality; and the conflict between equality and liberty will at once present itself. Liberty must stand its ground and needs no argument. Equality must justify every step taken in limitation of liberty, in the light of our two aforesaid principles. Inequality is a great help to liberty, for there is little liberty if there is little choice, and there is little choice if there is little inequality. The more inequality—not in the sense of injustice, but in the sense of variety, the more inequality in a society, the more liberty.

I think this example provides an excellent rule or an excellent form for showing a justifiable limitation of liberty. Suppose we grant that principle of inequality for the sake of liberty, but that we grant it immoderately. Through the play of the instincts of acquisitiveness which are the bane of society, the type of the excessively wealthy citizen will appear. On the day the excessively wealthy citizen is able to put his hand on the economic leverage of society, the economic bones of your liberty, your liberty is dead. So if we exaggerate the principle of liberty and of inequality to the point of granting sufficient power to the wealthy we will destroy liberty.

Common sense, the subtlety of nature, the complexity of society, the constant intertwining of the tendencies of man, should prevent us from exaggerating principles, however important, however essential.

A similar argument could be made for limitations of liberty designed to check an excessive amount of destitution.

These are, to my mind, the most important ideas that, so far as I am concerned, might be debated under the theme of "Liberty in Society," and now my time is up and yours begins.

A MATERIALIST ON FREEDOM AND VALUES

By J. B. S. HALDANE, F.R.S.

WE ARE MET TO CELEBRATE THE TERCENTENARY OF MILTON'S AREOPAGITICA, a protest against the censorship of books, but our main business is concerned with the relative importance of spiritual and economic values. Milton objected to a law according to which books, before publication, had to be submitted to a board of censors. This law was ultimately repealed. Unfortunately, as I shall try to show, what Parliament did not dare to do has been achieved piecemeal by lawyers and judges, and to-day we should be lamenting the liberties lost in our own day rather than celebrating those gained by our ancestors. I do not speak of the special conditions of war, when some form of censorship is inevitable, even though it has been grossly abused.

In the first place, the principle of censorship before publication, to which Milton objected so vigorously, is applied to the drama, the cinema, and the radio, of which the two latter, at least, reach a far wider audience than any book. As Shaw has pointed out, the censorship of stage plays was adopted as a purely political measure. Its most important application is still for the preservation of abuses. Had *Mrs. Warren's Profession* been performed when it was written, it would have accelerated the decline of prostitution in this country by several years. It was only shown when it had ceased to be immediately topical. Any play written to-day dealing with prostitution as it actually exists would meet with the same fate. The most realistic recent English book on this subject, *To Beg I Am Ashamed*, was banned. On the other hand *Darling Dora* was not realistic; so *Fanny's First Play* was not banned.

But at least we can read banned plays, and they can even be acted by private societies. The case of the film is far more serious. The costs of production are so great that every British film must be shot with one eye on the British Board of Film Censors. The British people find it difficult to understand the American people, and the results may be disastrous for the peace of the world in the future. One reason for this is that their ideas on the American people are largely derived from films filtered through the American Hayes film censorship. This remarkable organisation never allows wrong to triumph, or ministers of religion to appear as villains. If Sophocles had written *Antigone* as a film, the heroine would have retired to a cottage, or possibly risen to a throne, as Haimon's bride in the last act, while the Reverend Mr. Saygrace, to descend to a lower level, would have wrestled in prayer for Lady Touchwood's immortal soul. No wonder we are apt to think of the Americans as alternating incomprehensibly between violence and smugness.

The question of radio freedom is more difficult. Here we cannot give everyone a hearing, because enough wavelengths are not available, but once a month we could allow distinguished men to say what they think and write. I cannot believe that the British public would be corrupted, even if sections of it were annoyed, if they were allowed to hear what Shaw thinks of medical research, and Wells of Catholicism. In practice all scripts are rigidly censored, and those broadcasters who require more than occasional correction are regarded as nuisances.

The censorship of the films and radio has come about largely because writers did not do their duty in standing up for intellectual liberty. But the situation as regards books and periodicals is little better. Every newspaper and almost every publisher employs at least one lawyer to expunge potential libels. In practice, therefore, literature is now subjected, as it was in Milton's day, to censorship before publication. The great libel industry protects the rich rather than the poor. It is difficult for a bus driver to prove that a libel has done him £500 damages; it is easy for a company director to do so. The law is different in America. That is why everyone knows that big business in America is corrupt, and in England spotless. Our judicial system is equally impeccable. The law of libel prevents me from publishing certain facts about some of its leading members now alive, and the unwritten law of good taste protects them when dead. A publishing firm has recently refused to publish some remarks of mine on a late Lord Chancellor because they are in bad taste. They may be. So, in the opinion of the last speaker, were many passages in Milton's works.

At the present time the Home Secretary can suppress any newspaper "On his mere motion," as King Henry VIII would have put it, and recently suppressed the one with which I am associated. It is doubtless necessary that the State should have such powers in war-time. But I can see no justification for the grant of such powers without the right of appeal to a Court of Law. The *Daily Worker* is the only daily newspaper suppressed in England during the war. It is also the only paper which has had an editor killed fighting as a volunteer in battle against fascism. The two facts are not unconnected.

I must now turn to our second theme, the relative importance of spiritual and economic values. Here I am doubly handicapped. I object to the word value. I can only suppose that it means a quality in an action, a person, or a thing, of which someone approves. The important question is Who? Some authors appear to think that values are independent of men.

> "But value dwells not in particular will
> It holds his estimate and dignity
> As well wherein 'tis precious of itself
> As in the prizer."

Says Hector to Troilus. This is intelligible if they represent the opinions of a personal God. On no other hypothesis do I find it intelligible. In fact the notion of values divorced from individual valuers appears to me to combine, to a singular degree, the intellectual disadvantage of theism and atheism. I particularly object to the phrase economic values, simply because the word value is already used in one of several senses in economics, such as use value, labour value, or exchange value, and its use in a wholly different sense in the present discussion can only lead to confusion or worse.

Secondly, I am a materialist, and cannot see how to distinguish between economic and spiritual values. Let me give a concrete example. Sir Philip Sidney wrote *Astrophel and Stella* which, in the terminology that I must unfortunately use, embodied certain aesthetic values, which I suppose are taken to be spiritual. Later on he got a bullet in his thigh, and refused a drink of water in favour of a comrade, saying, "Thy need is greater than my need." During the last two months the value behind these words has been exemplified by the actions of many quite ordinary men and women during the bombardment of London. Sir Philip was actually enunciating the basic principle of Communism, "To each according to his needs," and was acting on the principle as well as uttering it. But when an attempt is made to apply this principle in a broad manner, for example in the Beveridge Report, we are given to understand that this is a matter of economic rather than spiritual values. I begin to harbour the suspicion that, in controversy, spiritual values are those to which the speaker attaches importance, while economic values are those supported by his opponent.

This is probably unfair. Perhaps we shall approach nearer to the truth by considering what most people would assess as an economic value, namely cleanliness. This is something you can get if you have money, and cannot if you have not. It was certainly a prerequisite for science. Chemistry and physics demand a higher standard of cleanliness than cooking or cosmetics. It is probably a prerequisite for many kinds of art. I do not see how painting with clean lines and pure colours could have' developed in an atmosphere of squalor. And I do not hesitate to say that for the men or more probably women who started the ideal of cleanliness it was at first an aesthetic value, presumably therefore a "spiritual" one. A neolithic woman who swept her floor, polished her pottery, and washed her face when her neighbours did not, was making a far more important contribution to civilisation than if she had loved her neighbours, or attributed a somewhat unusually merciful character to the local idol.

Once, however, cleanliness is established as a generally respected value, one can often realise other values by going against it, for example by going without a bath for weeks in war, by dissecting human corpses, by feeding lice on one's body, and so on. New values are often made by overriding the old ones.

In fact when a spiritual value is sufficiently widely accepted in a community it becomes an economic value. The clergy, who claim to be special custodians of spiritual values, are paid for their work. So are authors and artists who enunciate spiritual values which are accepted, if not acted on, by the community in which they live.

> "The True, the Good, the Beautiful,
> These are the things that pay,"

as the Rev. Charles Dodgson put it; and he had been well paid for his literary output. It seems, then, that we must recognise, either that the dichotomy between spiritual and economic values is false, or that a value ceases to be spiritual when those who enunciate it are rewarded by cheques, chairs, or benefices rather than rotten eggs, libel actions, or crucifixion. Though I am a strong critic of most existing societies, I am not prepared to go quite as far as that. I think that, in so far as any meaning can be attached to the words, a spiritual value may also be an economic value. This is doubtless rather a rare coincidence in an evil type of society like our own, but we should endeavour to make the two coincide, as, for example, Ruskin devoted much of his energy to raising the market value of what he regarded as good pictures, and Lenin to raising the market value of creative labour and lowering that of what he (and Ruskin) regarded as dishonest practices.

I object to the term "spiritual values" for another reason. The word "spiritual" is taken over from the terminology of religion, and it appears to be tacitly assumed that a spiritual value is a good. But yet most religions admit the existence of evil spirits. Consider the value embodied in the words (from the *Götterdämmerung*):

"Lachend lass uns verderben,
Lachend zu Grunde geh'n.
Fahr hin, Valhall's leuchtende Welt;
Lebe wohl, prägende Götter Prächt,
End' in Wonne, du ewig' Geschlecht."

These words are probably inspiring thousands of Germans at present. I think they must be said to express a spiritual value, but an evil one. The same is true of many of the spiritual values put forward by the Churches. Here is the papal encyclical, *Quadragesimo Anno*, published in translation by the Catholic Truth Society. It contains attacks on capitalism and socialism which would not have displeased Carlyle or Ruskin. When we turn to the index and look up "Fascist Corporative Regime," we find reference to such passages as this: "Little reflection is required to perceive the advantage of the institution thus summarily described: peaceful collaboration of various classes, repression of socialist organisations and efforts, the moderating influence of a special regime." If these are spiritual values, they are no more wanted than the spiritual values which urged the then Archbishop of Canterbury to his famous defence in the House of Lords of Hitler's annexation of Austria in 1938. It was apparently such values as these that inspired the present Archbishop of Westminster, in his first public speech, to demand a censorship of books. The Romish hierarchy, and those clergy of other sects who imitate them, are as great a danger to intellectual liberty to-day as they were when Milton wrote.

After these unfortunately necessary preliminaries we come to the core of the discussion. There are those, and I am one, who hold that the intellectual aesthetic and moral ideas current in a society, its spiritual values, if you like that phrase, are primarily determined by its productive forces and relations, matters with which economists deal. This, of course, applies not only to the orthodox ideas, but to the unorthodox ones, and particularly to those held by revolutionary minorities who may be about to change the economic system, or at least to accelerate and to some extent guide a change when this becomes inevitable. My opponents say that it is the ideas which make the society. I cannot attempt to argue the case here in detail. I leave that to Marx and Engels. I would simply point out that such seminal ideas as those of Newton were unacceptable in the Middle Ages, and that it is reasonably certain that had Newton died in infancy almost all his scientific ideas would have arisen in other minds during the century following his birth. Society produced these ideas through the agency of

Newton. It could have produced them through other agencies, notably Leibniz and Hooke.

If this is correct, we cannot hope for great improvement in our spiritual values without improvement in the economic structure of society. We need not be Marxists to believe this. The Dutch statesman, John de Witt, was not a Marxist when he wrote of "trade and navigation, which are the very soul and inner substance of our State." It is noteworthy that Ruskin demonstrated it both by precept and example. For his failure to produce or inspire great architecture amid his economic surroundings is at least as instructive as *The Seven Lamps of Architecture*.

The opposition to historical materialism arises largely from the false belief that when you have stated the conditions for a human activity you have explained it away. Bach could not have written his music for a five-stringed lyre, but the theory of organs does not explain Bach away. However, musical progress is impossible without technical progress. Nor is moral or intellectual progress.

Another reason is the fear of men and women engaged in intellectual pursuits that, as a result of changes in the economic system, they will have to do work judged to be of immediate economic value. I have little sympathy with this view. I have been doing applied science during the last five years, and find that it raises problems of great intellectual interest. I think that everyone should do work judged by the community to be of economic value, but that everyone should have leisure for other work. If the community will pay for intellectual work, so much the better; if not—well, St. Paul, Spinoza, and the *douanier* Rousseau, to take three names at random, earned their livings in other ways. I should like every scientist to devote part of his or her time to applied science, in the interests of pure science as well as that of the community. Conversely I should like to see every applied scientist given facilities for some "pure" or fundamental research.

It is alleged that where, as in the Soviet Union, almost all research is paid for by the State, the free expression of scientific opinion is checked. Thus on p. 135 of *Phoenix*, published in 1942, Mr. H. G. Wells wrote:

"In the last ten years young biologists have had to make a hasty departure from the country because they published their belief in Darwinian survival of the fittest, and that was judged to be contrary to the dogma of the dictatorship of the proletariat."

As a member of the Academy of Sciences of the U.S.S.R. I should have protested had this been proved correct. I asked Mr. Wells for the names of any of the men in question. He did not know them, but stated that his information came from an American, whose name, but not his address, he remembered. I have been unable to confirm his statement, or other similar ones, from sources at my disposal, including "white" exiles. I rest my case.

I think that a very great deal of the opposition to historical materialism comes from a mixture of pride and misunderstanding, as did the opposition to Darwinism. It is as unpleasant to think that our intellectual activities are largely determined by economic causes as that we are descended from apes. But both may be true, and in my opinion are so. Marxists, at any rate, believe that this economic determinism is a temporary phenomenon from which man can and will liberate himself by producing a classless society in which there is plenty for all, and the present tyranny of things over people will end. They believe that the first step in overcoming an evil is to recognise its existence, and that those who lay claim to such superhuman virtue that their spiritual activities are uninfluenced by economic facts are doing a very poor service to the spiritual values whose champions they proclaim themselves.

A world of health, leisure, and plenty is technically possible. In such a world some people will be content with no more action than the minimum demanded of them. But others will develop the various faculties of man in the ways to which the term "spiritual value" applies. This is at any rate what the rare possessors of plenty and leisure have done in the past. But there will be two great differences. All will have opportunities of full "spiritual" development, and life will not be warped by the necessity to defend and justify privilege. Some will find their highest expression in asceticism, using the word in its original sense. No casual labourer, no monk, is exposed to such voluntary poverty as an arctic explorer, no worker in a dangerous trade to such concentrated risk as a rock climber. Pain, danger, and disease are rarely ennobling unless they are voluntary.

That is why I believe that the realisation of economic values is a necessary prerequisite to that of spiritual values. At every new cultural level new spiritual values emerge, at first in the minds of a few cranks, then of a minority, and finally of a majority. For example, in the nineteenth century the conditions of human existence rose high enough in a few European countries to make the idea acceptable that animals as well as men have rights. If by spiritual values you mean those values whose existence is only discerned by a small minority, I say that that minority will only be increased when you have satisfied needs which were once spiritual values in this sense, and are now expressed in economic demand, for example, the needs for cleanliness and travel.

Man is a noble and insatiable animal. I believe that he will always make fresh demands on the world and on himself, and thus create new spiritual values. Let us frankly admit that we writers are mostly champions of values which have been current for some centuries, and have now perhaps less claim to spirituality than when they were first perceived. Let us beware of claiming to be gifted with inner light, and of rejecting the claims of those less fortunately placed than ourselves in the name of spirituality. If there are spiritual values, there is also such a thing as spiritual pride. By that sin fell the angels.

THE JEWISH SCALE OF VALUES

By Aaron Steinberg

I.—Principles

THE INSTITUTE OF JEWISH LEARNING REPRESENTED AT THIS COMMEMORATION Conference by Dr. Kobler and myself is very grateful for the opportunity given to us by the London Centre of the P.E.N. to put before you a Jewish view on the crucial question:

What is the true perspective in which we, at this fateful juncture, are called upon to visualise the relation between Matter and Spirit?

For this, I believe, is the kernel of the problem before us.

In taking the liberty of stating the theme of our conference somewhat differently than the official formula, I am putting, I am fully aware, a certain construction on the point in question which anticipates the answer. But in so doing, I feel I have on my side both the high authority of the immortal patron of this assembly, John Milton, as well as that of the unbroken tradition of Jewish thought and learning. To Milton, not less than to the Jewish creed, things economic could qualify as human values only after Paradise had been lost; only after Adam—lifted in the act of Creation by the force of the Spirit above the "Adamah" (the ground)—has first come under the full sway of gravitation, bound "to return unto the ground."

It is indeed this verse 19 of Chapter 3 of Genesis which impresses upon Adam's mind, in the same breath, Man's earthly origin, the material aspect of his existence, and his dependence on the daily bread and the many exertions indispensable to gain or earn it. To keep body and soul together is, accordingly, not merely the minimum of economic achievement, but at the same time the fulfilment of a divine command which certainly appears to be a curse, a curse, however, apt to be turned into a blessing, if only the balance between Matter and Spirit, between the sub-human and superhuman in Man, could be restored in conformity with the original design.

History is, in this view, the incessant attempt of the B'ne Adam, the children of Adam, to regain—by their own effort, and in the clear light of consciousness—the control of the human spirit, of Man's "portion from above," to say it in Job's phrase, over the material conditions of life and living which are, within human society, based on its economic structure.

To participate in this great work of liberation, the liberation of the human spirit from the fetters of economic gravitation, i.e., from the purely earthly and physical conditions of human life; to contribute to the elevation of the human being to that dignity which is conferred upon Adam since his creation, the dignity of a free citizen of God's Universe; to keep this goal of universal history in untarnished clarity before the eyes of humanity; to remind it again and again, by word and by exemplary deed, that the sons and daughters of Adam are born into this world to be always and everywhere on the move—this is what Israel is for among the peoples of the world.

Looking around and ahead at this critical, but not less inspiring, moment in human and Jewish history, one cannot help feeling that despite all the contentions of the devil's advocates, the sowing was not in vain. As ever before, Israel is still a living exhortation—a stumbling-block to some, a stepping-stone to others, an enigma to all, including itself. And yet, in the endeavour to assign to the values of the spirit their proper place alongside the economic, those values which are capable of being adequately expressed in quantities of ponderable matter—in this bold undertaking of readjusting the primary correlation of Spirit and Matter for the generations to come—where can we turn for a guiding light? Surely not to the twilight of some present-day myth. Shall it be the searchlight of modern science which can well do without the hypothesis contained in the word "spirit," and would not know what to do with it? Obviously there is no other light to guide us, if not the unextinguishable light of our civilisation's sunrise, *ex oriente*, or in Hebrew, *me' Misrach*.

Whether the present Jewish generation is worthy to take an active part in the universal work of the rehabilitation of man's prime dignity is beyond the scope of our judgment. The future will show. The past (which Dr. Kobler is going to survey) leaves us in this respect, to say the least, not without hope. That much seems, however, certain that no exploration of mankind's promised land would be complete, should the explorers not avail themselves of that instrument which Israel applied throughout the ages as an unalterable scale of values.

May I therefore, Mr. Chairman, give now a brief description of this ancient but by no means obsolete instrument? The fundamental principle underlying all the markings on this Jewish scale of values, its whole gradation, has by implication already been touched upon in the introductory remarks. It is the spirit, man's "portion from above," which, or shall I say, who prevails. What makes man man is the bond of likeness linking him with his Creator, who is the Maker of all things perceptible, thus Himself beyond sensual perceptibility, beyond space and time, pure spirit. Man is man in so far as he incarnates spirit, by definition supernatural. Consequently, human values in the proper sense are all without exception spiritual values; real objects of free human will governed by reason, because, to put it in the Miltonian way, "reason is but choosing," the faculty to choose between good and evil.

That is why we are entitled to say that economic values are either related to the human will and subject to valuation under the moral aspect of good and its opposite, thus representing only a particular variety of spiritual values; or, they are not human values at all, something which in point of value is quite neutral and indifferent. On the Jewish scale of values this reasoning is symbolised by zero point.

Real things, life itself and even existence in general, are to the traditional Jewish view in themselves quite irrelevant. Let me explain this truly essential point, "by what is contrary" to put it again in a phrase out of the *Areopagitica*. There is a widespread belief that to the Jews endless continuation of life, stubborn persistence, unconditional survival is an end in itself, a belief embodied in the well-known medieval legend of the "eternal" *Wandering Jew*. Nothing is farther from the truth. The paradox of Jewish survival is actually the test case in human history destined as it were to prove that life attains its highest intensity only when it is stripped of all its tempting qualities, when it becomes a means to an end, which has nothing in common with life in the purely biological meaning of the word; when it is entirely subordinated to that value which is supreme on the Jewish scale—to holiness. "Ye shall be Holy; for I the Lord your God am Holy," thus is introduced the Chapter of Leviticus, wherein we find the command, "Thou shalt love thy neighbour as thyself" (19, 18).

From the Holy One, the Pure Spirit, the Value of Values, all their gradation must needs derive. The criterion is holiness, and only owing to the faculty of sanctifying life conferred upon man does life derive its value and dignity. But then—in all its length and breadth. Holy may become a land, its inhabitants, their laws and customs, their language, even their daily bread not to speak of their writings. It is perhaps fitting at this *Areopagitica* Conference to say a few words more on the last point.

How strangely familiar sounds to the Jewish ear the famous passage on the "Potency of Life" contained in books! Is the *Sefer Thorah*, the "Book of the Law," not a living entity to the Jews? The copying is a holy craft. The accomplishment of every copy is marked by a feast as if a child were born. Later it is provided with a luxurious girdle, clad in satin and velvet, and adorned with a crown. Before and after reading it is kissed, and when, after a long and useful life, it begins to disintegrate, it is carried in solemn procession to the graveyard to be buried to the sound of Psalms. So deep is the love of holiness, and so holy and innocent is the face of love.

Here is the point from which it can be clearly seen where, according to the Jewish table of values, the economic activities find their proper place. If they are put into the service of sanctification of life, if they are subordinated to the sacred principles of social justice, human solidarity and brotherly love, they reflect immediately the dignity of the spiritual values guiding them; if not, if these activities are a law unto themselves, they go down on the scale of human values, at the best, to zero. But they may fall even below the moral freezing point.

For there is yet another alternative, apart from holiness, to the point of moral indifference, namely—unholiness, and it is, I believe, essential for the Jewish scale of values, that it points not only upwards to the highest possible degree of human achievement in the service and emulation of the divine Spirit, but also to the bottomless abyss of human depravity and wickedness. Evil is as bad as good is good. Hence the "choosing" of good must imply the active and forceful rejection of evil. This is what probably accounts for the remarkable fact that at all critical turns in human history the Jewish table of values was a bone of contention not only to evil-doers but also to the lukewarm, those who try to disguise lack of purpose as love of peace.

They failed to notice the place peace occupies in Judaism and in Jewish history. When Israel, scattered all over the world, lives in peace, the whole world enjoys it. World-peace and "Schalom al Israel," "Peace over Israel" are identical. So all our prayers culminate in the word "Schalom." But craving for universal peace with passionate impatience we know full well that the way to God's Kingdom of Freedom is as long as the way back to the Garden of Eden. To deserve it, we have yet to conquer ourselves, our own selves.

"We" means, of course, all dwellers of this earth. The Value of Values, the Holy One, is not the God of Jacob only. His image is impressed on all children of Adam, from "sunrise to sunset," wherever they may be. Potentially all life is holy. However, *the potential of holiness* is not evenly distributed, and it is perhaps still a blessing to humanity that in a continuous succession of a hundred generations a human community *preserved* the original meaning and *sound* of the word: *"Kedoshim t'hiyou,"* "Ye shall be holy." If all of us unite in the common endeavour to *observe* it, the Divine Tragedy of human history will come to a universal *Kátharsis*.

THE JEWISH SCALE OF VALUES

II.—Historical and Practical Applications

By Franz Kobler

THE FOLLOWING THESIS MAY BE TAKEN AS ESTABLISHED BY OUR PREVIOUS examination: Jewish values are spiritual values *par excellence*. But, incidentally, the feature of these concepts shows a specific character by an intimate and inseparable relation to action, the actual human life on earth. Their application to the personal, social and economic life of man belongs to their very essence, while, on the other hand, life becomes worthless if not permeated by them. Thus the spiritual values are, above all, the driving force of that unique phenomenon called Jewish History.

The wanderings of the Hebrew tribes and the reign of the kings who ruled over Israel and Judah had never emerged into the limelight of history but for the law giving on Sinai and the appearance of the prophets. Powerless as they were, they rose above the people, the kings and their conquerors by spiritual force in order to secure the realisation of the divine rules. Thus they changed even the times of defeats and destruction into eras of sublime victories. Ever and ever again spiritual values shaped the character of this three-thousand-years history. The imperative "Justice, justice shalt thou pursue!" proclaimed in the Torah, became the directive for the ages. It moulded the social structure of the people, it decided the destinies of the kingdom. For the sake of this task, not by lust of conquest or expectations of economic advantages, the men under Ezra set out on their expedition from comfortable Babylon to devastated Jerusalem. About three centuries later, resistance against an aggressive Hellenism, sprung from the depth of a religious desire, inspired the Maccabees to deeds without which neither Judaism could have been preserved nor Christianity born. The spiritual impulse on Jewish history, far from ceasing, actually increased, when a dispersed people had to fit its life to that of various nations in many lands. A new synthesis of learning, law and ways of life was brought about by the fathers of the Talmud, a sacred tradition of thoughts and habits grew from generation to generation, and was not interrupted, when, in the middle ages, philosophy entered the field. The greatest representatives of this new Jewish philosophy, Saadya Gaon and Moses Maimonides, as well as the "God-intoxicated man," Spinoza, reflect in their theories and lives the synthesis of thought and reality.

Nowhere, however, did the innate Jewish yearning for an utter deletion of the frontier between spirit and action manifest itself more triumphantly than in Jewish mysticism. In striking contrast to the Christian and oriental mystics aiming at redemption from the passions and shortcomings of this earthly existence, Jewish mysticism as it appears in the Kabbalah and the various kinds of Hasidism is an active mysticism, a spiritual force driving man to an approach to God's holiness by exhortation to a godlike life here on earth. No teaching is more remote from any escapism than that of these Jewish mystics who appear in Jewish history by no means as single eccentrics but as leaders and members of great influential communities. These Jewish mystics, whether daring travellers like the medieval Abraham Abulafia, inspired teachers like Isaac Luria in the sixteenth, or venerated heads of Hasidic communities like their founder, Israel Baal Shem, in the eighteenth century—they are all fighters. What they fight is passivity, laziness of the heart, quietism and complacency; what they are fighting for is the broadening of the realm of the spirit, the joyful unity with God by deeds co-ordinated with the plan of creation, deeds of justice, love and mercy. The lives of the just men, the Zaddikim, who perform such deeds, constitute, in the view of these mystics, the true history of mankind. The destiny of the world, the coming of the Messiah, the redemption of the exiled Shekinah, the Glory of God, rests on them.

Thus Jewish mysticism joins the Messianic hopes. They had been the guiding stars of the Jewish people through the ages. The predictions of the prophets, the expectations of the days, when "all nations shall flow to the mountain of the Lord's house, and out of Zion shall go forth the Torah, and the word of the Lord from Jerusalem," these visions of a coming Kingdom of God, where "nation shall not lift sword against nation, neither shall they learn war any more," were never considered by the Jews as Utopian dreams but as certain realities which are the final goal of history. But it happened just on the threshold of modern times, while the great Jewish settlements in Spain and Portugal were doomed to destruction, and a new dispersal set in, that the hope for the redemption of Israel and mankind was being re-shaped into a mystical doctrine which became the inspiration for a religious upheaval of the Jewish world, and a historical power working, like in biblical and ancient times, immediately upon the actual development of mankind.

This turning point of Jewish history coincided with a fateful hour of the Western World which, fifteen hundred years before, had received its decisive and lasting impulse by Christianity, the pre-eminent progeny of Judaism. Now again the spiritual forces radiating from the living body of the ancient people began to gain a remarkable influence on the Western civilisation. That the expansion of the Western World to the Western Hemisphere was initiated partly by the tragic fate of the Spanish Jews, and that, if we accept the convincing arguments of Salvador de Madariaga, even Colon was a Jew by origin, is only one, though a most fascinating detail. But not only Hebrew Scripture re-vived and re-edited became a mighty ally of the Christian fighters against religious and moral degeneration: the very existence of the Jewish people, its mysterious survival, providential fate and everlasting hope proved a very effective inspiration in the great struggle of Humanism and Reformation. The new school of Millenarians, above all among them the English Puritans, who looked forward to the establishment of an evangelical Kingdom of God, drew their strongest arguments from Jewish Messianic predictions, particularly from the prophecies which applied to the restoration of the Jews themselves. On the other hand appeared the own future of those generations to them in the image of the Jewish Messianic hopes. They had a new vision of a New Jerusalem as the goal of their fight and pilgrimage. Zion became the symbol of their ideals.

"Why else was this nation chosen before any other, that out of her as out of Zion should be proclaimed and sounded forth the first tidings and trumpet of Reformation to all Europe?" This, of course, is a quotation from the *Areopagitica*. And there exists, indeed, no representative of that epoch who is more indicative for all the new Hebraism and especially British Hebraism stood for, than John Milton. We possess exhaustive studies on the subject of Milton's Hebraic reading and owe particularly to Professor Denis Saurat a most illuminating insight into the kabbalistic elements of Milton's thoughts. The more we penetrate into Milton's philosophy, poetry and life, the more we are struck by the overwhelming reflex of the prevailing Jewish values. He speaks of the "living intellect" and of the active soul; Truth ranges to him next to the Almighty, and a knowing people, a nation of prophets, is his political ideal. Nothing else than Adam's freedom to choose is the focus both of *Paradise Lost* and of the magnificent plea for the liberty of the word. Moreover, it is the very essence of the *Areopagitica* which points to the deepest roots of the connection between Milton's intentions and living Judaism. A sentence of the great Christian scholar, Travers Herford, may be recalled: "Let it be merely said that Judaism for its heroic maintenance of the position of dissent towards the Christian Church in the days of its pride, has had a large share in teaching the lesson of liberty of thought and conscience." The victorious defence of the inherited spiritual values put up by the Jews against the Church and Inquisition was indeed a prelude to the great battle for Nonconformity and Tolerance then inaugurated within the Christian world.

Now, once again, like three hundred years ago, the Western World faces the living Jewish people amidst a tremendous crisis. Again the destinies of both are bound together. But never before was this unity made so apparent as in these days. Both the Western Civilisation and Judaism have been attacked by a common foe, the future of both is threatened by a common danger. The very existence of this common foe and danger has a single cause: the sharing of spiritual values which came from the same source. Unalterable in their essence, they have to be re-established against new conspiracies, re-interpreted against future cynicisms. And as in the age of Milton, Judaism and the Jewish people, the origin and the witness of those values may still be blessed to play their part in this task.

Once again this task will be focused by the notion: Man—God's Image. The lesson of this basic biblical idea must, above all, be re-read and re-learnt by mankind. No generation paid so high a price for its disregard as ours, not only with millions of dead and tortured men, women and children, but with the deepest fall, the most shameful humiliation of man in the heart of Europe. This degradation was caused by the utter negation of any permanent values, by a complete nihilism which made man worthless and placed him not under the beast only but—what was by far more dangerous—under the machine. A kind of thinking and feeling became possible which changed man into a thing helplessly exposed to the satanic technique of the gas chamber and the flying bomb. Nothing could be more symbolic for this state than the circumstances under which the present conference is being held. We shall have, indeed, to go back to Adam, as Milton did, to regain a paradise we have lost: the paradise of the man who has confidence in himself, in his dignity and spiritual forces. We shall have to get rid of all kinds of Racialism and Spenglerism, and to view history in the sense of Scripture, as a unity which "has a meaning and definite direction," as Erich Kahler said and did in his recent book, *Man the Measure*. And we shall need another *Areopagitica* in defence not of the word but of man himself. It may happen that as a reverse of

Milton's immortal sentence this warning will be found there: "Who kills the Idea of God's Image kills man and all he stands for."

No bill of human rights will have any lasting effect lest it will be preceded by a statement of eternal value like the first sentence of the decalogue. No political or social freedom, no kind of post-war reconstruction, no economic order will secure humanity, if there will be not the man, put by the Creator into the midst of the world, as the great humanist, Pico della Mirandola, another Christian student of the Kabbalah, saw him: the man believing again in his freedom; the responsible man who reflects God's unity in the indivisible responsibility towards the inner and the social life, towards personality and community, the single nation and entire mankind, that co-operative responsibility which was emphasised by Mr. Rennie Smith in the discussion yesterday. There is a prototype for this man in Judaism where that unity and indivisibility are by no means idealistic notions but preconceived realities. A leader of the British socialist movement once remarked that perhaps no code of national law and custom has observed the balance between group life and individual life more successfully than that of Israel. This genuine tendency to link social welfare with the sanctification of the individual life lends a specific colour to Jewish economic legislation. The holiness of the Sabbath inserted in the working week is perhaps the most beautiful specimen and symbol of this synthesis. To master the antinomies of the intellect by a creative unity is, however, a general feature of Judaism. The Messianic perspectives are bound together with the past, love of Zion with an affection for the homelands of the Diaspora. An ardent desire for justice does not interfere with compassion and mercy, nor readiness to action with a daily, hourly uttered wish and longing for peace. This ability so characteristic for Judaism, of mastering the contradictions of the intellect may prove of help in an epoch which is looking for a new world where personality and society, freedom and planning, spiritual and economic values will have to be reconciled.

THE PHILOSOPHICAL BASIS OF TOLERATION

By the Very Rev. W. R. MATTHEWS, K.C.V.O., D.D., D.Litt.,
Dean of St. Paul's

"GIVE ME THE LIBERTY TO KNOW, TO UTTER, AND TO ARGUE FREELY according to conscience, above all liberties." These famous words express with incomparable force the idea of intellectual freedom and sum up the reasons why the publication of the *Areopagitica* is a memorable event in the history of our culture. I shall, therefore, be strictly in order if I take

Milton's book as a text on which to base some observations on the philosophy of toleration. The *Areopagitica*, as we all remember, was written in 1644 as "a speech for the liberty of unlicensed printing," and its immediate purpose was to protest against a censorship of books which had been introduced by the Long Parliament then dominated by the Presbyterian Party. I suppose it is one of the marks of a great man that he invests trivial controversies with universal significance just as it is the habit of small men to degrade large issues to the level of their own triviality. Perhaps from the standpoint of history the occasion was of no great importance— a question of the publication of some Left-wing Protestant pamphlets—but the principle which Milton laid down in dealing with this question was that of intellectual freedom.

We must own that Milton's conception of the nature of tolerable books was limited, and it appears that many who have not recently read his book have an exaggerated notion of what he urges as reasonable liberty. He claimed no toleration for the writings of Roman Catholics, Anglicans, Atheists or non-Christians. "I mean," he writes, "not tolerated Popery and open superstition, which as it extirpates all religious and civil supremacies so itself should be extirpated, provided first that all charitable and compassionate means be used to win and regain the weak and misled; that also which is impious or evil absolutely either against faith or manner no law can possibly permit, that intends not to unlaw itself." It is clear that Milton himself would have excluded not only the overwhelming majority of Christians but the greater part of the human race from the benefit of his tolerance. Are we wrong, then, in venerating Milton as a pioneer of intellectual freedom? Certainly we are, if we regard only what he himself intended, but we are right if we regard the arguments he used, for they carry us beyond the limits which he would have imposed.

It is of more than merely exegetical interest to discover what Milton really meant. All readers of the *Areopagitica* must have noticed the importance of the phrase, "the unity of the Spirit" in his exposition. The idea is in fact fundamental. The tolerance for which Milton pleaded is toleration within a community or fellowship in which certain fundamental beliefs and judgments of value are taken for granted. In his version of the unity of the Spirit the beliefs and values are those of the Protestant religion in its Puritan form, but we may abstract the conception from the particular interpretation which Milton gave to it, and think of his essential doctrine as being that where there is unity of the Spirit, there tolerance is possible and right. I shall suggest that this is in fact the most reasonable form of a philosophy of toleration.

We must not expect that Milton will do justice to the arguments against toleration, for, after all, his book is a speech for the prosecution. The arguments for intolerance are strong; we have only to look into our own minds to understand how strong. Probably no one is really prepared to grant unlimited toleration. It may be that we should draw the line at different places, but we should all draw it somewhere. Would you be willing, for example, that propaganda for the theory and practice of the Thug religion should be allowed among people whose grandfathers had followed it? Would you be quite satisfied if a wealthy society established schools to inculcate the flat-earth theory? Or to come to a question of really practical importance, is it incumbent upon us to tolerate those who preach the need for intolerance and set before their adherents the duty of abolishing the "effete liberalism" of freedom of discussion? Perhaps we may see in the present disasters of civilisation an object lesson on what happens when the evangelists of intolerance are tolerated.

The great names among the thinkers of the world are not all on the side of freedom. Indeed, I should say that, if they are weighed, the preponderance would be with those philosophers who oppose toleration. First is the weighty name of Plato. (Milton glances at him, but does not attempt to meet his argument.) Not only in the *Republic* but also in the *Laws* he maintains that the State dare not tolerate opinions, or emotions, which are subversive of its nature. The city must be bound together by a common belief concerning the Good and the Just; nay, it must have a common worship. We have learnt of late that there was more freedom of discussion in the Middle Ages than used to be supposed, but the overwhelming majority of the scholastic philosophers would agree that the propagation of heresy ought not to be permitted in a Christian State. We must not imagine, however, that only those who can be described as religious thinkers are against toleration. The most consistent of materialists, Thomas Hobbes, at the very moment when Milton published *Areopagitica* was meditating his *Leviathan*—that sketch of a totalitarian State in which what men shall believe is determined by the Government. It would be difficult, I think, to claim that Hegel was on the side of unlimited freedom of discussion and still more difficult to enlist Marx and Lenin, who "stood Hegel's philosophy on its head," in the army of intellectual liberty. These are great names—and the list could be indefinitely enlarged. Can we discern any common factor in men and systems so different? It might be suggested that they are all thinkers who hold that the society, or the State, is more important and of higher value than the individual. Perhaps this is too sweeping; it is at least controversial. We may safely say, however, that they are all men who were deeply concerned with the problem of the society and the State. What they meant by the "beloved community" no doubt differs enormously, but whether they are concerned with the Universal Church, the national State, or the socialist world-community, they are all thinking of some society, of the necessary conditions for its existence and welfare. And they have apprehended a most important truth—that the coherence of any society, its stability and its viability, depend upon some general agreement about values and aims. And division of opinion on these fundamental assumptions must be dangerous.

Is there an answer to this? Can we defend intellectual freedom and the "liberty to utter and to argue"? Not, I think, by denying the force of the contention that such liberty is dangerous, but by falling back upon that principle which is really the presupposition of Milton's plea—the unity of the Spirit. But it is precisely unity that the opponents of toleration seek to secure by their methods and, if the unity of the Spirit is to be the basis of free discussion, we must add to it what I can only call one of the most audacious of all acts of faith—that unity of Spirit can be gained by persuasion, reason and love. If this faith is justified, then certainly the spontaneous unity arising from personally apprehended truth will be far stronger than "the forces and outward union of cold and neutral and inwardly divided minds."

In contrast to this view we may note the widespread idea that there is some necessary connection between intolerance and a belief that there is such a thing as absolute truth. The "reign of relativity" in the sphere of knowledge is hailed as a guarantee of the spread of intellectual freedom. To me this appears an unfortunate misunderstanding. The proposition that there is no such thing as absolute truth easily leads to the conclusion that any assertion may be "true" in some circumstances, but false in others, and that there is no final court of appeal open to the intelligence and conducted according to its principles. This was the situation as Thomas Hobbes conceived it. He rejected the appeal to "right reason" to decide controversies, but since some controversies at least must be concluded for practical purposes to avoid the disruption of society, some external authority must be called in—and there can be only one really effective: the governor, whether the governor be some dictator, the majority, or the clique in power. There is no basis for intellectual freedom in scepticism. Its true foundation is the conviction that there is an Absolute Truth and that it is so majestic, so vast and many-sided that all sincere human minds together can grasp only a part. This at least was Milton's thought, as we may see from his pregnant words on the method of knowing: "to be still searching what we know not by what we know, still closing up truth to truth as we find it (for all her body is homogeneal and proportional), this is the golden rule."

The prospects for toleration and intellectual freedom are not rosy. The last twenty years have seen the suppression of free speech and unlicensed printing over great areas of the world. When the Government owns all the printing works or controls them evidently we have the precise opposite of unlicensed printing. The causes which have led to dictatorships of various types are complex and it would be naïve to imagine that they will be removed by victory in the war. On the contrary, the desperate need for unity in nations profoundly disturbed and convulsed will tempt the governing type of human being to impose uniformity of thought and emotion by all the formidable means which science has put into their hands. The defence of intellectual freedom will be with the "clerks," the writers and intellectuals. If they abandon the cause, it will be lost.

It is my conviction that the defence of intellectual liberty can be securely based only on a philosophy or religion which places persons above the community and above the State, which affirms that a person is something more than a citizen, having relations with Realities and Values which transcend all temporal societies—in short, that a person is, as Christians put it, a "child of God." If we hold a philosophy of this kind, we must also hold that the person has rights and claims even over against the State. Milton was speaking on behalf of one of these claims when he said, "Give me the liberty to know, to utter, and to argue freely according to conscience, above all liberties."

A THEOSOPHIST'S VIEW

By JOSEPHINE RANSOM, F.T.S.

IT IS A PLEASURE TO SPEAK TO THE TITLE CHOSEN FOR THE CONFERENCE, AND to share thoughts with those deeply concerned with and anxious for the welfare of mankind in the future.

It must, of course, be taken for granted that what each speaker says, has, in all probability, occurred to every other speaker, for each ponders over the same problems, which have a magnitude at the present time, and an urgency, beyond all other problems in the past. If, then, my ideas seem familiar, you will note that it is a familiarity supporting or running counter to your own conclusions.

Each of the speakers taking part in this conference has, of course, his or her own special background of experience, thought, aspiration and conviction which brings certain conclusions. You will recognise behind my own contribution that my views are coloured, not only by a lifetime's study and effort to understand the spiritual life of the world, and the ways in which spiritual impulses urge individuals and groups, but also by a lifetime's study of Theosophy. By Theosophy I do not mean just a cult or a society, but use the word in its true meaning, i.e., the effort to understand the Divine Life, Love and Will in action in a very varied universe, where divine laws are fundamental in all its ranges, and where those divine laws have also special application, as, for instance, in the human kingdom. This kingdom (like all others in their own measure) stands witness to its past, and now in the midst of unprecedently violent changes, faces a future which may seem uncertain to many, but to a theosophically-minded student, holds a destiny far more wonderful than ever before. So, seeing life from this angle my views may appear different from your own, but, I trust, are none the less useful.

Long observation of human society has convinced me that growth in the understanding and practice of spiritual life is the constant, inevitable prelude to growth and change in the social order. There are many historical events which bear witness to this fact. For instance, the Hindus look back to a long past time when spiritual awareness and wisdom directed the social polity into a form which has lasted through many centuries to the present day. One can still discern in modern Hindu conditions, however debased, the traces of a just, yet firmly based organisation, so adjusted to variable human needs that each individual could be fitted with considerable convenience and happiness into the whole fabric. Lovers of India do not hesitate to urge Hindus to emulate again that noble past, and in her revivification to put again at the disposal of her own and the world's life her spiritual knowledge, which might influence us all to seek more fully the exercise of those spiritual powers which are the only safe basis of all policies.

There is constant reiteration in all Hindu Scripture that for the sake of the real self in each are all others dear. That inner self is made in the "divine image", and it is utterly necessary to shape all human affairs worthily to express that self in full and unhindered beauty and relevance. Too often it is thought that the Hindu teaches escape—utter and for ever—into a tideless, timeless, Nirvāna. Closer study convinces one that the true escape has always been truly known as the escape from the bondage of ignorance into the release of perfect knowledge. That is, the escape from the bondage of Karma, the "wheel of the law", or birth and rebirth is the changing of inharmonious outward affairs into conformity with the harmonious life of the spirit. Hence we find that of old the ideal "caste" system with its plan to fit each individual into his appropriate place was so valuable and fundamental that it impressed itself upon the whole world. We have our own "class" distinctions. The term class has fallen into disrepute in the West and has come to mean barriers of one kind or another.[1] In the ancient system "economic values" were seen as what constituted the wealth of society, to be used to the advantage of all. And those inherently suited, by right of type and past Karma, to handle finance were expressly enjoined by the ancient Law Giver of our whole race— the Manu—to use wealth to bring content and happiness to all and not merely to the few. Monopoly was regarded as reprehensible, even impossible, and wherever wealth was accumulated, it was distributed at regular intervals.

[1] Many now speak of a "classless" social order. Actually, distinctions among people are entirely unavoidable. We all come to birth with more or less capacity owing to our long past growth. So we drift naturally into broad divisions, and, as long ago in India, capacity takes us into one or the other of the divisions. The modern Trade Unions with their unity and diversity would have been a "class" or caste of "workers" of all sorts. All administration, including kings, the Civil Service and all military establishments would have formed another class. All financiers, bankers, stock exchangers, traders and shopkeepers another caste, and all priests and teachers yet another caste. As long as these natural distinctions last there can be no question of a classless society. What we have lost, and need restoring, is the ideal of *service* to the whole, which should replace any aim at domination of the whole by one group. We may have to find another term than "classless" with which to describe the future social order.

Each caste or class type has been distributed over the whole world and to-day the financial caste is more powerfully concentrated in this country or that. Some of the type has the true sense of the use of wealth in general service, many have strongly the determination to use it for their own ends. It is our task to convince them their gifts should be used to benefit, not to destroy. I take it that this ideal was in the minds of those who chose the title under which this conference is discussing economic problems, that what this gift for handling finance—whether by individuals, groups or nations—should have to inspire and direct it is indeed a spiritual inspiration which we could all trust. We should be able to rely upon it to ensure that "material security" so ardently advocated. Then surely the dark clouds of fear and oppression would begin to dissolve away, and leave chances for a fairer civilisation based on certainty of no more poverty (which is but the result of the abuse of wealth) and all its sad accompaniments.

Had we time, we might consider also from the same point of view, the spiritual impulses of other religions and trace how those impulses have, in the long run, brought about social attitudes. We might not like these social attitudes, because of our own bias, we might even—rather presumptuously—deny the validity of their spiritual origins. But there they are, full of value to humanity, and offer precious lessons to all.

We note in all these matters the difference between the spiritual impulse —which leads to change and betterment in thought and aspiration, the yearning to fulfil an ideal—and the drive of outer circumstances, which impels to a standard which might or might not have true ethical value. We are apt to think that to change our economic system will lead to beneficial and lasting social improvement. One might concede a great deal to this point of view, but closer consideration of all that is involved would make us say, I think, that life becomes arid with only material contacts to satisfy it. There might be much contentment for a while that the economic sorrows have been eased, but very soon our hearts would cry out: But what is it all for? We need constant assurance that our lives are to be spiritually enriched by all that happens. Man has never at any time been content with material security only. His spirit breaks through to demand as well, and more urgently, the blessing of spiritual fulfilment.

What is this spiritual value, or life, of which we speak so easily? The answer to this question will be given differently by each great religion, which holds sacred some method of expressing divine revelation, or realisation of inner verities.

Here in the West, we think we have but two general conditions with which to contend—the physical and the spiritual. We are gradually learning that there is much more content to both these categories than we imagined. There is, roughly, man, the *person*—active, emotional, thoughtful; there is also man, the *individual*—intuitive, universal in intent, and with will rooted in Godhead. To me it is these three latter qualities which indicate "spiritual life," for the reason that they are fundamental, and it is they which reflect themselves in the personal three qualities. If we can realise the nature of the spiritual, we can, then, direct the personal to express the spiritual. The person is concerned with its own small affairs, urgent and *self*-centred. The spirit is concerned with universals, with the harmony of the many and not only the satisfaction of the few.

We know that some individuals have attained to realisation of spiritual principles and have communicated them to the world to change its thought and consequently its activities. They have taught us in no uncertain terms that spiritual principles in action constitute the saving of man from fear and misery. They urge us to practise the spiritual will in action, which will not try to dominate or exploit; the spiritual wisdom that guides emotion to right expression in happiness; the spiritual intuition that illumines thought and shows what are true ideas to follow.

The medium of communication between spiritual and personal qualities is seemingly an "entity", whom we call the Soul. It is the storehouse of personal experience and the transmitter of spiritual life to the evolving personality. It is naturally of extremest importance that the Soul should be supplied with experience which can be best co-ordinated with spiritual principles. Hence the high importance of the nature of our social organisation. We must indeed strive to make it fit the demands of spiritual universals, the beauty of which all Scriptures try to enshrine in some measure. For the West the Christian Scriptures at their best offer a spiritual doctrine about worldly wealth which is at once drastic and bed-rock—one towards which we move reluctantly because it runs counter to our personal fears for what we call "security".

What, then, are the social forms which we should aim at in order to ensure in some measure a spiritual civilisation?

Ponder on the treatment recommended in the Gospels for the hungry, the thirsty, the stranger, the naked, the sick and those in prison. What more delicately beautiful direct instruction have we for the ordering of a world struggling towards social security than that all of us, for we are all bound together in action, feeling and thought, should receive from one another treatment "as unto the Lord".

For backing up the forms thus created we are given a few more instructions—to love our neighbours, to serve them without distinction, as did the "good Samaritan"; to see in them God at work shaping a perfection, the Sons of God; and the nature of the Sonship is magnificently outlined in the Beatitudes—the portrait of the Spiritual Self.

We are asked to face the facts of personal (self-centred) life and the facts of spiritual (God-centred) life, and to hearken to the words which make clear how the two may be so co-ordinated as to bring about the splendid social forms which release the high-powered, dynamic forces of the Self through a cultured, creative Soul with safety, balance and harmony. Thus may there be hope of embracing in justice and mercy the humblest and last as well as the greatest and first of our immense group of human pilgrims, toiling so courageously throughout the ages along life's highway. In other words, bring about a brotherhood on earth which is the circumference of the Unity of the Spirit at the Centre.

We know so well that to bring about any great changes in society it is necessary first of all to change the individual's outlook, so that he may move in a given direction with others like-minded. This, I take it, is the objective of this conference with its important and comprehensive title. We know we need a new outlook to create a new world—another and happier civilisation; we know *how* it should be done, have we the will to move to its accomplishment? We do need to try to create a civilisation recognising clearly that spiritual values brought into play to a degree never before attempted are the *real* forces which shape outer circumstances. Because life is one and indivisible, we do seek the opportunity of testing more fully our beliefs about this, and of finding out how we can be outwardly and universally served in as lovely forms as we imagine spiritual life to be served in divine splendours.

ECONOMIC STABILITY AND ETHICAL DEVELOPMENT

By H. LEVY, M.A., D.Sc., F.R.S.E.

PROBLEMS OF VALUE, IN PARTICULAR THE PROBLEM OF HOW AND WHY ethical judgments vary from one social period to the next, and the linkage if any between this and the economic structure of society at each stage, appear to lie in a field into which any individual, whether qualified or not, may enter. I belong to a profession in which those who are not qualified to speak hold their tongues. Only those who are expert are allowed to speak. On this occasion I have agreed to speak on a field on which I cannot claim expert knowledge, but may I plead in justification that the field does not yet appear to be one so clearly analysed and understood as other branches of scientific study. Why indeed should one regard it as falling within the range of science at all? After all, science is concerned with the determination of facts, their ordering and arrangement, the recognition of regularities among them and the formulation of laws to describe these regularities, and theories to explain and link them together; and finally the application of these laws to experiment and to social life. Judging, estimating and valuing hardly enter. Ethical ideas of right and wrong, good and bad are extraneous issues, except that basically scientists must tell the truth, otherwise science becomes impossible. That, broadly speaking, defines the field in which science operates. Now, if we look at our particular problem, the changing relation between judgments and economic stability, we find that in point of fact this is a field very much akin to that. It is a fact that judgments are made and values held. In society economic processes occur. It is not my function to say, for the moment, that this particular judgment is better than another; for example, that it is better to be tolerant than intolerant; but rather to accept the fact that some people maintain that tolerance is better than intolerance, that at certain periods in the history of man tolerance of a kind has been practised, and at other periods intolerance has been practised; to record those facts and examine whether, seeing them in the background of social and historical change, setting them alongside the economic situation in which they have been practised, there is any kind of regularity, any consistent pattern or relationship which shows itself. If we are successful in this, then we can describe it as a regularity in social behaviour and to that extent we will have dealt with this field in a scientific way. We can then go on to consider how the laws and regularities which show themselves are explained and how they can be used by people like ourselves, in social practice. In doing that we shall be following, step by step, the kind of process a scientific man follows, who, having studied his facts, formulates them in the form of general laws, then seeks to apply them to social change, using them as a guide to action. Such action will be on the social plane and may be implemented through political activity.

The first point to which I want to direct your attention is that if one looks at social history one can see that during periods of social crisis, during periods of economic confusion if you like, there has also been ethical confusion, a war of judgments, a war of valuations, when individuals have set themselves up into separate camps and have struggled against each other physically. During such periods also each section has provided for itself ethical or moral justification for the action it has taken. When in the physical field groups make war on each other you are dealing with a socially chaotic condition; you are seeing at the same time reflected in the world of ideology, in the world of thought, a chaos of judgment and ideals. Let us look at one or two illustrations of this. Take, for example, the story of anti-Semitism, the attitude to the Jewish people throughout the past two thousand years. We find that anti-Semitism has reached a climax in successive waves in different parts of the world at different times of social history. When we study the situation geographically and the exact time at which each of these crises took place, we find that where anti-Semitism reached its height, there also was a point of social crisis and economic struggle. Here is a regularity showing itself in the behaviour of men. Nobody is going to deny for a moment that when a section of the population turns on the Jews to exterminate them it does not seek to offer a justification. It does. We are not discussing whether that justification seems well founded, i.e., whether we believe in it. But the fact is that a justification is formulated and, as far as the Governments which profess it are concerned, is believed in; and the persecution, following the formulation of the justification, has been practised always in that particular time and in that particular area where social crisis has developed. The greatest climax in the history of anti-Semitism has been during this past five years in Europe, and no one can deny that those five years have witnessed the greatest social crisis in the history of civilised man. This is an illustration of the particular regularity to which I am directing attention.

Take again the history of Germany between the two wars. Here was a country choked economically, unable to get on her feet in the situation in which Europe was placed, a country with a capitalist structure, with an unemployment problem more intense than in any country of the world at that period, caught in an economic impasse, socially decaying. Inflation, hunger, starvation, class struggling against class, judgments and justifications put up for this action and that action; and finally, out of this chaos, the coming of the Hitler regime. Here then is a period of social crisis and, seen from our present standpoint, one of false valuations and judgments, the ethical level steadily falling, until finally Nazism comes. Out of that, again, comes war, which spreads outside the boundaries of Germany and draws in the whole of European and Western civilisation. Here is an illustration of economic chaos, social collapse, giving rise to ethical chaos and ethical collapse.

Take now the history of this country. I think sufficient time has now elapsed for us to go back to the betrayal of Czechoslovakia. I think it is true to say we have now got to a stage where those of us who underwrote the betrayal can now see that it was a betrayal. Yet look at the justifications we produced at that time. We were prepared to see Chamberlain shake hands with Hitler, knowing full well he was leader of a monstrous Government. But some of us could then find a justification, in that worse things could thereby be avoided. We were prepared to tolerate that particular evil, even to see it as a good, because of the economic and social dangers threatening Europe. We can look back on that now and see the kind of fever which had seized us because of the peculiarity and danger of that time. It is not for me to judge here whether it was good or bad, but looking back on it we recognise that we ourselves in our judgments and valuations were sharply conditioned by social and economic difficulties.

That is the first point, that when you have economic chaos you tend to have ethical chaos.

The next point is that when you have a period of contracting economic welfare, that is to say when you are passing through a period of scarcity, side by side with that comes deterioration in the level of our ethical valuations. Let us turn to the period of 1926-7-8 in this country. You remember the march of the unemployed, the hunger marches, the conversations that used to be held about the "won't-works," the "unemployables." They were scum! Those who had jobs, who were drawing dividends, who belonged to the more fortunately placed section of society could find all manner of justification why unemployment, which was falling so heavily on that other section of the community, was a punishment for some kind of mysterious moral crime. We look back to-day and see into what a fever we had fallen. We can see, of course, quite easily now that Europe, and England in particular, was in a period of economic contraction. We were in a slump. Instead of recognising that this was likely to have an effect on our moral judgments, we took our moral judgments as absolute at the time without realising how relative they were to our economic and social situation. We can look back now on that particular piece of history and see how we have changed.

During war we are living in an economically expanding period, and to-day we make all sorts of high moral judgments, such as those we have just implied about our past judgments. When the war ends and this particular form of expansion comes to an end, unless it is followed by a new period of expansion, we may expect to contract ethically and morally again. We may disapprove of these high moral judgments or become cynical of them. We may find ourselves justifying fascism. A period of economic expansion reflects itself ethically in one way; a period of contraction reflects itself in turn in another way. It does not follow that economic expansion will correspond necessarily to a "rise" in our moral judgments: that depends on something else. Let us look at this country in the nineteenth century. Britain was becoming rapidly mechanised, factories were being constructed and manufactured products turned out at an enormously increasing pace. Sections of the population became wealthy; there was the *nouveau riche;* colonies were absorbed, new markets found. Production expanded at a rate never previously excelled in the history of any country. We can see all this reflected in the cry for a certain kind of individual freedom in economic enterprise, the philosophy of *laisser faire*, the belief in the "self-made man," and the judgment that those who did not succeed were necessarily of poorer clay. It was also a period, in the early stages, when men, women and children worked for enormously long hours in mines and factories, and when all sorts of moral arguments were forthcoming to justify this exploitation. Men and women ranged themselves on opposite sides of the ethical and ideological front. Out of the class war on the material plane emerged a war of values on the ethical plane.

Here, therefore, is an expanding economy, but when it is class divided, when one section is being exploited and the other benefits from that exploitation, it does not follow that you necessarily have a uniformly widening ethical outlook rising from one level to the next. It does not follow, if society itself is class divided.

So the three points are: that where you have economic confusion, you tend to have moral confusion; that where you have economic contraction, there you have moral depression; and that where you have economic expansion you do not necessarily have a uniform rise in moral sensitiveness if the society is class divided. Social history provides plenty of other illustrations of the type I have mentioned that underline these points.

On the other hand, if the society is not class divided, economic expansion goes side by side with a growing richness in moral sensitiveness. Let us take the case of the Soviet Union. It has had a very short period in which to expand economically. This expansion clearly dates from the early 1930's. After the first struggle to survive as a Union, in the teeth of many invading armies, had been resolved, when electrification and industrial planning began to be introduced, when universities grew and technical skill developed, when education came to the people, a new sense of unity emerged. Men and women began to display a real creative interest in their work. Peoples, speaking different languages and with diverse cultural heritages, yet feeling that they were linked together as brothers, began to create new values, to exercise new moral judgments. Gradually they awoke to an understanding of what social unity could mean. They felt they had control over life. And whereas, at that time, outside the Soviet Union other peoples were saying: "Well, I may have a job to-day, but the slump has come. The bottom has fallen out of everything; something has happened over which we have no control; we are the victims of this mysterious market that has slumped," in the Soviet Union they were planning their own economy and therefore creating their own market inside the country among their own people, building up a solid structure of society, something they could see and understand, whose planning and development they could appreciate. While we were reviling the unemployed as "won't-works," they were combining together, developing all sorts of new capacities and moral values, building crêches, sanitoria, concentrating on child welfare. When the testing time came, when the Union was attacked by Nazi Germany, at Stalingrad, Moscow, Leningrad, Odessa, Sevastopol, then we saw the new moral fibre at work in the heroism of the people. Men and women of all nationalities sacrificed themselves for the common good. It was not simply a case of these individuals believing that they were less important than the State, or that the Soviets believed this. Marx and Lenin never believed anything so childish; neither does Stalin. Only in an individualist society does such an antithesis present itself. To the Soviets, the State, as they understand it, that is to say, the Soviet State, the Workers' State, is in fact the people and the two link together. If one looks at the past history of States objectively, one recognises that they have functioned to maintain the power, and press the interests of the dominant class. Hence the ideology that justifies the sacrifice of the individual to that State. But when you have a proletarian society in which the State is actually the people self-organised, in which they play their part in the planning of their own economy so that the burden of organisation falls on their own shoulders, and the responsibility is theirs in their own workshops and factories, then they *are* the State. The individuals express themselves in the State which they are building, and in the direction and control of this new organic body. The individual says: "I have reached my greatest consummation in sacrificing myself for this historic thing which I have helped, myself, to bring about. It is my own creation." In this way the unity between the individual and the State expresses itself in the purest patriotism. It is this, not the spirit of pan-slavism that lies at the root of the present rise in patriotic fervour. It is a practical expression of something profoundly ethical.

We have to recognise that there is this vital difference between social life, and its values, under a capitalist economy and under a socialist economy, or we shall not understand the linkage I am seeking to point out. People do not realise how the economics of a society colour every aspect of one's life. Fundamentally it arises in this way. An individual in capitalist society sells his labour for a wage. I do not mean to say that he makes a definite object, and sells it for a price. If I have the energy to labour I can go out on the market and sell myself as if I were a commodity. I say: "Give me a wage and use me as you require." It is my *labour power* that I offer for sale; my labour power ranks as a commodity, because it is bought and sold. The price varies according to whether there are many of these commodities on the market. If there are many, the price comes down; if few, it goes up. I naturally go with my labour power. Under capitalism, in this respect I am like a piece of material. There are no human values intrinsic to these operations of capitalism. If I work in a factory it is not my business to inform the management if there is waste or inefficiency of any kind. That is not my responsibility, and because of this my values are affected. My function is to carry through a certain allotted task, to come and go at specified times, to work at this task steadily between these times, and not to think of other matters that do not concern me. Fundamentally this settles the value placed on human labour under capitalism, except in so far as organised labour has forced a change. Hence it is to be expected that in capitalist society human beings will tend to be treated and valued as commodities, as inanimate objects. This must reflect itself in other aspects of human valuation. Why give tolerance to a section of society that you can buy and sell? What can a commodity know of truth, beauty and goodness? So there arises this sharp division in standpoint between the "machine-owner" and the "machine-minder." The latter sees life as one who is treated like a piece of a machine, seeking always an escape from his environment; the former as one who owns and controls the destiny of others, and who is concerned whether he will continue in that position of power. They have different values, different judgments of what is significant.

So society is split; just as the week is split into six days of commodity production, and a Sunday where human values force their way to the front. The contradiction inherent in this separation mirrors the values of a class-divided society.

Now you may say, that is all very well. If we get rid of a society that uses human beings as instruments of profit, there appears to be this possibility of a rise in values, seen with the eyes of to-day. But this still leaves us without any standard of value to give meaning to the phrase "a rise in values." It is true that I have been speaking of higher and lower levels as seen by us here and now, and in doing so have stressed their relativity to the social and economic situation. Is there any absolute sense in which it is possible to say that it is wrong to walk out into the street and, for our own amusement, to strike a child across the face? There is plenty of evidence that the Nazis have done this sort of thing. You and I, in common with many generations behind us, say it is wrong, but to-day we have a social situation in which some people feel otherwise. We need not stretch our imaginations very far for other illustrations in which this conflict of values shows itself in ourselves. We are dropping bombs on the Germans. They are dropping bombs on us. We are both doing worse than strike a child across the face. We are both maiming and killing children. At one and the same time we tell airmen not to strike children across the face, and to drop bombs with the fair certainty that some children will be maimed or killed. It is felt to be wrong as an individual action, but right as a social action. Europe is at present rent asunder by this contradiction because it is rent asunder socially and physically, in very much the same way as a capitalist country is rent by a dichotomy of judgments side by side with its dichotomy of class. In such a welter of rights and wrongs is there something more fundamental, more stable to which we can appeal? The fact is that we do appeal to something more fundamental. Let us see what it is and how it arises.

The Marxist, at any rate, would say that because of the nature of its make-up, capitalism is changing, sometimes slowly, sometimes with increasing speed, towards a classless society. It is moving towards socialism. However you may try to squirm out of it, you will find yourself bringing it about. Hitler may try to establish in Germany, and throughout Europe, a capitalist dictatorship—misnamed National Socialism—but in doing so he raises such a flare-up that for five years he pushes Europe along its economic path with accelerated speed. One hundred years ago, Marx began his Manifesto with the words: "A spectre is haunting Europe." That spectre has already become flesh and blood. Will Germany go communist? Will Poland go Soviet? What is to happen to Czecho-slovakia? Is Europe going Red? These are the questions people are asking. Europe is undoubtedly moving Leftwards at a tremendous pace through the actions of Hitler and his capitalist backers who sought to prevent it from doing so. Those who work for a particular end, sometimes find they have done the opposite to what they intended. The logic of economic change was against them, and in resisting this logic they have merely accelerated it, and coupled it with endless bloodshed. It was not a question of personal preference but social and economic necessity.

If this is the case, I do not ask you to accept it from me, but suppose for the moment that it is so—if it is the case that the West is moving towards a socialist society, then it means that we must expect that in the classless society about to emerge, there will develop new ways of living, changed attitudes of people one to another, and to the society in which they are being brought up. From this must emerge new values in conduct, new concepts of what is and what is not important and significant. These are social and moral compulsions to which we will become conditioned, accepting them as we do the law of gravitation. We shall have discovered the laws of social living. To take these as a standard when they belong to the future would appear to be impossible. This is, in fact, untrue. A large number of these rules of conduct has already emerged from the cream of the experience of the past. Many religions have taken to themselves these values; and that very fact is in itself evidence of a recognition that to that extent at least have we found something which is approximately a permanent feature of social life. The whole concept, for example, of the brotherhood of man, and all that it implies as regards race and nationality, verbally accepted as it has been, is clearly an anticipation of a moral outlook that can have practical meaning only in a future classless society. Yet, men have arrived at this idea by their recognition of an "opposite," in the Marxist sense, to oppression, exploitation and the use of one being by another as an instrument of private profit. It is not only, therefore, in the ultimate classless society that our moral standards of a more permanent nature are built up, but it is also *in the struggle to attain that classless society*. For, in that struggle the justifications that are forthcoming to energise us, borrow their meaning and their strength from the realistic vision of the future as seen against the torture and bloodletting of our own time. It follows that even to-day we are already building up the basic standards of judgment that can act as a frame of reference. Those who can see, however dimly, the kind of society which will be developed in the future, can also sense the judgments and values we may then have, and can act to-day on the basis of these. Those who do not are to that extent ethically blind. They react in a mechanical way in relation to the economic and social state of the period through which they are passing. Those who hinder the coming of socialism, act counter to what will ultimately be regarded by human society as good. To the Marxist the immediate evidence that such actions are immoral lies in the fact, that while in the long run socialism is inevitable, the consequence of these actions is to delay it and to increase pain and suffering unnecessarily. The agony of capitalism is merely prolonged. It follows that a primary test of good social conduct must lie in whether or not such conduct is conducive towards the achievement of a classless society in a way most economical of human sacrifice.

SOME PRESENT-DAY SIGNS

By KENNETH WALKER, M.A., F.R.C.S.

AS YOU ALL KNOW, WE SURGEONS ARE ACCUSTOMED TO FUNCTION WITH our subjects under the influence of an anaesthetic. This effectively suppresses their sensibilities and their critical faculties, a great advantage not only to our victims but also to ourselves. How different are the conditions under which I begin to operate this afternoon, when those in front of me are in full possession of their senses! You will forgive me, therefore, if I show some slight reaction to these unusual circumstances and do not display the unruffled calm with which we surgeons are generally credited. It is no light undertaking to address a distinguished gathering of men and women of letters. Although the description of the members of my craft given by William Clowes, Queen Elizabeth's private physician, namely, that we were "no better than runagates, or vagabonds, shameless in countenance, lewd in disposition, brutish in judgment and understanding," may no longer hold true, it is still a fact that we cultivate our hands rather than our minds. I would find it easier to operate on you than to talk to you. I confess also that at this moment I miss the comforting anonymity that is conferred on the wearer of an operating mask, and the additional reassurance that comes from the knowledge that the subject of my attention cannot possibly answer me back.

The theme which the P.E.N. Club has chosen to discuss is an immense one, a theme in which we speakers are likely to be lost, or else to be caught up in some small part of it which provides us with the opportunity of giving vent to our own particular enthusiasms and prejudices. I shall endeavour to avoid both these dangers. What will be the place of spiritual and economic values in the future of mankind. When I looked at this imposing title my mind became a blank, and feeling that I did not perhaps possess the necessary equipment for peering into the future, I consulted a friend. "What," I asked him, "will be the nature of man's future spiritual and economic values?" His reply was very revealing. "Describe to me," he answered, "man's economic future, and I will deduce from this his spiritual values." I realised then that he was a Communist and that instead of talking to him I might just as well consult Marx and Engels at first hand. For it will have been realised by those who have attended these meetings that dogma is not confined to the Churches but is engendered in the very bones of man. Now I will put it no higher than this: dialectical materialism does not appeal to me intellectually, emotionally or—yes, despite Professor Haldane, I shall use the word spiritually. And it is not only the materialists who fight shy of this word, as shocking to scientists as the adjective nude is to Mrs. Grundy, for there are a great many educated people who look upon man as being an economic, sociological and biological unit rather than as a spiritual being. For such people man's economics can never be determined by his spiritual aims, but his spiritual aims will always be shaped by his economics. They believe that if we can organise ourselves in such a manner that everyone of us is provided with a living wage and with a house equipped with all the paraphernalia of modern existence in the way of central heating, refrigerators, washing-machines and, I now gather, with milk laid on from a municipal dairy, our souls will be secure. With the help of all these ingenious contrivances we shall undoubtedly have more leisure, but leisure for what? Leisure for earning more and for adding new interesting machines to our collection would be the only logical answer. Ruskin once summed up the spirit of his times in these words: "Whatever we have—to get more; and wherever we are, to go somewhere else." If this was true of the nineteenth century, it is still more true of this. Efficiency and speed are for many of us criteria of progress.

Before attempting to forecast the future it will be necessary to orientate ourselves by looking at the present and the immediate past. During the last hundred years there has been a rapid fall in the power exercised by religion, and a corresponding rise in the influence of science. Alfred Loisy wrote: "The world has two faces, one that is visible, phenomenal, material and directly observable which is the domain of science; the other invisible, interior, spiritual, felt rather than perceived, sought rather than observed, which is the domain of faith." From the earliest times we in the West have shown a preference for the investigation of the world's visible and phenomenal face, and in our intensive study of physical laws some of us have reached the conclusion that this visible and phenomenal face alone exists. To many people the invisible world of the spirit is only a derivative of matter, an epiphenomenon of particles in motion. The failure of the biologist to account for life along physico-chemical lines has not shaken the conviction of those who hold this view that all higher phenomena will eventually be explained in terms of lower phenomena, life in terms of chemistry, thought in terms of life, and consciousness in terms of thought. There are a great many people who have developed a fanatical faith in science, believing that in time the scientists will not only supply all our material needs, but will also provide us with a metaphysic and a *religio vitae*.

As a medical man I am fully aware of the immense gifts which science has brought to the art of healing, for the whole of Western medicine rests on a scientific basis. Had it not been for the devoted work of the scientists, medicine and surgery in its modern form would not exist. It is, of course, true that the discoveries of the scientists have been used as freely for the destruction as for the saving of human life, but the purpose to which we put their discoveries is our responsibility and not that of the scientists. It is not the fault of the chemists that at the present moment their energies are being directed principally to the devising of new explosives and novel means of destruction. The scientists have provided us with knowledge which gives us an immense power over our physical environment, a power which we are not fitted to handle. If they eventually teach us how to explode the atom, and we use this knowledge to destroy ourselves, this is our affair and not theirs. As F. L. Lucas, a member of your club, has put it:

"We have invented the petrol motor—and Caliban has climbed into it, and Europe flares red in the wake of panzer armies. We have invented the aeroplane—and Caliban soars in it, dropping on our clever heads the two-ton bombs we have likewise contrived for his amusement. We have invented wireless, and from the Propagandamium Ministerium comes—the voice of Caliban. For His are the Kingdoms, the Power and the Glory." (F. L. Lucas: *Critical Thoughts in Critical Days*.)

Personally I think that this is rather an affront on Caliban but let that pass.

But we are faced with another and more immediate danger, the danger that the knowledge given to us by science may be so misused that it brings us into a state of spiritual as well as material confusion. Science speaks the language of matter, and its knowledge is derived from sense data and from sense data alone. Scientists have, therefore, no means of determining the value of a poem, the significance of a picture, the merit of a sonata, or the truth of a religious doctrine. At one time this was so obvious to those who followed the teaching of science that they never presumed to step outside the material sphere and to pass judgment on that invisible, interior and spiritual world which is "felt rather than perceived, sought rather than observed." It was clearly recognised that science, philosophy, art and religion all had their contributions to make to the sum-total of human knowledge. But with the pushing forward of the frontiers of science so that they embraced also the study of the mind, and with the adoption of such new techniques as the statistical method of research there has been a growing disposition on the part of many to believe that science is capable of dealing with all forms of human experience. For some scientists, and for still more of their followers the word "science" has nowadays become synonymous with the word "knowledge." The devotees of science are as firmly convinced that humanity will ultimately be saved by scientists as the devotees of economics are convinced that it will be saved by economists, and I believe that this growing disposition to look upon the scientists as the future spiritual leaders of men to be a very real danger.

How do the priests of the new religion intend to deal with our spiritual difficulties? I quote from Julian Huxley's book, *Religion Without Revelation*:

"Once we have rid ourselves of this doctrine of a Divine Power external to ourselves, we can get busy with the real task of dealing with our inner forces. These are largely subconscious or latent: any developed religion must find ways of helping the individual to face his subconscious and to realise the latent possibilities of his spirit."

How is this to be achieved? In this work Dr. Huxley does not tell us how we are to be helped to face our subconscious, admittedly a very unpleasant part of ourselves, and to cultivate the spirit, whatever that means to him, but at a meeting at which he was a principal speaker I gained the impression that it would be by means of a judicious blend of Freudism and the study of patterns of animal behaviour. With the help of a visit to the Zoo with a notebook and with Freud's convenient catalogue of complexes, we would apparently obtain all the guidance that was necessary for our future welfare. But perhaps I am doing Dr. Huxley an injustice in this description of the synthetic religion of the future, for there are suggestions in his writing of other ingredients in his recipe. There are hints that something might be added to the mixture in the way of extracts from yoga and because man is clearly an emotional as well as an intellectual animal, sustenance will have to be provided for this part of him by the cultivation of literature, music and art. Allowances will have to be made for the peculiarities of different people, but it is essential that of the faith of the future should be reasonable, systematised and under scientific supervision. This idea that a rational religion can be concocted by a number of clever men sitting in committee is no new one in the history of human thought. It is reported in Indian literature that the Mogul Emperor Akbar summoned to the city of Fatipur Sikra the finest scholars of the day. A special hall was built for them in which long philosophical and religious discussions took place. Finally, dissatisfied with their teaching and anxious to produce something better, the Emperor decided that the time had come for devising a new and reasonable religion which should combine the best contributions from everybody. This new eclectic religion was eventually synthesised, but it did not survive the Emperor's death.

To realise how ridiculous it is to believe that science can ever supply us with a metaphysic and a way of life, we have only to examine the particular analytical technique which it uses. Scientists begin by isolating the object of their study from its surroundings and they then abstract from it only those qualities which they are able to study. All the human and personal features of their study are discarded in the hope that a residuum will be left behind which will not be personal and human, but absolute and invariable. By this process each science is reduced to its lowest terms; ethics becomes a question of utility and inherited experience, and political economy, stripped of all conceptions of justice and charity, a matter of self-interest. Physical phenomena are interpreted in terms of matter and motion, life in terms of physics, and thought in terms of life. Science thus professes to start with something which is simple, invariable and exact, and from this to proceed step by step until it reaches man. But actually science has never left man, for it is impossible to see the world except as a human eye sees it, or to interpret it otherwise than as a human mind interprets it. We may attempt to explain the world by means of impersonal forces, or particles in a state of agitation, but it is we who have visualised these forces and we who devised this concept of frenzied electrons. We cannot struggle out of our human skins and find a *locus standi* outside of ourselves from which to view the universe as some disembodied being might see it. It may be useful to concentrate our attention on certain abstractions and to simplify the complicated phenomena which we are studying, but when we do so we must bear in mind that this is being done for certain limited purposes. And we must remember also that the intellect which we are using is an instrument which always works towards utilitarian ends; it is the toolmaker of man, the lens which focuses his attention on those aspects of his environment of which he must take stock if he is to adjust himself successfully to it. Used in its proper sphere this instrument, the intellect, gives excellent results, but used wrongly and to the exclusion of all other faculties, it leads to confusion. Even when employed in the interpretation of physical phenomena the concepts of matter and motion prove serviceable only on a certain scale, on the scale of man. In the investigation of the great world of the stars and the minute world of the electron, they are of limited use. As a means of explaining the phenomena of life and consciousness they are valueless.

We must accept the fact that our knowledge of the universe and of ourselves is limited and subjective, and we must realise that science cannot answer any of those questions which most nearly concern us. Science "is only a makeshift, a means to an end which is never attained," and the answers which we find to all those questions which lie outside the province of science must come not from the intellect alone but from all our faculties working in harmony. Knowledge is derived from the whole of our experience, and it is significant that Socrates, our prototype of wisdom, was both a man of the world and a poet, a rationalist and a mystic, a soldier and a lover of music. He combined in his person that harmony and balance of mind and body which constituted the Greek ideal. Whether there be knowledge of a higher order than that which is based on sense data, it will be for each of us to decide. Personally I am in agreement with Dr. Julian Huxley when he states that there are latent forces in man, but in disagreement with him when he writes that they lie in man's sub-consciousness. I would prefer to use the word superconscious, for they are the forces to which we owe the world's sacred books. It is for this reason that I regard the title of his own work, *Religion Without Revelation*, as being a contradiction in terms. Religions, as I have tried to make clear, cannot be the product of ordinary thinking, but must be based on thought of a higher order and all the great world faiths are derived from revelation, in other words, from the knowledge gained by the great religious teachers on higher levels of consciousness. It is because language is only suited to the expression of ordinary thought that this higher knowledge must often be conveyed in the language of symbolism.

Whenever I have attempted to discover the trends of present-day thought by such criteria as private conversation and the books which people are reading, I have been given the impression that during the last few years these trends have begun to point in a new direction. I note in people an uneasiness and a growing conviction that all is not so well with them and their world as they had formerly believed it to be. Thought is becoming more serious and more adventurous, veering from the trivial and the familiar to what for most people is a new quarter. There is a reawakening of interest in books on philosophy and on the comparative study of religion, and a deepening realisation of man's need for some gospel of living. There are signs, in other words, of a spiritual revival, but of a revival which is more in evidence outside than within the Churches. The doors of the Churches are open to all who care to enter them, but these ecclesiastical gateways are narrow and certain conditions are demanded of those who pass through them, conditions to which all are not prepared to agree. Moreover, those inspired words which were uttered in the open air of Judea two thousand years ago, would appear to have lost much of their magic in the process of being translated, reinterpreted and brought into line with ecclesiastical views. When a religion enters into partnership with the State, the partnership is an uneasy one which can only be maintained by means of compromise. The teachings of religion must be watered down lest they offend Mammon. As Michael Roberts has pointed out:

"The State aims at the immediate preservation of its own life and the material well-being of its citizens. Its best servants are often those who sympathise least with the ultimate purposes of the Church, and who in their pursuit of material ends are not distracted by thought of spiritual values."

It is not surprising therefore that in course of time the supernatural essence of a religion is lost and that many of those who have crossed the thresholds of the temples of institutional religion retrace their steps, complaining that Christianity has had its day, and that they are in need of a new message and of a new Messiah. And for the undiscerning and the superstitious there are many new Messiahs to be found, leaders of new movements, drawing-room yogis, facile teachers of the occult and purveyors of all classes of supernatural phenomena. Never was it easier than at the present time for anyone with a striking personality and a few high-sounding phrases to collect around him a circle of credulous disciples.

In times of war, spiritualism and other forms of pseudo-science and pseudo-religion flourish, but I believe that the turning of present-day thought in the direction of the supernatural is something more than a war phenomenon. For the last hundred years science has dominated our thinking, and because science attempts to explain everything in terms of matter, we have become materialist in our outlook. But as history clearly shows, epochs of materialism and idealism alternate with each other, and I am inclined to think that we are witnessing the beginning of a reaction to the thought of the last century. The recent advances in physics and the discovery of *quanta* have necessitated the abandonment of Newtonian physics, and with it of a purely mechanistic interpretation of the universe. After breaking the world up into smaller and yet smaller pieces until electrons have been reached, the physicists have discovered, somewhat to their dismay, that all the time they have been engaged not in the study of reality, but of the shadows which reality has cast on their minds. Their predecessors were so convinced of the reality of matter that they built out of it a model of the world in which their minds had no independent existence. Now that the material out of which this model was made has been scrutinised more carefully, it is found to consist chiefly of mind. It is not mind that is in danger of disappearing, but matter. The discoveries of the twentieth century physicists have produced a first-class dilemma, and they will eventually lead to a revolution in science. By breaking through the plausible façade erected by their predecessors, they have reached that bewildering hinterland of science in which the philosophers have long been groping for knowledge, to the amusement of the scientists. But it is no longer possible for them to poke fun at the metaphysicians for by force of circumstances the scientists have become metaphysicians themselves. They are compelled to swallow their constitutional dislike of philosophy and to study epistemology, for not only is it necessary to investigate matter, but to discover the nature of the knowledge which we obtain about matter.

I am not suggesting that the startling discoveries of the physicists will have an immediate effect on contemporary thought, for much time is required for the diffusion of knowledge. My sole object in referring to the recent changes in physics is to draw attention to the fact that at the present day we are probably witnessing the beginning of a revolution in thought. Classical scholars have indeed drawn a parallel between our own times and those of Socrates and Plato, and undoubtedly they have many features in common. The old Greek atomists, like the Victorian scientists, believed that they had explained everything by means of a theory of particles in motion. Socrates and Plato also lived in a world the foundations of which were disintegrating from the erosive action of wars, revolutions and conflicting ideologies. Thucydides gives an excellent account of the condition of Greece at that time, and his description might be applied to our own:

"The seal of good faith," he wrote, "was not divine law, but fellowship in crime. . . . Any agreements sworn to by either party . . . were binding as long as both were powerless. Neither faction cared for religion; but any pretence which succeeded in effecting some odious purpose was greatly lauded. And the citizens who were of neither party fell a prey to both; either they were disliked because they held aloof, or men were jealous of their survival."

Then, as now, there were no fundamental principles on which all men agreed.

The present war is not merely a conflict between rival political ideologies, but it is a struggle between different values and manners of living, and it is almost banal to point out, at this moment, that the basis on which the whole of Western civilisation rests is being subjected to an enormous strain. We are no longer sure of any of those values the soundness of which our forefathers accepted as confidently as they accepted the stability of the earth, and there is no agreement even amongst the so-called free nations on the subject of man's temporal good. Can the foundations of our civilisation be saved, or is it necessary, as the Communists would have us believe, that the whole edifice should be brought to the ground? Personally, I am of the opinion that in a chaotic world deliberate acts of destruction are best avoided. What better foundations could be laid on which a civilisation can be built than those on which Western culture rests? These are usually described as being Christian, but actually they are much broader and more fundamental than that adjective would imply. They are constructed out of those basic principles which are not only Christian, but are common to every great faith. It is possible for all men whatever their upbringing and their creed, whatever their nationality and their colour, to accept them as fundamental. Let us cease, therefore, to bother ourselves any longer about the subsidiary beliefs which divide men into different religions, Churches, sects and factions, and let us attempt to work together for the common good. Already there are a few signs that men of entirely different ways of thinking are searching for and even discovering some common ground for action. In his Conway Memorial Lecture Gilbert Murray pleaded for closer co-operation between all who accepted Christian values whether or not they subscribed to the creed and the mythology of the various Churches. In his last book Jacques Maritain likewise counselled the Catholic Church to combine with non-catholics for the attainment of certain limited common objectives. It is a good omen.

LEAVEN IN THE LOAF

By RICHARD CHURCH

THESE OCCASIONS WHEN TIME COMES ROUND, LIKE A REMEMBRANCER, TO summon us to a particular recollection of great events and characters, are not merely mechanical, Time itself is a great character, a perpetual event. Indeed, time is the greatest critic amongst us; and in the long run, after we have tried out many experiments and rebellions, it is time to whom we listen. It has been the custom, during recent years, those pre-war years of unhappy questioning, to be sceptical about the institutions built after listening to the advice of this arch-critic, Time. It seemed as though our progressive thinkers looked upon time as a reactionary, an ally of the obstructionists. I don't know why that should be. I don't know how the idea has arisen, unless it be from the simple fact of man's impatience. For when enthusiasm, reforming zeal, comes in at the door, patience is apt to fly out of the window. And once patience is gone, then Time no longer looks like an ally. It becomes really bearded, really elderly, really one of the diehards, a Right-winger of the deepest dye.

Now the truth is, that Time is just the opposite of all this. Time is the most revolutionary experimenter. It has always got all sorts of processes in operation, both short-term and long-term. Its ingenuity in the mechanics of trial and error is beyond the grasp of our imagination. It plays about with genes and chromosomes; it interferes in human politics and philosophy; it changes the perfume of certain flowers and elongates the necks of certain animals; and all in such a way as though to suggest that it is groping after perfection as ardently and progressively as the most Left-wing member of the P.E.N.

That being so—and much more could be said about this matter of the genius of Time (perhaps somebody will say something during the discussion afterwards)—it being accepted that Time is a lively revolutionist, then we must take his reminders seriously and not be sceptical or cynical about those mementoes which come as chronic guides from the past, through the present, and toward the future.

We can agree, then, or at least I hope we can, that to stand piously in front of the manuscript of Thomas Hardy's *Tess of the Durbervilles* in the British Museum, or to stare at Victor Hugo's pen in the Cluny Museum in Paris, or to turn over the visiting cards on the grave of Chopin in Père Lachaise; I think we can agree that none of these acts is a mere gesture of sentimental superstition. They are symbolical acts, and have larger meaning and influence than our conscious minds can visualise at the moment of performance. Their value is eucharistic, like the Christian sacrament, and in warming our imaginations to thanksgiving they restore us to faith and a renewal of action.

It is the same with these birthdays and centenaries. I think that there is even no danger in believing a sort of destiny marks their recurrence. They come so aptly, with such dramatic moment. Isn't the present occasion an example?

In what way is it an example? Because the occasion which led Milton to write his famous pamphlet about the freedom of the Press, is almost precisely similar to the occasion about which we have reason to be cautious to-day, and if necessary to fight with our pens as Milton fought with his.

And what was that occasion? It was one which found Milton deeply committed as an official of that party in the English State which stood for democratic freedom. Milton, in fact, was committed to more than that. As philosopher and poet, he was a spokesman of something more universal than a national politic. But that is a matter too big for discussion here to-day. I might, however, refer you to Professor Denis Saurat's remarkable study of the roots of Milton's genius, in a book called *Milton, Man and Thinker;* a book that probes down into the esoteric sources of Milton's scholarship, and the strange demonism which pervaded men's minds during the Renaissance; a demonism that stank of the death of gods.

But as a political Englishman, here was Milton in 1644 faced with one of the inevitable results of the triumph of a democratic faction. An Order of the Commonwealth Parliament, dated 14th June, 1643, forbade the printing of any book without the licence of a censorship committee appointed by the House of Commons. Those who know the extreme pride and even arrogance of Milton's nature will realise how this must have shocked, indeed enraged, him. If ever there was an intellectual aristocrat, it was Milton. He was the prince of Highbrows, and made no secret of his royalty. And this attitude of mind was not one which grew upon him with advancing years, success and position. In one of his academic exercises written while still a student at Christ's College, Cambridge, he wrote as follows:

"To be the oracle of many nations, to find one's home regarded as a kind of temple, to be a man whom kings and States invite to come to them, whom men from near and far flock to visit, while to others it is a matter for pride if they have but set eyes on him once. These are the rewards of study, these are the prizes which learning can and often does bestow upon her votaries in private life."

That was the spirit in which Milton set out on his career. He never deviated from it.   Like so many Left-wing rebels, strugglers for freedom, he was in himself arrogant, contemptuous of the average man, horrified by the pleasures and purposes of the mob whose emancipation he had been fighting for.   Was he peculiar in this?   Or was he typical of all men of genius, all men of a single motive?   I recollect that Shakespeare had a word for the man in the street.   He spoke of the crowd "throwing up their sweaty nightcaps," and one feels that he shrank with disgust as he spoke. But I will say more about this matter in a moment.   Meanwhile, we see how Milton, many years after that picturesque confession of his aim as a scholar, returned to private life.   The appetite of ambition had been sated, perhaps, but the pride remained, though purified by suffering and experience.   He had gone the full round of political experiment, and after helping in the putting down of tyranny by force of arms, was now able to contemplate a greater purpose; a purpose which he could see was not being put into practice by the men by whose side he had fought.   Listen to what he said about this:

> My spirit aspired, victorious deeds
> Flamed in my heart, heroic acts; one while
> To rescue Israel from the Roman yoke,
> Then to subdue and quell o'er all the earth
> Brute violence and proud tyrannic power,
> Till truth were freed, and equity restored:
> Yet held it more humane, more heavenly, first
> By winning words to conquer willing hearts,
> *And make persuasion do the work of fear."*

That was the point he had come to.   He had learned to master his own irritable pride and impatience.   Years of contact with zealots, politicians, men of much action and little thought, men whose one impulse was that of appetite seeking the occasion for personal profit; all this disillusioning experience had somewhat humbled the princely arrogance, and taught him to "make persuasion do the work of fear."

But in the middle of that maturing treatment at the hands of Time, the master-critic, Milton found himself faced with an ironic situation. He found that not only the princely-minded scholar and poet can be arrogant. The man with the sweaty nightcap, the parochial-minded philistine, could be arrogant, too.   As soon as that little fellow, that typical John Citizen, by force of numbers came into power, he made an Order in Parliament forbidding the freedom of thought, and the interchange of ideas.

In response, Milton became a prince once more, and wrote *Areopagitica;* an action which apparently persuaded the new Presbyters that "we should be wary, therefore, what persecution we raise against the living labours of public men, how we spill that seasoned life of man, preserved and stored up in books; since we see a kind of homicide may be thus committed, some-times a martyrdom, and if it extend to the whole impression, a kind of massacre; whereof the execution ends not in the slaying of an elemental life, but strikes at that ethereal and fifth essence, the breath of reason itself, slays an immortality rather than a life."

So there was Milton, fighting once more against tyranny; but this time within his own democratic party, after he had conquered tyranny in his own heart, and overthrown it and the Government of a king who believed that he ruled by Divine Right. Milton disputed that Divine Right, being convinced that he himself possessed it. The drama of time works that way, by setting a thief to catch a thief. Time is a homeopathist, whose methods are usually slow.

Now that dramatic situation is likely to repeat itself to-day. I can say that without being in danger of falling into cynical defeatism. The danger is widely known, and has been as widely discussed since the days when Hilaire Belloc first began to talk about The Servile State. That Servile State is an ever-present threat, and will continue to be a threat so long as we delay facing the problem of what bounds are to be put to democratic control. How are we to state that problem? Can we put it this way: how far, in the interest of individuals as a whole, is the State to interfere with the life and liberty of individuals as units? That is the proposition. It cuts right through our human relationships, and it dictates the structure of our social organisation. It seems to be one of those fundamental questions which divides mankind into antinomian halves. Which are you; which am I? Do you believe in the all for the one? Do I believe in the one for the all? Men obviously believe that these are legitimate questions, because they make wars over them, commit crimes and deeds of desperate heroism over them. They consider that answers to these questions are ends that justify any means, no matter if they are drenched in blood.

But is it right? Is any statement of a case right, since it brings down the actuality of circumstances and cuts it into the pattern and dogma of words? It is a desperate state of affairs if human life is to be lived between two drawn swords; the swords of "yes" and "no"; of "black" and "white"; of "individualism" and "communism." How, in that constricted groove, is man to develop as he is inherently capable of developing? And of what use is freedom to him if that freedom itself becomes a dogma and a ritual to admonish him at every turn of his imagination and humour?

I've been asking a lot of questions to which I can give no answer. And I should fight shy of a man who proposed to give a cut-and-dried answer. I should know that here I was up against another zealot, who was out to convert me to his way of belief, and his system of cutting human nature to a certain shape. I should suspect him of being willing, if a crisis arose, of putting me in a concentration camp. He might be an ardent advocate for free enterprise, for unrestricted adventure within a capitalist State, or he might be a puritanical Communist, with Karl Marx as his St. Paul. And if, under either persuasion, he were to put his leading question to me, I should cough, and hesitate, and talk about the weather, and appear to be as thoroughly stupid as I possibly could. That is how I should prepare. For I know that there are such people. We all know it. And we know, too, that they are often the most well-meaning, intelligent and active members of the community. They are always to the front when any planning is to be done, or when society, having worn out one coat, is proposing to make another.

But I believe that they are invariably wrong. I believe that they can't see the wood for the trees. And am I justified in believing them to be wrong? I know that I am, because a man who insists on attacking a crisis of to-morrow with a law of to-day, or a crisis of to-day with a law of yesterday, is a man who is presenting me with a pig in a poke. His science is a clumsy one, and out-of-date. If he insists on using it, he will bring misery and disaster once again into the world, and freedom will once again be destroyed.

Rather than subscribe to such a man's methods, I would risk being called an anarchist, or a distributionist, or even plainly called a fool. I foresee the coercion that is likely to come into society as the rule of the majority supersedes the rule of the few. For there is this unescapable danger: the rule of the many must be a remote and centralised rule. It will therefore be a rule by regulation, and not by insight, the humane touch of the five senses and personal intuition. We already know that it is so. And how hateful, how degrading it is. Think what treatment a man or woman gets in a Labour Exchange or any other Government Office. You can't even go into a post office to buy a twopenny stamp without feeling that poisonous touch of dreary indifference, that implied contempt for the Holy Ghost in man. Something in the very administration of this departmental machinery seems to rob the executive of all human qualities. And this is not because they are servants of the State. It is because they are cogs in a top-heavy machine, something too big for any individual human imagination to operate except in a stiff, blunt and clumsy way that wounds and bruises every human spirit that it bumps into.

But all that is in the small, mechanical matters. How much more damaging is this centralised rule of the many when it legislates in the world of culture, taste—all the subtle and precious things of the mind. "My mind to me a *kingdom* is!" A kingdom, not a side-street branch of some sordid Government Office where every idea is either endorsed with a rubber stamp or thrown into the wastepaper basket by a stunted little clerk who in his spare time is concerned only with keeping six chickens in a backyard! But unless we are careful in our legislation, it is this little man who is to administer our lives. It is this little man who by his local interpretation of an intricate network of laws will decide whether or not some genius of to-morrow may publish his masterpiece, or attack the Government in a local newspaper, or exhibit a piece of sculpture showing superbly the love-gestures of the gods.

We see this dreadful state of affairs closing round us. More and more the mechanics of society are becoming a menace to the variety of human growth. The very benevolent and philanthropic intent of modern government threatens us. We are likely to be smothered by it. Free birth, free milk, free schooling, free health, and sickness, and death. Free! But at what a cost! Our very identity will be the price. For the old crowd-emotion, the primitive superstition and intolerance of subtlety and the finer, more exquisite tropes of the mind and spirit; this old coercive force of inertia which has always made the mob suspicious of the artist and the prophet, has to-day a most powerful machine by which to implement its obstructive nature. It has the unification of school methods, it has the cinema, the radio. It has, above all, the swift means of transport, by which noise is substituted for quiet, confusion for separateness, sameness for local distinction. In a few years' time, a man will learn nothing by making a journey from London to Chungking, for Chungking will have the same advertisements, the same foods, films and radio items, as London. And the people of Chungking will be unaware that a stranger from the Occident is in their midst, with something new and exciting to teach them.

These are our dangers to-day. But they are not new dangers. They are the permanent demonstration of that time-lag in consciousness between the crowd and the individual. That mob in its "sweaty nightcaps" which Shakespeare contemplated with such loathing, consisted of a number of individuals amongst whom probably Hamlet and Perdita might be found. And that acidulated little Government clerk with the six chickens in his backyard, whom I mentioned so snobbishly a moment ago, will probably go home to-night and neutralise his acidity by the alkali of privacy, assuming his own particular royalty in the kingdom of the mind.

The danger, therefore, of government is an eternal danger. It will always produce a tyranny, even though it may be a benevolent tyranny. And thus it must always produce its rebels. Milton wrote, in *Paradise Lost*, the biography of the first of these rebels. And when he wrote *Areopagitica*, he was such a rebel himself. For Government, like Justice, is blind, and treads clumsily. That may be why Christ, and all other mystics of religious genius, turn away from it in disgust, just as the artist turns away in disgust from the crude and clumsy æsthetic demands and assertions of the majority.

The fact is that adventure, with all that it implies in fear, surprise and rapture, is always breaking out, like the human nature which it sustains. And it is always against the law, especially when the law is paternal. The poet Robert Frost sums up this eternal conflict in a poem about a brook that runs through a city:

"The farm house lingers, though averse to square
With the new city street it has to wear
A number in. But what about the brook
That held the house as in an elbow-crook?
I ask as one who knew the brook, its strength
And impulse, having dipped a finger length
And made it leap my knuckle, having tossed
A flower to try its currents where they crossed.
The meadow grass could be cemented down
From growing under pavements of a town;
The apple-trees be sent to hearth-stone flame.
Is water wood, to serve a brook the same?
How else dispose of an immortal force
No longer needed? Staunch it at its source
With cinder loads dumped down? The brook was thrown
Deep in a sewer dungeon under stone
In fetid darkness still to live and run—
And all for nothing it had ever done
Except forget to go in fear perhaps.
No one would know except for ancient maps
That such a brook ran water. But I wonder
If from its being kept forever under
The thoughts may not have risen that so keep
This new-built city from both work and sleep"

We have yet to resolve the conflicting claims of that brook, and that new-built city. Meanwhile—and this may sound old-fashioned to many impatient people—we can listen to what Milton had to say about the bridge between the two extremes—the individual and the community. And what Milton had to say is something he learned from Plato:

"He who reigns within himself, and rules
Passions, desires, and fears, is more a king;
Which every wise and virtuous man attains:
And who attains not, ill aspires to rule
Cities of men, or head-strong multitudes,
Subject himself to anarchy within,
Or lawless passions in him, which he serves.
But to guide nations in the way of truth
By saving doctrine, and from error lead
To know, and knowing worship God aright,
Is yet more kingly: this attracts the soul,
Governs the inner man, the nobler part.
That other o'er the body only reigns,
And oft by force, which to a generous mind,
So reigning, can be no sincere delight.
Besides, to give a kingdom hath been thought
Greater and nobler done, and to lay down
Far more magnanimous than to assume."

It is only by this grand paradox of winning power in order to relinquish it, that great men and little men alike may bring their private virtues into their public life and service. As Milton said in a letter which he wrote in the same year as the famous pamphlet whose tercentenary we are now celebrating, "being perfect in the knowledge of personal duty, men *may then* begin the study of economics." That is as true to-day as it was three hundred years ago. It is the only way in which we can keep the Fabian dust from choking us.

CAN ECONOMIC CONDITIONS AND INTERNATIONAL RELATIONS BE BASED ON CHRISTIAN ETHICS?

By Rev. M. Davidson, D.Sc.

IT MAY ASSIST IN CLARIFYING THE TREATMENT OF THE SUBJECT FOR discussion to-day if I make a few preliminary remarks on my own position. As an official representative of the Christian religion, and in particular of its tenets as embodied in the doctrine of the Church of England, some of my audience will probably think that my answer will be an emphatic affirmative. Perhaps there is the suspicion that a cleric cannot approach such a problem with an unbiased mind, but I want to assure those present that the subject will be treated in an impartial spirit, so far as I am able to do so, and for the present I shall endeavour to regard myself as one almost outside the Christian faith. I may anticipate what follows by stating that my answer is no, but it is not an unqualified no, and I hope to show that not only Christianity, but other religions as well, can play an important part in helping to solve many of the problems of a distraught world.

It would be quite in accordance with precedent if I took a text this evening, and it will be very appropriate if I adopt a text emanating from my own Bishop—the Bishop of Chelmsford. In *The Sunday Chronicle*, 6th August, the Bishop dealt with the Churches' plans for peace, and laid down three points which are essential if organised Christianity is to establish itself and win an adherence of at least a considerable minority of the people of our Churches. The first point laid down was as follows:

"Ordinary people want the proclamation of a truth about which the preacher is dead certain. They want, not what he thinks, but what Christ has said."

For the sake of argument we shall accept the Bishop's statement which probably referred more to the ethical than to the social implications of Christ's teaching, though the latter are by no means excluded. I cannot believe that the Bishop had in mind anything relating to Institutional Christianity which depends, not so much on what Christ said, as on what St. Paul wrote. It is probably true to say that without St. Paul Christianity would not have survived, and yet we should scarcely say that the ethics of St. Paul are anything of which Christians need be proud. Canon Barry in *The Relevance of Christianity* says: "St. Paul's moral judgments about marriage, master and slave relations, fall below the level of the best contemporary Pagan sentiment." It is unnecessary to enlarge on this point which is obvious to any who study St. Paul's teachings, and for the ethical implications of Christianity we must turn to Christ Himself.

When we appeal to the Gospels for the ethical teaching of Christ we are confronted by the most serious difficulties which it would be fatuous to ignore. These difficulties are numerous but they can be divided into three main headings, each of which will be separately considered.

(1) Have we the authentic record of Christ's sayings?

(2) Assuming that we have the authentic records, are we quite certain about their interpretations?

(3) Admitting the authenticity of the records and also admitting a consensus of opinion regarding the interpretation of Christ's sayings, are we certain that His teaching is applicable *in toto* to the complicated problems of twentieth-century civilisation?

That these difficulties are very real is shown by the fact that Christianity includes well over three hundred sects, many of them extremely antagonistic to one another, though, generally speaking, there is a consensus of opinion, with some exceptions, on ethical questions. Every Christian must deplore the existence of these sects, and if only we were certain that we had the *ipsissima dicta* of Christ, what a help it would be in healing our unhappy divisions! Let us deal more fully with the first point.

Looking at the matter from the point of view of the ordinary people of to-day who want to know what Christ said, the natural conclusion would be that we must appeal to His close followers if we wish to discover His mind, and of course those close followers were His twelve disciples. The remarkable thing is that the disciples have left very little to help us. Not only have their records been scanty, but practically all the disciples disappeared very quickly from the scene soon after the establishment of the early Church, and we hear nothing more about them. In the accounts of the primitive Church how little we hear about the disciples, with the exception of two or three. The need for compiling trustworthy records of the life and teaching of Christ was felt during the second generation, and it is extremely difficult to believe that all the accounts supplied by the Synoptists are historically accurate. It is, of course, unnecessary to consider St. John's Gospel in the same category because it is a symposium of the corporate experience of the early Church and contains very few of Christ's actual words. It is generally conceded that many of the events recorded by St. Mark in the second Gospel were narrated by St. Peter. St. Matthew and St. Luke used the second Gospel and an earlier source, Q, now lost, in compiling their narratives, and probably St. Mark's version must be considered the most authentic of the three. St. Matthew's version, assuming that Matthew the disciple and former tax-gatherer wrote the Gospel, displays a most irritating habit of showing the fulfilment of prophecy where there is no connection between the prophecy and the events with which the writer associates it. A more serious fault is the number of interpolations in the text, obviously introduced to support certain views. The most flagrant of these is in xvi, 18-19, an interpolation which has split Christendom in twain. (Compare the version in St. Mark, viii, 29, where there is no account of such extraordinary powers delegated to St. Peter.) Are we certain that we have always got the words of Christ when interpolations in the records are so obvious?

Origen, born about A.D. 185, adopted a very liberal view in his interpretation of the Evangelists' writings. He believed that their object was to give the truth, where possible, both spiritually and corporeally, but if this were not possible, the spiritual was to be preferred to the corporeal, the true spiritual meaning being often preserved in the corporeal falsehood. If one of the early Fathers was prepared to entertain such a view we need not be surprised if modern exegetes are very doubtful about the accuracy of the records. It would be tedious to enlarge on this point with which every student of New Testament criticism is conversant, but one quotation seems to sum up the present position which many are prepared to accept. In the Bampton Lectures for 1934, R. H. Lightfoot says:

"It seems, then, that the form of the earthly no less than that of the heavenly Christ is for the most part hidden from us. 'For all the inestimable value of the Gospels, they yield us little more than a whisper of His voice; we trace in them but the outskirts of His ways. Only when we shall see Him hereafter in His fullness shall we know Him also as He was on earth."

Even if it is assumed that we have the words of Christ, are we quite certain about their interpretation? This is the second point which, in some respects, is even more important than the first. Should we take Christ's sayings literally, as the Fundamentalist professes to do, though I suspect he is sometimes prepared to compromise where his material interests are at stake? A few examples of the difficulty of interpretation will suffice for our purpose.

The Sermon on the Mount contains some very hard sayings. Incidentally, it probably was not a continuous address but was compiled from a number of Christ's sayings at different times and places and under very diverse circumstances. Note the moral paradoxes in some of the sayings. Dean Matthews in *Christ* tells us that they are not merely the condemnation of a brutal society; they condemn any society which has existed or could exist. "The use of force to restrain anti-social individuals is forbidden. Some have solved this difficulty by the 'two standards' theory, that is, the commands of the Lord and counsels of perfection."

Even in the days when these moral paradoxes were spoken (assuming that they were spoken by Christ) their literal fulfilment would have led to the disorganisation of a society which was much less complex than it is to-day. Is there any explanation for these very hard sayings? One obvious explanation is found in the apocalyptic view which was held by Christ at various times, though on some occasions, if we are to judge by the writings of the Evangelists, it was not held so strongly as on others. This in itself would partly explain some of the paradoxes though it should be remembered that many of the sayings from the "Sermon on the Mount" are by no means original but are paralleled in the Old Testament, the Talmud, and even in the precepts of Buddha. This fact need not detract from their value so long as they were precepts which were not merely *ad hoc* counsels for people in a world which was soon to pass away to be replaced by the new and better order; it would seem, however, that eschatology was often in the mind of Christ.

In the account of the mission of the twelve disciples there was the note of urgency about their work. They were not to waste time in saluting people by the way—an Eastern custom which required more time than our method of salutation at present. They were encouraged by the promise that they would not have gone through the cities of Israel till the Son of Man had come. We are not informed what was the outcome of this urgent mission, but St. Luke, who describes the appointment of seventy others to travel through the places where Christ was to follow, tells us that these returned with joy. Judging from the text, however, the only result of their mission seems to have been the casting out of devils, and we hear nothing more about the seventy. Throughout a great part of His career Christ spoke of the coming of the Kingdom, and even at the time of His trial He assured the High Priest that henceforth he would see the Son of Man sitting on the right hand of power and coming on the clouds of Heaven. The view that the old order was to pass away very soon in a catastrophic manner had a profound influence on the early Christians, and it is not surprising that they had little interest in social and economic problems when they believed that the end of the world was imminent. These facts should be taken into consideration by those who think that the ethics of Christianity are relevant to economic conditions and international relations. The matter is not of mere academic interest; it is of the utmost importance, and my fervent hope is that no attempt will be made in our country to construct an economic system on the so-called Christian ethics.

It should be said, in fairness to those who can cite evidence from the Synoptists to show that Christ was not always influenced by the eschatological view, that on some occasions He seemed to forecast a long period of struggle and then ultimate triumph for His followers. In many of these cases, however, there are obvious interpolations, and the evidence that Christ spoke the words is very meagre. Take, for instance, the charge to the disciples to preach the Gospel to the whole creation, mentioned at the end of St. Mark's Gospel. If we accept this as authentic we must be prepared to believe that Christ took a longer view of the existence of the world than appears from some of His other utterances. It is now admitted, however, that the last portion of Chapter xvi, 9-19, is a later addition and did not form part of the original manuscript. Few of us can seriously suppose that the disciples were encouraged by the promise that believers should be able to take up serpents and drink deadly things with impunity, as recorded in verse 18. The authority delegated to St. Peter after the confession of his faith suggests that Christ foresaw the existence of a Church, though it is doubtful if this view can be sustained from the records of the Evangelists on the whole. As we have already seen, the charge to St. Peter is an obvious interpolation and cannot be taken seriously, and it is certain that throughout the greater part of His earthly life Christ believed in the imminence of the new order. In such circumstances we should exercise the greatest care before accepting His mandates on economic conditions as binding at all periods and amongst all nations of the world.

Let us now proceed to the third point. Suppose we admit the authenticity of Christ's sayings and also a consensus of opinion regarding their interpretation, and we further assume that the apocalyptic view had little influence on His precepts, are the ethical principles advocated by Him applicable to the problems confronting us to-day? It will be advantageous to deal with a few specific cases.

We are enjoined to love our enemies and to pray for those that persecute us. How far are we able to practise this precept, and if we were able to practise it, what would the net result be? At this point some comments on Christ's own methods for dealing with His enemies may not be out of place. Ignoring the prayer on the Cross for His persecutors, where do we find any special love displayed by Christ towards His enemies? The words of Dr. C. G. Montefiore in this connection are apposite. In his *Rabbinic Literature and Gospel Teachings* he asks whether, as a figure calculated to inspire men to heroic acts of self-sacrifice, the figure of Jesus, detached from what Christians have believed about Him, is adequate. He adds: "What one would have wished to find in the life story of Jesus would be one single incident in which Jesus actually performed a loving deed to one of His Rabbinic antagonists or enemies. That would have been worth all the injunctions of the Sermon on the Mount put together. Even if such a deed were only reported, and it were of dubious authenticity, how valuable it would be. . . . Towards His enemies, towards those who did not believe in Him, only denunciation and bitter words. The injunctions are beautiful, but how much more beautiful would have been the fulfilment of those injunctions by Jesus Himself?"

It may be argued that, while Christ denounced the methods of the Rabbis and religious leaders, nevertheless He still loved them though He hated their ways. This argument, however, loses some of its force in view of the fact that, on the whole, the influence of the Jewish religious leaders in the days of Christ was beneficial and they were not so bad as they are sometimes pictured. There is something to be said for Dr. Montefiore's view that there was nothing but denunciation towards Christ's enemies, and the injunction to pray for our enemies is a counsel of perfection. Very often, too, we find that our enemies display little signs of requiring our love.

While praying for our enemies is not necessarily anti-social or a public or national menace, the same thing cannot be said about other precepts, such as, "If a man smite thee on one cheek turn to him the other also," or,

"All they that take the sword shall perish with the sword." These and similar statements have been taken literally by a number of people who have, in consequence, refused to bear arms even in times of grave national crises. Most people realise what such doctrines would lead to if acted on by a majority of the people. Dr. Inge's words are a fitting warning to the pacifist, and few of us would accuse Dr. Inge of being a warmonger. In his *Christian Ethics and Modern Problems* he says: "If Christians had been as pacific as Buddhists, or if Western Europe had been as well suited to hordes of cavalry as Russia and Hungary, there is scarcely any doubt that the legacies of Greece, Rome and Palestine would have been finally and totally extinguished." Wm. McDougall deals with this problem in his work, *Ethics and Some Modern Problems*, and points out that the acceptance of a universal or Christian Ethics would tend to the general degradation of human nature and to the destruction of civilisation and all the higher culture. It would allow the peoples of lower culture to settle in white men's countries and so reduce the standard of living. He expresses the opinion that the dysgenic factors in modern civilisation are increased by humanitarian ethics—a view with which some of us would certainly not agree though most of us would probably feel that there was some justification for his first opinion regarding universal ethics.

Let us face the position honestly. Can we adopt the "Christian" ethic (though it is not characteristically Christian) which seems to forbid the use of force, not merely in acts of aggression but even in self-defence? If so, then we must be prepared to see vast portions of our planet revert to a comparatively few migratory tribes living on the product of the hunt, and most of the advantages of civilisation eliminated from many parts of the earth. At this point we can hear the old platitude about the "brotherhood of man"—a theory to which we do lip service, but which few of the democratic nations practise or intend to practise. (Some of the nations under the regime of dictators make no pretence of observing the injunction.) We are all aware of the fact that our treatment of the so-called "inferior" races belies our profession, and it is an amazing thing how a policy can be advocated from the pulpit, based ostensibly on Christian revelation, which its exponents know perfectly well to be impracticable.

Let us look at another side of Christ's teaching which has led to a lot of confusion in the economic world. For many centuries the Church waged war against usury—not only against exorbitant rates of interest, but against interest in any form on money lent to those in need. It is certain that a mistranslation of St. Luke, vi, 35, was partly responsible for the opposition of the Church to money lending where interest was payable, but how many people to-day would say that a fair rate of interest was unethical or anti-social? If this attitude were adopted towards lending money it is difficult to see why the same attitude should not be adopted towards rents for houses, lands, etc., and the abolition of such would produce the utmost chaos in our economic system. There is no intention of entering on a controversy in support of any particular economic system, though the attitude of the arm-chair critic who has an assured income and who can find nothing good to say about the system which allows him to live in comparative ease and comfort is, to say the least, very exasperating. Some of my clerical colleagues have assured us that Communism is in accordance with the mind of Christ and that it is only under such a system that human nature can find its highest expression. It is true that the early Christians practised a community of goods for a time, but their system was as ephemeral as were some of Robert Owen's communistic colonies in America or as was the modern Russian experiment which ended in something utterly different from its earlier communistic schemes. Whether Christ taught that such a system was essential for those who were His true followers, or whether there is nothing in His teaching to indicate the ideal economic system, seems rather irrelevant. "By their fruits ye shall know them," is the best criterion to apply, and up to the present the fruits of communistic systems have not proved entirely captivating. It seems possible that many reforms could be grafted on to the present system without demolishing it completely, as some are anxious to do. Such a demolition would probably involve us in "blood and tears and toil and sweat," and no doubt we should be able to endure the ordeal if only a Utopia were the reward, but it is much more probable that the end would be bitterness, recriminations and disappointment.

Up to the present the substance of my remarks has been directed against constructing economics upon what some people believe to be the teaching of Christ. The perplexity in the Christian world will, in any case, probably prevent such an attempt; it is certain that no consensus of opinion will be found on the matter. A few quotations from those with the Christian outlook will show the terrible confusion that exists in Christendom when we come to deal in detail with some of the problems that vex our souls.

In his *Progress and Religion*, Christopher Dawson points out the danger of civilisation losing its cultural traditions. He says:

"To-day few thinkers would be so bold as to identify the material advance of modern European civilisation with Progress in the absolute sense, for we now realise that a civilisation may prosper externally and grow daily larger and louder and richer and more self-confident, while at the same time it is decreasing in social vitality and losing its hold on higher cultural traditions."

We should have liked some details about a system which would obviate this loss of cultural traditions, and in particular, examples from some countries which are maintaining their hold on such traditions. Perhaps Mexico, where the Church had such an enormous influence until recent times and where the great majority of the people were illiterate, might be cited as an instance, but many of us might feel dubious about Mexico as an illuminating example. What system is going to prove ideal? Listen to Christopher Dawson again in his condemnation of certain countries.

In his *Enquiries into Religion and Culture* he informs us that "mass-civilisation can only be made spiritually tolerable if subordinated to a principle of the religious order which the individual can serve freely and wholeheartedly without becoming either a slave or an automaton. Mass-civilisation either of the American or Russian type will destroy human personality and hence all the higher cultural values."

A statement of this kind leaves us bewildered. The civilisation developed by our powerful allies will, we are informed, destroy human personality. If so, for what are we fighting? Is Russia going to save her soul by returning to something like the old Czarist regime when she was one of the most religious countries in the world? Did her religion imply progress "in the absolute sense"? While these quotations are instances of the utter chaos in Christian thought, the next and last instance is a revelation of such confusion that one is almost tempted to despair of the Christian religion ever effecting anything for the human family.

During the 1914-18 war various reasons for the moral collapse of Germany were advanced by religious leaders and others. Some blamed the teaching of Neitzsche, some attributed the trouble to the influence of the Roman Catholic Church in Germany, some to the German higher critics, and others were convinced that it was the evil influence of Lutheranism which caused the moral collapse. Dr. Inge, in some of his works written after that war, poured contempt on such puerilities, and so far we fully agree with his attitude. But what has altered the opinions of Dr. Inge that he should now adopt the very argument which he previously denounced? In a recent article in *The Church of England Newspaper* he informs us that the Lutheran religion has been responsible for all the moral débâcle in Germany. It is remarkable that he did not extend his argument to some of the Scandinavian countries where Lutheranism is the State religion, but apparently Lutheranism has not yet sapped the moral fibre in these places. The trouble with Lutheranism has been, according to Dr. Inge, that the emphasis has been placed on the Atonement instead of on the Incarnation, in accordance with Luther's teaching. As this emphasis cannot have been a modern development, one would like to ask why Luther's pernicious teaching has required four centuries to materialise in Germany and how long it will be before its influence will be felt in other countries. No doubt the theologically minded would have a ready answer to such questions, but the condition of the world at present demands some more drastic remedy than speculation in puerilities.

The main thesis of my address this evening has been that the lack of certainty on Christian doctrine and more especially on Christian ethics should make us very cautious before we start constructing an economic system on a foundation of sand. No clear line of demarcation has been drawn between economic and international problems, because the latter very often depend on the former. The economic conditions in one country are often a fruitful source of irritation to other countries and such conditions can lead to war even if we could eliminate racial antagonism. The truth is that what we call Christian ethics is a misnomer; it may be more humanism than Christian, and when we speak of people displaying a Christian outlook it is often nothing more than showing that good feeling and spirit of kindness frequently found in human nature, in spite of all its defects. This does not imply that Christianity has no part to play in our social or international life, and it is now necessary to see whether the Christian, and indeed other religions, too, have any place in the modern world.

In his comparatively recent work, *God and Evil*, Dr. Joad says that deterioration in man's conduct has often been associated with a decline in Christianity. I am aware of the fact that this statement may be open to various interpretations. For instance, does it imply a causal connection—first of all a decline in Christianity, followed as a natural consequence by a deterioration in conduct? While this undoubtedly does take place, it is certain that in some cases both the decline in the outward observance of Christianity and deterioration in character are effects of one cause. That cause or causes may not be directly connected with any particular form of belief but may be due to economic or social factors or even to international crises. For instance, a serious depression in trade with the inevitable hardships of unemployment often embitters a large section of the community. The outbreak of a war has devastating moral effects and in the aftermath we discover how badly the social fabric has been torn. A decline in religious observance and a loosening of the moral ties in such circumstances may both be effects of a common cause. The experience of those who are closely associated with religious work is that, generally speaking, those who observe the outward forms of religion are well-disposed people who in any case, whether they observe religious practices or not, are not likely to indulge in the grosser vices. The unfortunate thing is that religion so often fails to lay hold of the very people who appear to need it badly. However, allowing for all this, there is much to be said in favour of Dr. Joad's contention: "With the decline of Christianity something has faded out of Western civilisation; a vitalising, humanising, refining, and restraining influence has been withdrawn. We may not be able to go back to Christian orthodoxy, but the world stands desperately in need of something that we have come to know as the Christian spirit."

If I may cite a few instances of the influence of Christianity in comparatively recent times it is only necessary to refer to the Wesleyan revival which, many think, and perhaps with some justification, saved England from collapsing into utter depravity, anarchy and chaos. It is irrelevant to the point to say that Wesley's methods would make no impression to-day; indeed it is difficult to say what method of presentation of the Gospel will make any impression at present. The work of Shaftesbury, Wilberforce, Maurice, Kingsley, Barrett, Westcott, Scott-Holland, and others is so well known that comment would be superfluous. How far the representatives of Christianity should continue interfering in public conditions is too great a question to attack, but briefly, it seems that the creation of a healthy public conscience is more the function of religious leaders than is advocating special economic systems. Dr. Jacks pointed out twenty years ago in the *Hibbert Journal* that once theology waxed eloquent over the depravity of human nature, and that as much harm was being done then by the doctrine of the total depravity of the social system. The question remains, "Can society maintain its stability without religion?" Malinowski's words in this connection are worth pondering. Speaking of modern political movements, Communism, Fascism, etc., he says that none of these "can take the place of a religion which satisfies man's craving for the absolute, answers the riddle of human existence, and conveys the ethical message which can only be received from a Being or Beings regarded as beyond human passions, strife and frailties." Elsewhere he says: "The affirmations of an eternal Providence, of immortality, of the transcendental value of human life, are the eternal truths which have guided mankind out of barbarism to culture and the loss of which seems to threaten us with barbarism again."

How far can men of science co-operate with religious leaders in re-making a world that is drifting or has already drifted into chaos from which it will be extremely difficult to extricate it in spite of all the promises of better conditions under the post-war regime? My own personal view is that the future lies largely with men of science, so long as they are endowed with the right spirit—whether it springs from religion, humanism, or any other forces. Perhaps some will consider the implication that men of science could ever be endowed by anything only the right spirit is a malicious suggestion, but it is only necessary to look at the German scientists who have acquiesced in the extraordinary doctrine of the pure Aryan descent to realise that the innuendo is not so malicious as it may appear. It is true, as Sir Richard Gregory has urged, that, apart from its vocational value, science contains instruction which was at least as broadening and humane as any that could be learned from the classics, and its influence on social affairs has been enormous in recent times, not only in our own country, but in others as well (the case of Russia is an out-standing example). I have no sympathy with the view advocated (seriously, I suppose) by the Bishop of Ripon at the meeting of the British Association at Leeds in 1927, that every physical and chemical laboratory might be closed for ten years without reducing the sum of human happiness, outside scientific circles. I am of the opinion that human happiness would suffer much more from the experiment than it would do if the various squabbling sects in Christendom declared a truce for ten years.

It must be admitted, on the other hand, that the position of the scientist in the industrial world is not an envious one. It is pointed out by J. G. Crowther in *The Social Relations of Science* and also by J. D. Bernal in *The Social Function of Science*, that the scientist who transfers from academic to industrial work, or from research to the selling side of business, is often struck by the lower tone, which makes him feel uncomfortable at first. But he generally becomes used to it, and forgets the difference as he becomes absorbed in the exciting game of outwitting competitors. At the end of

Crowther's work eight points relating to the social responsibilities of scientists are laid down, amongst which the following seem to be of great importance:

(1) The exposure of errors in science, such as racialist theories, and the exposure of scientific errors in the ideas of destructive social movements.

(4) Descriptions of what social improvements are desirable for the advancement of science, and explanations of how science is thwarted in bad social systems, and how this thwarting is liable to produce still worse social systems.

(5) The persuasion of scientists who keep their scientific and political ideas in separate compartments to support constructive movements on the ordinary political grounds of economic interest and social justice (note the last two words).

(7) In peace, to co-operate with all constructive, social and intellectual movements, expand science, and remove the causes of war.

Do men of science require the inspiration of religion (using the word in its wider sense) to achieve these ends? Sir Richard Gregory deals with this point in *Religion in Science and Civilization* and shows the influence of religion as a social force. If it is true, as he asserts, that religion expresses the collective ideals of a society, and that all categories of thought, including that of science, are regarded as of religious origin, there is ample opportunity for co-operation between religion and science. Just as the exponents of religion feel that they have a responsibility to society, so should men of science realise that a solemn responsibility is also entrusted to them. Point 4 just quoted from Crowther's work is important in this connection.

An instance of the influence of scientific progress on social customs and even on potential legislation is found in the case of the so-called transmission of acquired traits. As we are all aware, the evidence for such transmission is most unsatisfactory, yet some eminent biologists have believed the case to be conclusively proved, amongst which may be mentioned the late Prof. E. W. McBride. As Prof. J. B. S. Haldane points out, this belief led McBride to advocate sterilisation of the unemployed to prevent their acquired traits from being transmitted! A great many other implications are found in the view of the transmission of acquired traits, and political parties could easily make use of the doctrine for almost pernicious ends. Prof. Haldane's rebuke is a good illustration of the truth that we do not require a holiday from scientific research, as some have advocated, but more research. In the words of Sir James Jeans at the British Association at Aberdeen in 1934: "The country which called a halt to scientific progress would soon fall behind in every other respect as well—not least important in its culture. Better, like Icarus, perish while flying too near the sun, than be slaves of a social system like that of the bees and ants."

SCIENCE, CULTURE AND FREEDOM [1]

By JOHN R. BAKER, M.A., D.Phil., D.Sc.

I

A SCIENTIST, IN ADDRESSING A SOCIETY OF WRITERS, IS AWARE THAT HIS ideas of freedom differ from those of his audience. To you writers, freedom of publication is the primary liberty. Censorship is to you "the greatest discouragement and affront that can be offered to learning and to learned men," as Milton wrote. Still, if you lived under a dictatorship (in Hitler's Germany, for instance, or Stalin's Russia), although you would have no freedom of publication, yet at least your imaginations would be free. Now for a scientist it is useless just to imagine: it is his job to find out demonstrable truth. His primary liberty, more fundamental to him even than freedom of publication, is freedom of inquiry, the freedom to choose the subjects of his research in accordance with his own judgment. Without that he is as you would be if a dictator could control even your imaginations. The scientist's most fundamental liberty is gravely threatened to-day by the would-be central planners of his subject.

Scientists do not have freedom of inquiry in the U.S.S.R., and that country, therefore, provides us with an object-lesson from which we can profit. A group of British scientists never ceases to praise Soviet science, but the praise may seem unmerited unless one favours the political regime. It is very difficult to assess the science of one country in comparison with that of others, but it is unlikely that any scientist who was free from political bias would place Soviet science on a level with that of Britain or America. This is confirmed by a test I made recently. I asked seven of my colleagues at Oxford to prepare a list of the two dozen greatest scientific discoveries made between the two wars. All seven are lecturers in science in the University (in physical chemistry, organic chemistry, botany, zoology and physiology), and are themselves engaged in scientific research. I gave them no hint of the reason for my request. They provided me with a list of twenty-seven items, which I am publishing elsewhere.[2] It suggests what is likely to be the general opinion of scientists, namely, that in the chosen period Great Britain, America and Germany were pre-eminent in discovery (though towards the end of the thirties totalitarianism was beginning to interfere seriously with German science). Different groups of scientists would, of course, have produced different lists, but it seems significant that despite all the propaganda for Soviet science, the list contains not a single item from the U.S.S.R.

[1] The address was delivered from short notes. The author subsequently wrote this article from the same notes and in the same colloquial style in which he delivered the address.

[2] *Science and the Planned State*, by John R. Baker. George Allen and Unwin (1945).

When scientific autonomy is lost, a fantastic situation develops; for even with the best will in the world, the political bosses cannot distinguish between the genuine investigator on the one hand and the bluffer and self-advertiser on the other. A good example is provided by the appointment of one Lysenko to be an Academician in the U.S.S.R. and Director of the Soviet Academy of Agricultural Science. Much propaganda has been made for this man, and he is credited with the discovery of what is called "vernalization," or the treatment of grains and seedlings to affect the time of development. (Vernalization was actually practised in the U.S.A. before the Civil War.[1]) This man, Lysenko, has strongly attacked the whole sub-science of Mendelism or genetics. He has used the authority of his position to prevent the publication of translations of foreign books on this subject, and has also insisted that the research workers at all agricultural stations shall carry out their investigations in conformity with his own belief in what is commonly called the inheritance of acquired characters, a belief that is not shared by the scientists of the rest of the world. The case of Lysenko provides a vivid illustration of the degradation of science under a totalitarian regime.

It is sometimes argued that the success of the U.S.S.R. in war is evidence of high standards in scientific culture, but this argument results from a misunderstanding. Only relatively small and isolated parts of science form the basis for modern advances in the technology of war. Engineering and medicine are much more important than science if you want to kill a lot of people quickly. It is not the purpose of science to provide military might. Many of the greatest scientists have been very unwarlike men and their work has not been adapted to violent applications. It has long been recognised that totalitarianism is an effective system for the prosecution of war, because armies cannot be democracies and because in war nearly everyone in a country earnestly desires one and the same thing above others—to defeat the enemy. (In times of peace, on the contrary, people's inclinations and aspirations are extremely diverse, and there is no evidence that totalitarianism can satisfy diverse desires.) Military might depends largely on the amount of money and energy that have been devoted to preparing for war. If one were to judge scientific or any other culture by military might, one would have to place Nazi culture very high. Germany is at last being defeated, but her military might has been astounding and is now collapsing only because she is assailed by overwhelming odds in man-power and material. It would be absurd to judge Nazi culture by Nazi military might, and it is equally absurd to judge Soviet culture by the same criterion.

II

The theme of this conference is "The place of spiritual and economic values in the future of mankind." I find it very encouraging that someone is still worrying about spiritual values, for the would-be central planners

[1] See Sax, K., 1944. *Science*, Vol. 99, p. 298.

of science seem to deny their existence. For them, the purpose of science is to give us material things—food and health and shelter. Run this idea out to its logical conclusion, and you arrive at nonsense. If food and health and shelter are our objects, we are living so that we may have these things, so that we may live to provide them for others, so that those others may provide them for yet others, and so on, endlessly and senselessly. You may object that there are valid ends for which people want to live, and you may cite great literature, art and music as examples. Certainly those are valid ends, and many scientists recognise them as such; but if a scientist uses this argument, he is saying that he practises science because he wants to provide food and health and shelter so that people may keep alive so that they may appreciate literature and art and music. His object, then, is the fostering of literature, art and music. This house-that-Jack-built rigmarole is nonsense. He may, indeed, want earnestly to foster these forms of culture; but if his dominating interest were not science, he would be a poor scientist. Science is as much an end in itself as literature or art or music.

Science does not exist only to serve material wants by forming a basis for technology: that is only one of its functions. It exists because man has an innate desire for demonstrable truth, a tendency to regard truth as an ideal and to work towards it as an end in itself. It is not necessary to tell this to anyone who knows anything of the history of science, for it shines forth in the biographies of the great scientists, and it is seen also in the daily lives of one's colleagues in the laboratory; but so little do people understand the nature and purpose of science, that it is important to make these facts known as widely as possible.

III

The rest of this address will consist of some general remarks about liberty. I want to suggest that the cause of liberty is being systematically undermined by stealth. It is happening in many ways. For instance, we are not told how a censorship is applied to our national daily newspapers so as to prevent outspoken criticism of the Soviet Union. Any editor who wants to malign the Polish Government is free to do so: he can even suggest deliberate falsehood by claiming that the men of the Polish Government are comparable to the men of Vichy. But the anti-Polish propaganda can only be effectively and truthfully answered by an adverse criticism of the Soviet Union, and such criticism is not published in any of our daily London papers to-day. Milton's cause, in fact, has been lost, and its loss has nothing to do with the safeguarding of military secrets.

There is one special way in which our liberties are being systematically undermined by stealth, and to this I wish to call your careful attention. *Liberal organisations are being infiltrated and permeated by those who wish to destroy liberty*. Believers in totalitarianism are supporting liberal organisations. The National Council for Civil Liberties, for instance, receives communist support, and so does the Radio Freedom League (although, of course, both these organisations would be illegal bodies under communism). Never were liberal organisations more urgently needed than they are to-day, and it is presumably for that very reason that they are being rendered useless by communist infiltration. The result is a situation that can only be called absurd. The National Council for Civil Liberties actually organised *opposition* to the setting free from prison of a man against whom no charge had been brought. Of course one may argue that Oswald Mosley would have imprisoned people without trial if he had gained power, but if so, then at any rate, those who opposed his release were in this respect no better than he. It is fantastic to see a Council founded for liberal ends trying to set aside what may justly be called the most fundamental of our liberties (because the others depend upon it), the freedom implied in *habeas corpus*.

Those of us who value liberty should separate ourselves sharply from those who do not. Societies founded for liberal ends should exclude Communists by requiring all applicants for membership to sign a statement that they believe in free speech, free publication, free association, the freedom of *habeas corpus*, and all the other freedoms denied to the citizens of communist, fascist and national socialist States; and that they regard these freedoms as permanent necessities in a civilised State.

Although the U.S.S.R. is our ally, we who value liberty must no longer be silent about what we regard as the defects of the Soviet regime. It is right that believers in totalitarianism should praise what they believe to be good and should give their reasons, but it is wrong that they should affect opinion by stealth: and that is what they do when they make propaganda for communism and preach liberty at the same time. Those who group the Soviet Union with Britain and the U.S.A. as a "democracy" and a "freedom-loving country" are deceiving the public, who are ignorant of the actual conditions of life under the Soviet regime.

IV

Those who uphold liberty fight against heavy odds. They provide a platform for people who would destroy liberty. If the platform is used effectively, so that for a time a majority of our people believe totalitarianism to be good, then that temporary belief will have a lasting effect; for the moment the totalitarians have gained power, every contrary opinion will be ruthlessly suppressed. When that happens, only bloody revolution can restore freedom—and revolution is pretty hopeless when all the technological devices of modern war are in the hands of the holders of power.

The people of the democracies are being fooled by subtly misleading propaganda suggesting that the central planning of our social life is consistent with the retention of liberty. We must act before it is too late. A mass swing of opinion is in progress. Many who could have been leaders of thought have swum with the tide and gained popularity and influence as a result.   Men and women of integrity and intellect are needed who will try to check the movement before it is too late.   They will need courage. Low motives will be ascribed to them and they will be vilified in every possible way.   They must not mind that.   The people must be made to understand that liberty and central planning are incompatible.   What can we expect if our liberties are gradually lost?   Milton himself has told us very precisely, in referring to what would happen on the loss of freedom of publication.   "We can grow ignorant again," he wrote, "brutish, formal, and slavish."   Note his choice of adjectives, for it would be difficult to improve them: ignorant, brutish, formal, and slavish.   That is what has happened and is happening in other countries.   Let there be no doubt that it can happen in ours.

ON MILTON'S *AREOPAGITICA*

By HERBERT READ

THE SPEECH WHICH MILTON ADDRESSED TO THE PARLIAMENT OF ENGLAND in 1644, "for the Liberty of Unlicenc'd Printing," was provoked by the particular circumstances of the time. Those circumstances had their pattern in the past, most notably in the Spanish Inquisition: but Milton could not have foreseen that they would recur in the future, and that three hundred years after the appearance of his pamphlet, his words would be as apt as if they had come hot from the press. The *Areopagitica* is Milton's greatest prose work, and this rank is given to it on account of its inherent qualities of fervour and style: but it is great also because of its wisdom, its logic and the universal application of its argument. Every newly established tyranny brings its pages to life again: there is no encroach-ment on "the liberty to know, to utter and to argue freely" which it does not anticipate, and oppose with unanswerable reason.

The public measures and commercial practices which to-day threaten the liberty of printing will not be far to seek, but before I review them I would like to draw attention to some features of the situation which provoked Milton's speech that find their counterpart in our own situation. It is sometimes assumed that the questions which agitated our country in the seventeenth century, and particularly those which broke over Milton's head, were so theological or doctrinal in their nature that they no longer concern us. Milton is one of the chief protagonists of the Reformation in England: the Reformation is past and done with, and the dust has settled on ten thousand tracts. If we exempt one or two of them from oblivion, it is for qualities of style which we manage to enjoy while remaining indifferent to the underlying argument.

That this is a mistaken and superficial attitude is made very clear in the present instance. We now realise, more clearly than ever Milton could have done, that revolutions have their evolution: they are caused by an irreconcilable conflict of wills, but from the victory of the revolutionary party there emerges, not unity, but a reflection of the old conflict. It seems easier for men to unite to destroy than it is for them to unite to construct. Just as the French Revolution gave birth to the violent struggle of Girondins and Jacobins, Dantonists and Robespierrists, and just as in our time in Russia we have seen revolution succeeded by the fratricidal strife of Menshevik and Bolshevik, Stalinists and Trotskyites, so after the Reformation in England there was a bitter dispute between Presbyterians and Independents. What was the precise doctrinal difference between these reforming sects we need not stop to inquire; but the Presbyterians were for the establishment of a new orthodoxy, and were the immediate object of that most bitter taunt of Milton's, that "new presbyter is but old priest writ large."

In the exercise of the liberty to argue freely "according to conscience," Milton had not hesitated to argue freely where his own conscience pricked him most keenly—that is to say, on the subject of divorce. The Order of Parliament requiring all publications to be licensed for press by an official censor, and to be registered in the books of the Stationers' Company, had already been in force for two months when Milton issued his pamphlet on *The Doctrine and Discipline of Divorce*, uncensored and unregistered. The printing might have been in train before the Order was promulgated, but to make quite clear that his defiance was deliberate, Milton issued a second and enlarged edition in February, 1644, and addressed it openly to Parliament and the Assembly of Divines.

We must remember that England was in a state of civil war. Milton belonged to the ascendant parliamentary party, and enjoyed the patronage and protection of its leader, Cromwell. The outraged Presbyterians could not hope to succeed in a personal indictment. They therefore tried to catch Milton in the net of the law, and for this purpose entered into alliance with the Stationers' Company. In August, 1644, the Company was induced to petition the House of Commons to take action against all writers who were showing contempt of the printing ordinance. It was then that Milton roused himself to a defence of unlicensed printing, addressing his remonstrance direct to Parliament.

The Order of Parliament of 14th June, 1643, is drafted for a far-reaching effect. The Preamble recounts that "many false . . . scandalous, seditious, and libellous" works have lately been published "to the great defamation of Religion *and Government*," and complains that many private printing-presses have been set up, thus infringing the monopoly rights of the Stationers' Company. It then orders, among its several provisions, that no Book, etc., "shall from henceforth be printed or put to sale, unless the same be first approved of and licensed by such person or persons as both or either of the said Houses shall appoint for the licensing of the same."

In plain words, every manuscript must be submitted to official censorship, and licensed, before it can be printed. But even then the copyright—that is, the right to copy the manuscript in printed type—is vested in the Stationers' Company; that is to say, it is their monopoly, an interest vested in them "for their relief and the maintenance of their poor," and the Order of Parliament gives them full power to enforce this right, and calls upon all "Justices of the Peace, Captains, Constables and other officers" to assist in the search for unlicensed presses, and to break them up; to search for unlicensed books and to confiscate them; and to "apprehend all authors, printers and others" concerned in publishing unlicensed books and to bring them before the Houses of Parliament or "the Committee of Examination" for "further punishments."

It was against this totalitarian edict that Milton hurled his scorn and eloquence, his learning and logic. Again he defied the regulations and issued his pamphlet unlicensed and unregistered. He took Parliament by storm, and though its deliberations on the subject are not recorded, he won the day. He was never prosecuted, and the Order of Parliament became a dead letter. It is true that it was not the end of the attempt to impose a censorship on printed books. That attempt is made whenever a sufficient excuse is discovered in war or revolution: we have seen it made in our own time. If our vigilance continues armed with invincible weapons, it is mainly because Milton forged them in his *Areopagitica*. His arguments are immortal, but it is the duty of every age to review them, to burnish them till they shine in a new light, and sharpen them for a present use.

There are four principal arguments in Milton's speech. All I intend to do is to restate them in our current phraseology, and give them application to our current affairs.

There is first what we should now call the pragmatic argument. Milton's way of expressing it is simple, and we perhaps only add complications of no value if we convert his words into our modern jargon. "Assuredly," says Milton, "we bring not innocence into the world, we bring impurity much rather: that which purifies us is triall, and triall is by what is contrary." Trial by what is contrary suggests the dialectical theory of the progressive development of thought which Hegel introduced into modern philosophy, and which has played such a part in the social philosophy of Marx and his followers. But I do not think Milton can be claimed for dialectical materialism. Truth might not be wholly revealed to human nature, but he did believe in its absolute nature or existence. He did not suppose that it was something which was being *discovered* by a continuous process of trial and error: he would have said, rather, that we have an intuitive knowledge of truth which must, nevertheless, be continually proved by the process of trial and error. The doctrine of free will, so foreign to dialectical materialism, is involved: "what wisdome can there be to choose, what continence to forbeare without the knowledge of evill?" It is a philosophical distinction and may therefore seem of little importance to some people: but it might, nevertheless, explain why the practical exponents of dialectical materialism have shown such a readiness in our time to suppress what they consider false or evil: why they have become reincarnations of those "glutton Friers" and dour Presbyters against whom Milton directed his arguments. *not true*

Milton was, above all, a Humanist—the greatest representative in England of that movement which had abandoned the dogmatism of the Middle Ages and was seeking for a natural or empirical basis for its beliefs. That is why I have called his first argument for the liberty of the press pragmatic. He would have subscribed to William James's definition: "True ideas are those that we can assimilate, validate, corroborate, and verify. False ideas are those that we cannot." But how can this process of assimilation, corroboration and verification go on unless there is the freest circulation of the relevant facts? And facts are facts independently of our discrimination of them: we cannot wish them away, or legislate them into oblivion. They are the dust and heat, through which the race for the immortal garland is to be run. And if your aim is a philosophical one, the relevant facts are in controversy, and in our days controversy is in books. "Since, therefore," concludes Milton, "the knowledge and survey of vice is in this world so necessary to the constituting of human vertue, and the scanning of error to the confirmation of truth, how can we more safely, and with less danger scout into the regions of sin and falsity then by reading all manner of tractats, and hearing all manner of reason? And this is the benefit which may be had of books promiscuously read."

There are plenty of people to-day ready to give their assent to this first argument of Milton's who yet boggle at some specific application of it to present circumstances. They say that Milton was generalising from theological or philosophical premises, and that he did not have in mind, for example, questions of public morals or provisions for public safety. Milton, however, made no exceptions. He did not exempt books from the normal incidence of the law, he admitted that their authors should be punished if convicted of libel, scandal or blasphemy. But the punishment is always *ex post facto*, and there is no prohibition of the means available to the delinquent. Indeed, Milton discusses at some length those scurrilous writers of antiquity, and is clearly of the opinion that there never was a case for suppressing any of them, not even "that Petronius whom Nero call'd his Arbiter," nor "that notorious ribald of Arezzo, dreaded and yet dear to the Italian Courtiers."

Milton's tolerance of the printing even of obscenities follows more logically, perhaps, from his second and third arguments, to which I now pass. These two arguments are connected: one points to the extreme difficulty of knowing where to draw the line between what is true and what is false, what is good and what is evil; and the other points to the impossibility of finding individuals competent to draw such a line, supposing it to exist. Generally, on the first of these scores, Milton argues that the kind of control contemplated in the Order of Parliament is impossible of application: "this order of licencing conduces nothing to the end for which it was framed." If your end is the restriction of heresy, why stop at books? "If we think to regulate printing, thereby to rectifie manners, we must regulate all recreations and pastimes, all that is delightful to man. There must be licencing dancers, that no gesture, motion, or deportment be taught our youth but what by their allowance shall be thought honest. . . ." We could extend the list to-day, for though we have an illogical censorship of the theatre, and a farcical censorship of the cinema, the means of propagating heresy, corruption and all other mental errors through the press and broadcasting are limitless. But the complexity of the task of censorship does not deter our legislators, and in many parts of the world Milton's arguments are needed, not so much for the liberty of unlicensed printing as for the liberty of any kind of expression. Perhaps it would be more realistic to say that the truth of this particular argument of Milton's has been recognised, but in countries where liberty is an inconvenience to a tyrannous Government, no limit is set to the scope of censorship. Milton thought he was asking a rhetorical question when he said: "And who shall silence all the airs and madrigalls, that whisper softness in chambers?"; but we have lived to see these, and other fancies he thought absurd, come to pass throughout most of Europe. Not knowing where to draw the line, our modern tyrants have made it all-inclusive: it is the totalitarian logic.

Totalitarian government has an equally effective answer to Milton's third argument. In his innocence of our modern efficiency, Milton imagined that though licensing were imposed, writing would still continue, and that men would freely submit their manuscripts to the official censors. He therefore found it difficult to imagine a body of men with either the patience or the competence to carry out such an enormous task. His description of such a judge will strike a modern publisher's reader as painfully apt: "If he be of such worth as behooves him, there cannot be a more tedious and unpleasing Journey-work, a greater loss of time levied upon his head, then to be made the perpetuall reader of unchosen books and pamphlets, oftimes huge volumes. There is no book that is acceptable unlesse at certain seasons; but to be enjoyn'd the reading of that at all times, and in a hand scars legible, whereof three pages would not down at any time in the fairest Print, is an imposition which I cannot beleeve how he that values time, and his own studies, or is but of a sensible nostrill should be able to endure." But this, of course, is not what happens in modern censorship. There is, no doubt, a thin trickle of unsolicited matter which must be read by some poor drudge. But the modern method is to print only what is initiated by the State, and entrusted to reliable servants to execute. The totalitarian censorship operates on the mind of the public, not on the manuscripts of its writers.

But all this makes Milton's final argument all the more relevant to our present circumstances. "I lastly proceed," says Milton, "from the no good it can do, to the manifest hurt it causes, in being first the greatest discouragement and affront, that can be offered to learning and to learned men." This is partly a psychological argument. A man does not become learned without acquiring a certain sense of dignity or self-respect. If the State infringes this delicate structure of confidence and freedom, the intellect itself suffers—recoils and atrophies. In his travels Milton had found and visited "the famous Galileo grown old, a prisoner to the Inquisition, for thinking in Astronomy otherwise then the Franciscan and Dominican licencers thought," and that sight and its significance had been deeply impressed on his youthful mind. In other countries, "where this kind of inquisition tyrannizes," he had "sat among their lerned men . . . and bin counted happy to be born in such a place of *Philosophic* freedom, as they suppos'd England was, while themselves did nothing but bemoan the servil condition into which lerning amongst them was brought; that this was it which had dampt the glory of Italian wits; that nothing had bin there writt'n now these many years but flattery and fustian."

In his first argument Milton has said that truth must be tested against error: what he is now saying is that truth nevertheless can never be stabilised or defined. It is in a continuous state of emergence, the issue of ceaseless mental strife. "Truth and understanding are not such wares as to be monopoliz'd and traded in by tickets and statues, and standards. We must not think to make a staple commodity of all the knowledge in the Land, to mark and licence it like our broad cloth, and our wooll packs." Or, as we might say to-day, truth cannot be rationed, or standardised or cut to a pattern of utility. Truth cannot be controlled in any way: it is the unpredictable outcome of the exercise of free will, a harmony of colours which are discordant as they lie juxtaposed on the canvas, but mingle and cohere in the vision. Milton himself uses a vivid architectural metaphor: "when every stone is laid artfully together, it cannot be united into a continuity, it can but be contiguous in this world; neither can every peece of the building be of one form; nay rather the perfection consists in this, that out of many moderat varieties and brotherly dissimilitudes that are not vastly disproportionall arises the goodly and the gracefull symmetry that commends the whole pile and structure." "There must be many schisms and many dissections made in the quarry and in the timber," he says, "ere the house of God can be built."

Milton welcomes the free circulation of schisms and heresies. Let every man, he says, be his own prophet. If the root be strong, what matter how we branch out. He then indulges in that greatest metaphor with which his tract is adorned: his picture of the City "besieg'd and blockt about, her navigable river infested, inrodes and incursions round, defiance and battell oft rumor'd to be marching up ev'n to her walls, and suburb trenches" and the people within this city "wholly tak'n up with the study of highest and most important matters to be reform'd . . . disputing, reasoning, reading, inventing, discoursing, ev'n to a rarity, and admiration, things not before discourst or writt'n of." And this, he continues, far from being a sign of weakness in that city or nation, "argues first a singular good will, contentedness and confidence in your prudent foresight, and

safe government, Lords and Commons." It is a sign of organic health.
"For as in a body, when the blood is fresh, the spirits pure and vigorous,
not only to vital, but to rationall faculties, and those in the acutest, and the
pertest operations of wit and suttlety, it argues in what good plight and
constitution the body is, so when the cherfulnesse of the people is so
sprightly up, as that it has, not only wherewith to guard well its own
freedom and safety, but to spare, and to bestow upon the solidest and
sublimest points of controversie, and new invention, it betok'ns us not
degenerated, nor drooping to a fatal decay, but casting off the old and
wrincl'd skin of corruption to outlive these pangs and wax young again,
entring the glorious waies of Truth and prosperous vertue destin'd to become
great and honourable in these latter ages." Then follows that supremely
beautiful passage envisaging "a noble and puissant Nation rousing herself
like a strong man after sleep, and shaking her invincible locks."

Such are Milton's arguments for the liberty of unlicensed printing.
Not one of them is without its aptness to-day, and though in our state of
siege we have not wholly abrogated this liberty above all liberties, there is
a dull acquiescence in the many restrictions that have been imposed, and
a tolerance of their abuse. We have not come through this time of trial
without some cause for doubting whether England is still a place of
philosophic freedom. Refugees from foreign tyranny have been imprisoned
on suspicion of their opinions, and not on any proven transgressions of law.
Englishmen who have too openly expressed their sympathy with the false
and illiberal philosophy of our enemies have been arrested and detained
without open trial. A specious sophistry has been used to arrest and
imprison men whose moral objections to war were as strong and as sincerely
held as any which could be brought under a religious rubric. But these
are blatant and occasional infringements of our liberties which will, I hope,
disappear with the state of war which has given them their only sanction.
What I feel more concerned about are certain tendencies which prolong
their dark shadows into the time of peace and reconstruction. I refer to
the growing power of trade associations, and to the proposal, freely
canvassed, that such associations should be entrusted with what is called
a planning or rationalisation of their particular trade. For the printing
and publishing of books is a trade, and there have not been lacking voices
to call for its regimentation.

In Milton's time, as we have seen, the task of censorship was to be
entrusted to the contemporary trade association, the Stationers' Company.
Since Milton's time those corrupted remnants of the free guilds, which
tried their best for many years to restrict trade and to immobilise labour,
came under the control of Parliament and for the most part only continued
to exist as picturesque survivals of a past economy. But within recent
years—and largely as a counterpart to the organised associations of workmen
—these bodies have been revived, though generally under new names and
with new functions. That they are a necessary feature of the totalitarian

State is not to be denied: a centralised economy must have institutions through which it can transmit its rigid control of the lives and actions of its citizens. This is not the occasion to discuss the economic aspects of the question: there is undoubtedly much to be said for the planned production and distribution of the material necessities of life. But the control of material is apt to give the controllers consequential powers whose abuse cannot be prevented. This is particularly the case in publishing. The materials of publishing cannot be treated as ordinary merchandise, for the control of the materials cannot be easily distinguished from the control of the words and thoughts which they disseminate.

This wider threat has no sanction in war: it is a proposal for peace. Our publishing trade must, it is said, be planned, and if publishers cannot put their own house in order, the State must intervene. Liberty, we are told by one of our leading publishers, is a barren intellectual concept. "Books and authors, the literary art and science of a great nation, are too important to be left to the unrestricted scope of private enterprise." Publishers as a corporate body "should find a way of discouraging the minority from actions dangerous to publishers as a whole."[1] These may look well as the pious sentiments of a tidy mind: but the field of truth, as Milton describes it, is not tidy: it is a battlefield. We may deplore the waste of paper and labour on tracts that are pernicious, on books and periodicals that cater for the lowest levels of taste. But prohibition is no cure for the evil. The prettiest of flowers are a culture from the wilderness of weeds, and a garden in which only red roses are allowed to bloom is not only monotonous: it is a cemetery in which all adventure lies buried.

I am not recommending that we should let things be—that we should stand aside in idle indifference. But it is public taste and public sensibility which should be improved, by education, by example, by the abundance of beauty and the free intercourse of creative spirits. These manifestations come spontaneously from the groundwork of a free community, and because they are spontaneous, they seek and find many and diverse channels of expression. For this reason I would not strive to prevent the establishment of a State publishing house, or a guild of publishers, or a guild of authors publishing their own works: I would add to private enterprise any institutions of co-operation and mutual aid which promised diversity and ease of communication. It is the character of restrictions that they breed and multiply, until, as Milton so vividly says, we "fall again into a grosse conforming stupidity, a stark and dead congealment of wood and hay and stubble forc't and frozen together." But Liberty is absolute: it suffers no limitation to its range, no definition of its measures. It is a reflection of the confident belief that when the dust of controversy has settled, and many subtle engines lie broken in the ditches, the divine image of truth shall stand, simple, radiant, and benign.

[1] Mr. F. J. Warburg in an address to the Publishers' Advertising Circle, 24th September, 1942.

CULTURE, LIBERTY AND SCIENCE

By GEORGE CATLIN, M.A., Ph.D.

I

THE SUBJECT OF YOUR CONFERENCE IS MILTON'S GREAT WORK IN FAVOUR of free speech—and, I have to add, free divorce. As a humble sharer, along indeed with Field-Marshal Montgomery, in the benefits of that famous school which Milton in his day shared, bred in the humanism instilled by the pious founders, Erasmus and Colet, I hold myself fortunate to have this opportunity of paying my tribute to a genius who was politican, pamphleteer and poet. His campaign for the freedom of books is not irrelevant in a period when both the great modern instruments of expression —yet mightier instruments than printing in his day—the radio and the cinema, are monopolistic; and the former a State monopoly where one tsar of opinion, suitably ensconced, can without accountability or appeal approve or disallow views and crush rivals. One of the best tributes we could offer to Milton would be to have a free radio in this country. The views of this great humanist and clerc—not always above the use of pretty strong invective—are especially precious in an age which will probably be known to history as the Age of the Tyrants, an Epoch of the Persecution of Free Speech by enthusiasts. For the enthusiasts free speech is a liberal delusion, and is disapproved of by the People's Courts as disloyal to the cause. Loyalty and truth are put in antithesis, Caesar and God. As one who was once treasurer of the Burned Books Library, I may say that this gratitude of ours to Milton's theme is of a very real and immediate nature, and no mere general phrase of rhetoric. We condemn with indignation the Nazi Burning of the Books, as we also condemn the stupid fanatics who publicly burned Colonel Lindbergh's book in Canada.

The subject of your present session is Science, Culture and Freedom. Culture is the expression of freedom of spirit, which is the highest excellence of freedom, if not its necessary groundwork. If economic freedom is for the sake of living, cultural freedom is for the sake of good living. It is the trait in terms of which humanity is human. Science as knowledge is part of that freedom; science as experiment part of that creative freedom.

II

Our task, which we have not performed, is that of *the subordination of applied science to this culture*, the living spirit of civilisation—just as means must always be subordinated to ends lest they twist, contort and defeat those ends themselves. *Cui bono?* A German military commentator, von Studnitz, says to his compatriots: "The question who wins or loses this war in the battlefield is meaningless." The Maquis has taught us that this is significantly true. An American politician says that "the war is already lost" if it is to end in the domination of the four great Powers over the powerless Powers; and, in deeper terms than those of power politics he is partly right. Victory, that is to say, is but a necessary step to an end which may yet be missed if civilisation is weakened. It was the victor Powers of the last war, Italy and Japan, who were the first to destroy the structure of peace in Corfu and Manchuria: that is one of the lessons of history.

Of civilisation the clercs, the heirs of Milton, if they do not betray their international trust, are the defenders. Chauvinism and national socialism of all kinds, including class-chauvinism, whether Tory or Marxist—and including our domestic variety of which we shall hear more—Chauvinism is their horse of Troy. Mazzini gave the correct formula for the humanistic combination of a legitimate nationalism and a warm-blooded internationalism.

Where have the clercs been tempted into error, and how has so-called "science" tempted them? We live in an age that worships the pseudo-scientific phrase "dynamic." The phrase is almost as sacred for some as "dialectical materialism," to which it is philosophically related. In an age when young men still ask with awe, "And didst thou see D. H. Lawrence plain?" it is a pleasure to turn again the pages of Croce's *History as the Story of Liberty* and see a criticism of "the dynamic." This dynamism was the core of troubles for Plato. And with its concurrent worship of unreason, whirlwind being King, it is the core of our nihilistic troubles, the black and the red nihilism to-day. For myself I am anti-dynamist; in this limited sense anti-romantic; anti-nihilist. I adhere to the old antithesis of reason and passion, and I desire an emotion recollected in tranquillity. Freud tells us that all life is tending to equilibrium, and I am content to conform to the law of all life. I might say of myself, with Carlyle, "By gad, I'd better." I revere Freud who has reduced so much wild, lawless freedom of the unconscious to the bondage of reason and to the service of Logos. But so many are stimulated by that sense of power—of which Mr. Somerset Maugham in his last book warns us—which identification with a dynamic movement gives, "all marching together." They cannot believe, with Koestler, that it is the duty of the humanist, the clerc, to differ. They are drunk with the poison of power which is the especial poison of our age. They feel that life, the life of instinct, should be, as Mr. Joseph Wood Krutch has suggested in his *Modern Temper*, like an exploding star, an exploding bomb, its parts rushing with great heat and glamour of light and blast, irrationally in all directions, good only to destroy but offering a fine time to all in the indulgence of this destruction. And, if applied science gives us power, then we ask for more and more, just to see how big an explosion we can make and how dynamic we can be. Here no ends, no values not relative, are admitted. What matters is not the fox but the hunt. What matters is only the enjoyment of the means themselves as instruments satisfying the insatiable áppetite for power.

I am not engaged in the popular and reactionary pastime of decrying machines. I am content to keep to the eminently judicious position of that brilliant Chinese, Mr. Hsiao, in his *Dragon Beards and Blue Prints*. I am prepared to accept the American slogan of the Century of the Common Man: Felicity through machines. Why make things more hard for ourselves just by inefficiency? Why waste human energy? Only after we have seen what machines can give our neighbour, can we invite him to share with us the pursuit of the sapphire tranquillity, undisturbedness, disinterested activity, *ataraxia*, *apathia*. I am only questioning the activity of those clercs who, in careless rapture, have sung hallelujah to the god of the flood that bears them on to the barbarism of uncritical power-worship; and I have read with the more profit that little pamphlet, *Why Don't We Learn from History,* of that good and inopportunistic humanist, Captain Liddell Hart. "The truth is," says Jacob Burckhardt, in *Reflections on History*, "that power is in itself evil." Let no one think that I am hitting at Communism. As will be clear in a minute, I am not. I am hitting at anarchism—not of the type advocated by such spiritual aristocrats as von Humbolt and Mill, Kropotkin and Herbert Read and Milton himself—but a brainless chaos satisfied with the dynamic glow of power. Power is of two main types, material by machines, and human by domination over men—and, *of all forms, the most dangerous is the first in the service of the second*.

I would call your attention to an article by Alexander Seversky, author of *Victory Through Air Power*, scientist and eminent aeronautic designer, written recently. He writes in the *Boston Herald*:

"Nothing on the surface of the earth will be able to survive the punishment dealt from the skies. . . . The paradox of modern technology is this: though its creation calls for brains of a high order, its operation does not. . . . The mechanics of mass demolition, brought into being by the most highly developed countries, can readily be taken over by backward peoples, with hundreds of millions of robots at their disposal and no civilised restraints to inhibit their use of the most terrible engines of destruction. . . . War hereafter will hold the threat of the end of civilisation. We need to realise this in all its brutal nakedness. Only then will mankind become aware that it must put its moral forces in balance with its technological forces."

What are we to do about this? It is the duty of the clercs who would not betray their trust and become addicts of the power-poison, the heroin of the masses and the intoxicant of megalomaniac leaders, to consider; and to constrain back the means to the service of the ends. It is our duty, like Milton in *Areopagitica*, to speak courageously and unpopularly, in a free and unpacific quest for truth. We must improve on Milton, who made the exception that (proximate danger to security apart) there was a right to persecute just one group—those who agreed with most of Christendom and disagreed with Milton. We must repudiate compulsory uniformity of thought, not only Fascist but even Marxist. We must not have a world where a Gestapo or Ovra or (grandam of them all) OGPU official can tap us on the shoulder when we disagree about liberty with the *New Statesman* or *Izvestia* (which, being translated, is *Truth*). I would not be with those who make a famine in the name of economic progress. Perhaps, indeed, the people will be with us. We will not tolerate Hitler's domination of the world and union of Europe. Having swept out this devil *we must yet not leave a void*. If civilisation is not to be broken up by violent anarchy, we must be humanists and internationalists, and not follow that tendency which Dr. Friedmann, of London University, tells us is almost inevitable, towards neo-imperialism. This is the first fight, the great fight, even more important than the economic fight, just as Power Analysis is more important and more true than the *démodé* Marxist Analysis. Otherwise the third and yet more scientific, more total war, comes. I have parliamentary acquaintances who are fixing already the date for it—1964, beginning in Sinkiang. Let us, incidentally, remember that *technical and scientific autarky*, economic isolationism for great areas, barbarous although it will be, is far more practicable to-day than forty years ago. Applied science is a moral neuter, save where it increases man's power for the good, truth, justice and mercy.

III

My trade is that of a political scientist. The fruit of my reflections, since I began them outside Mons twenty-six years ago, is that the bases of politics are three: geography, man-power, organisation. To-day we Englishmen live on a small island. Our man-power is not much larger than that of Java. We are politically in the same position as France, with its falling population, in 1920. Alone we can no longer sustain the role of Richelieu and Chatham. Nor is our geographic position any longer determinant. Admiral Mahan is dead and sea-power, as determinant, was an accident of Atlantic history; and the Atlantic, until Columbus, was a great waste of water. As Sir Halford Mackinder has shown, strategic dominance lies with the country that can control land power from Vienna to Mongolia. Mackinder wrote in 1918, but the coming of air power has underlined his argument. Air power rests on land power. Among oceans the Arctic is decisive, that great waste of ice. What, then, shall we do? Shall we try, with our scattered commonwealth, our black empire of Africa, and clinging to France, to streamline a heterogeneous area and seek to hold again for ourselves the Balance of Power between U.S.A. and U.S.S.R.? Our statesmen tell us that this is far from their thoughts. Or shall we have the vision to build a world organisation, so far as we may, in which science and power shall serve; and a Western organisation which we may build, of all the Anglo-Saxon and all the Latin peoples and of Western European culture, within this grand world frame of federation? That is so great a vision—where all offer co-operation to all who will take it, and the peoples are fused.

As, however, I survey this middle-class world of ours, now bleeding to death in Europe, I do not see this vision. I see the prospect of unpreparedness, depression, jealousy and (as ever in human history) war. I see the Marxists refusing to believe that we can build a pacific world order this side of universal Marxism, and resorting to the "expectation of violence" in the inevitable third war. I seek to avoid the fated recursus, and I find myself thinking that the future will belong to Russia—at least until such time as China recovers her own and the Land of Confucius leads civilisation —as lead it she worthily will. The Webbs compared the Communist control of the battle for power to that of the Jesuits and, for those of us who have known the Webbs, I do not believe that any of us will regard that, from the mouth of Beatrice, as quite a compliment. Professor Haldane has suggested that it might be a new and ruthless aristocracy, paid at rates that Plato might have approved for his rulers. It may be that we shall see a dictatorship; and, at this end of the second thousand years we shall see, as St. Augustine saw, power completing its course in total concentration as power—power human and mechanical, means as their own ends. New Rome will arise. Some will see in this the triumph of Anti-Christ. Not I. I do not regard a reconciliation of Christianity and Communism, or indeed Catholicism and Communism, as at all impossible, although I believe that this will mean first a persecuted Church and persecuted clerks, in whom Milton's spirit will be needed again. Rather than again using the resources of science for war or ever again urging the workers here to march against the workers there, I would choose this way. And in the end the world Church will triumph in alliance with a world empire. This is how I see the future, the Sickle replacing the Swastika and a hundred national flags. And, in connection with it, I turn the pages of Augustine even more profitably than those of Milton.

Nevertheless, I am not content at this moment that matters should rest there. The Anglo-Saxon Tradition, the tradition of Milton, contains great and free values for civilisation. And ultimately it is the cultural similarities that dominate the political relations, and not the reverse. Our task is to give institutional expression to the spirit of a culture, Anglo-Saxon, Latin, Slav, Chinese. The widest common culture is that of humanism, *a humanism that must be capable of understanding technics, and what technics and disciplined social sciences can contribute.* I trust that we shall not be partisans of East or West, or be drawn into the fanaticism of religious wars of ideology, or of those menacing fanatics and barbarians in spirit—the true causes of why this is the New Age of the Tyrants, the Age of Fanaticism, the Age of Torture—of whom John Locke says that "they are sure because they are sure." I recall a further remark of Jacob Burckhardt's. "Of all struggles the most appalling are the wars of religion. . . . Among civilised peoples they are the most terrible of all. The means of offence and defence are unlimited, ordinary morality is suspended in the name of the 'higher purpose,' negotiation and mediation are abhorrent—people want all or nothing." What the West can contribute is its empiric, tolerant and free spirit, the spirit of Erasmus, Montaigne and Goethe, *where science and technical functionalism are used, not as a weapon of competitive power for the domination of man by politicians (of course, for his good) but, like penicillin, as a solvent of objective human difficulties, science being harnessed to the international ends of culture.* Above all nations is humanity, and it is their judge.

IV

From one point of view man desires, as Freud has told us, death and war. He actively desires to persecute whether for freedom or for dogma; and he will always use science as a sword and a weapon. This is part of his cultural pattern as a carnivore. Man is a bad gorilla who would build Babel or conquer the stars from pride and rage. He is at best an adventurer with a torch, at worst a Hun and a Vandal, like those who, for their fanaticisms, have contributed to destroy irreplaceable material civilisation in these days. As Mr. John Betjeman has told us in the *Herald*, in the language of the day, in his review of Sir Osbert Sitwell, "the Little Man is a perfect stinker." There is another side to man, more recent biologically, more human, governed by Eros, not Eris, Strife, aspiring to tranquillity, mother of the creative arts and sciences. To master the first, we may contribute an international army; or to four great armies of the Powers that have power; or to one army, a Red World army, moving forward under the tocsin call of the Internationale, slaying its enemies in millions and liquidating its foes—*actum Dei per Russicos deposuit potentes de sede.* Let us yet, as humanists, never relax in fostering the second, the active spirit of reason, the reconciling spirit of the contemplative and quiet mind which holds the equitable balance of historic justice. We cannot resist the Nemesis of evil, as it works itself out in the thunder and whirlwind. But we can understand, mirror-like, the cause of the storm, the dialectic in this history, and hear the still voice of creative wisdom. We can use our courage as clercs to exercise a Miltonic free speech and to demand that the politicians shall listen to the voice of psychology and political science, or ignore its teachings at their cost. Now is, for this understanding, the time, and ours, as clercs, is the responsibility.

THE CONCEPTION OF LITERARY OBSCENITY AND THE FREEDOM OF LETTERS

By ALEC CRAIG

THE QUESTION OF THE SUPPRESSION OF BOOKS ON THE GROUND OF OBSCENITY is one very proper to be considered in connection with Milton because it is very closely bound up with the principle of intellectual liberty with which he was so much concerned. It is very proper to be considered along with the more general theme of the future relations of economic and spiritual values because we place intellectual liberty high among those entities which we call (perhaps for the want of a better word) spiritual. My subject is not, however, directly connected with the *Areopagitica* because that work is a statement of the case against legal censorship of books before printing and so successful was Milton's statement of that case that we have no such censorship in normal times in this country to-day.

There is, nevertheless, abroad in this country to-day the idea that writing can possess a quality called "obscenity" and an idea that writing possessing that quality should be suppressed. Furthermore, the law provides for this suppression by punishing people who write, publish, or print books held to be "obscene" and by destroying the books themselves. This law and its repercussions have results quite as serious as anything that could arise out of censorship in the strict sense of the word, that is, before publication.

In approaching this subject I am in a slight dilemma. I wish to argue a certain opinion about the matter, but I can hardly do so without expounding a very complicated set of facts—and there is not space enough to do both adequately. Well-read people are often very ignorant on this subject and even lawyers will sometimes say that the basis of the law under which books are banned in this country on the ground of obscenity, indecency, or sexual impropriety, is the Obscene Publications Act of 1857. In fact that Act only provided for the summary destruction of books whose publication constituted the already existing (and still existing) common law misdemeanour of publishing an obscene libel. But if this short paper is not to become a dry law treatise I must refer the reader who is interested in legal niceties to my book, *The Banned Books of England*, and content myself here with narrating a few examples of the action and consequences of the law. Some of these examples will be rather old and some quite recent, but they will be all equally topical. I shall relate nothing in respect of which law or practice has changed and nothing which might not happen again this very day.

First of all, let us go back to the year 1898. At that time there existed a body known as The Legitimation League whose principal object was the improvement of the legal status of children born out of wedlock. Not a very startling aim, perhaps, but it caused a great deal of sensation in those days; and the police were constantly snooping round the League's meetings and its office. One day a detective found a copy of Havelock Ellis's recently published book, *Sexual Inversion*, in the office. Ellis had no connection with the League, but the detective bought the book and the secretary, Mr. George Bedborough, was charged with publishing an obscene libel. The case caused the highest indignation in enlightened circles. A defence fund was raised and a committee formed, including Robert Buchanan, Bernard Shaw, J. M. Robertson, George Moore, and Edward Carpenter. The stage was set for a grand vindication of the principle of freedom. Before the trial, however, the police interviewed Mr.

Bedborough. They pointed out that in the event of a conviction it would not be the notables on the defence committee, or even Dr. Havelock Ellis, who would go to prison, but George Bedborough; and he was promised immunity if he saved them trouble by pleading guilty. Bedborough was a comparatively humble man with domestic responsibilities. When the great day came, without consulting either his counsel or the defence committee, he entered a plea of "Guilty." Of course, the defence scheme collapsed like a house of cards. Bedborough walked out of court to all intents and purposes a free man; but the judge vented a tirade of ignorant abuse on the book and Havelock Ellis stood branded as a common pornographer without a word said in his defence. His life-work, the great *Studies in the Psychology of Sex*, of which the book was the first instalment, had to be published in America and until recently could not be openly sold in this country.

The words "until recently" in the last sentence are important, because in 1936 a new edition of the *Studies* was openly advertised and has been sold here without interference. It is impossible to explain how the book became "unbanned" because nothing legal or official had happened in the interval. This mysterious "unbanning" process is even more remarkably exemplified in the case of James Joyce's *Ulysses*. The book was originally published in Paris. In 1923 the publishers consigned 500 copies to this country and the Customs authorities burnt 499 of them on the quay of Folkestone Harbour. Yet to-day this book is openly published by a leading London house in the ordinary way of trade and anyone can buy it for a very modest sum. At no time was there any intimation of change in the official attitude.

Just as banned books may become unbanned by the silent passage of time so, conversely, may books which have been immune from interference for years after their publication suddenly fall into the banned class and, furthermore, land those who handle them into serious predicaments. So recently as 1942 a man running a commercial lending library through the post from Cornwall included among the titles circulated to his customers three books. Two of them were redactions of a French encyclopædia of sexual knowledge, one redaction published nine years before and edited by Dr. Norman Haire. The other book was *The Power to Love* by Dr. Edwin Hirch, published by Lane in 1935. The man was prosecuted for lending these specific books and sentenced to twelve months' imprisonment. The sentence was confirmed by the Court of Criminal Appeal. It is a pleasure to relate, however, that as a result of representations made by Mr. T. L. Horabin, M.P., and others the Home Secretary authorised the prisoner's immediate release in August, 1943; but by that time he would shortly have regained his liberty under the ordinary rules.

Speculation may suggest that the gravamen of this man's offence in the eyes of authority was lending these books to people who could not afford to buy them. The idea receives some support from the history of James Hanley's *Boy*, a realistic but sincere account of the sufferings and death of a working-class lad who runs away to sea. The integral manuscript was published in a limited edition at two guineas. In 1931 an ordinary edition appeared at 7s. 6d. in which certain nautical expressions were represented by asterisks. The next year, on D. H. Lawrence's advice, the asterisks were replaced by "innocuous" words. All went well for two years more until in 1934 the 1932 text appeared at 3s. 6d. Then the blow fell and the publishers were heavily fined. An incident from *The Sexual Impulse* case is also perhaps relevant. The evidence of sixteen expert witnesses that this work was of considerable scientific, educational, and social value did not save it from condemnation in 1934. Janet Chance, who was among these witnesses, testified that the book was a helpful item in the library at her Sex Education Centre. The magistrate immediately asked her: "Have you ever given the book to a member of the working class?"

Let us now turn to foreign literature. The outstanding case is that of Henry Vizetelly, a publisher who at the age of seventy had to endure the rigours of a Victorian prison for issuing bowdlerised translations of Zola's novels. A few years later Zola himself, wearing the rosette of an Officer of the Legion of Honour, paid an official visit to London and was publically banqueted and fêted, "much like a visiting potentate!" Even to-day the English reader is denied translations of works by such writers as Pierre Louÿs and Karl Huysmans. A condemnation in 1934 covering these authors also included translations of the *Satyricon* of Petronius and of a book of the *Greek Anthology*. Even the most scholarly translations of the classics (many of the magnificent Loeb series, for instance) are incomplete.

Having touched on the international aspect a story of a conference on obscene literature held under the auspices of the League of Nations after the 1914-18 war may not be out of place. When the delegates of the various countries assembled, a Greek speaker suggested that it would be as well to start off by defining the subject of their deliberations. The British delegate (Sir Archibald Bodkin) immediately rose to object. He pointed out that there was no definition of indecent or obscene in English law and at his suggestion the conference resolved that no definition was possible. The uniform enforcement of obscenity laws all over the world became one of the minor aims of the League of Nations; and it is pretty certain that the issue will be revived by any similar institution. Had such uniformity existed at the time of Havelock Ellis's trouble his *Studies* would never have seen the light.

Well, there are the facts so far as space will allow: what of opinion?

If I were addressing myself primarily to lawyers I should suggest that a law so arbitrary in its essence and so uncertain in its incidence was unworthy of the name of law, and, indeed, was no law at all in any proper sense of the word. I should argue that this was not only a matter of remedying occasional injustices to individuals or of restraining occasional excesses of zeal on the part of individual officials, but that the law as it is now interpreted and administered is an intrusion on those principles of liberty of thought and of freedom of discussion which are the very life-blood of our Constitution and, what is more, that it is deliberately exploited for their own purposes by interests which explicitly or implicitly deny the validity of those principles. I should urge that the least that could be asked for was a return to the interpretation of the law as expounded by Lord Chief Justice Campbell in 1857 when he insisted that the law of obscenity applied only "to works written for the single purpose of corrupting the morals of youth and of a nature calculated to shock the common feelings of decency in any well-regulated mind."

If I were addressing myself primarily to sociologists, I should use the simile of the iceberg whose larger and more dangerous part is concealed beneath the water. I should show that the cases that come into the law courts and the books legally destroyed are of less account than the repercussions of this law on scientific investigation, on the education of the mass of the people, and on the libraries and the cheaper publications which provide the bulk of their reading matter. I should maintain that the resulting ignorance and sexual misery has done far more harm to the community and the race than any imaginable spate of pornography could have done.

But I am addressing myself primarily to writers and I would remind them of distinguished names from among them who, directly or indirectly, have suffered from this law. Besides those already mentioned are D. H. Lawrence, Shane Leslie, Radclyffe Hall, Richard Aldington, and Henry Miller. I say: that law and practice in this regard constitute an insult to the integrity of letters; that as a body they should demand reform; and that as a body they should rally to the defence of any one of their number who is a victim of this state of affairs, however obscure he may be.

Before concluding I wish to refer to another case in order to drive home an important point. In 1942 a doctor named Eustace Chesser was prosecuted in respect of a manual of sex instruction designed to meet the needs of people as he had found them to exist in his consulting-room experience. Dr. Chesser had the courage to defend himself before a jury of his countrymen and was acquitted. In subsequent editions of the book, however, he omitted certain passages out of deference to the views of other doctors and authors. This is important. Anyone who pleads for liberty is always accused of advocating licence. This is particularly so where any sexual subject is concerned. What I am advocating is not irresponsibility, but the view that the law is not a proper instrument to secure responsibility in this regard. That a man should defer to the judgment of his intellectual peers and of his fellow writers I hold to be good. I believe that there is such a thing as a literary conscience among us to-day; and I believe that those who outrage it in any way do so to their spiritual hurt and ultimately to their material loss. It is some satisfaction to me that I have written two books (*The Banned Books of England* and its companion volume, *Above All Liberties*) on this rather delicate matter without being reprimanded by any critic on a point of taste except when the reviewer of the organ of the

Rationalist Press Association raised one objection. Since it has been my purpose to modify the enlightened taste of my time, not to outrage it, I shall defer to his susceptibilities in subsequent editions of my work.

Having entered this caveat that liberty is not licence, I trust that I may conclude by securing some measure of agreement to the proposition: that the claim of policemen, lawyers, and officials, to sit in judgment on the works of scholars, men of science, educators, and creative artists is an impertinent tyranny; and that three hundred years after the publication of Milton's *Areopagitica* it constitutes an anachronism which should be swept away.

AN EDITOR'S VIEW

By KINGSLEY MARTIN, M.A.
Editor, *New Statesman and Nation*

THAT MILTON WAS A VERY GREAT POET NO ONE DISPUTES; WHETHER HIS voluminous writings on political topics show him to have been a profound thinker or a very long-winded bore, I have never quite been able to determine. It is in any case clear that he minded about civil liberty, and it is no reply to say that the reason why he cared about divorce reform was that he wanted to get rid of his wife, and the reason he wanted free speech was because he feared interference with his own religion or pamphleteering. We are all influenced in our opinions by personal experiences, and the body of civil rights of which we are rightly proud has grown up because different groups of people in society have objected to interference with their own freedom. We have religious liberty because the Puritans fought against authoritarian creeds, and the right of free speech because the intellectuals and the scientists demanded the liberty to inquire and to speculate, and the right of free association because it was only through the trade union organisation that the workers were able to stand up to their employers. Anyway, Milton minded about freedom; in our century he would have disliked Goebbels and Franco and Sir William Joynson-Hicks, and his attitude to Stalin would have been, I suspect, very much what it was to Cromwell—a mixture of respect for the great Puritan leader coupled with criticism when his domination threatened the freedom of people like Milton.

In one famous passage he argued that the general toleration he advocated should not be extended to Roman Catholics because they denied the right of other people to similar freedom, and would suppress them if they regained power in Britain. This passage has been widely criticised by liberal writers as showing a limitation in Milton's thinking, if not a defect in his character. In the nineteenth century, when Catholics in Britain seemed to be dwindling, this was an easy point of view. Toleration could be advocated universally because those who advocated it did not fear the success of any group who would destroy it. But in Milton's day, religious wars were still being fought. The triumph of Catholic authoritarianism in England would have meant the end of newly-gained civil rights. His words are again singularly appropriate in the twentieth century, when Fascism is an even greater menace than the clerical authoritarianism of the seventeenth century. For us the issue arises just as it did for Milton. If we insist that there shall be no exceptions to our tolerance, then we are running the risk of finding, as German Liberals and Socialists found, that the Fascist movement may make use of the liberty we permit to destroy the liberties of all of us. We move here, you see, out of the sphere of pure theory into the difficult pragmatic test of politics. There can be no cut-and-dried answer. We have to remember that the liberty of the individual is our aim, but we may find it necessary in a critical situation (as we have during the war) to accept a certain curtailment of liberty in order that we may maintain it after the crisis is over.

It is on this point that a dispute arises about the Soviet Union. Without the western tradition of individual freedom, the Soviet Union has carried out the great social change without which the modern community cannot prosper or grow. Until the test of what is produced is that it meets the needs of the common people, and the main resources of the community are in the hands of a central authority, our society is condemned to an uneasy state of class struggle. It is only too clear that in such a revolutionary period, civil liberty may be destroyed, and that in Russia, now that there is general acceptance of the new economic order, certain civil liberties which we mind about will have to be won by Russians who care about freedom. I am sure, therefore, that our right attitude is to support the Soviet Union and to seek its friendship with all the strength in our power, but our support must be a critical and constructive support. It is a mistaken subservience to think that those are necessarily anti-Soviet who are critical of some Soviet policies. I may cite as an example the introduction which Mrs. Webb contributed to a later edition of the Webbian masterpiece, *Soviet Communism*. Replying to those who were critical of some of the methods of the purges in Russia, she pointed out quite correctly, that after a revolution there was always a hangover, and that in England, for instance, we went on persecuting Roman Catholics for at least a century longer than was necessary to secure the new Protestant settlement. Historically she was quite right, and the illustration exactly serves my purpose. Surely it would have been better, if there had been people to criticise the State, when in the wave of anti-Catholic excitement, people accepted all the lies of Titus Oates. Many good people perished in that purge. So to-day the task of the man who keeps his head is to support revolutionary change and at the same time to remind people that every attack on freedom that goes beyond what is absolutely necessary is dangerous to the very object of the revolution.

We are now moving from the profound peace in which we have been living during the last five years into an era of strife and difficulty. This may sound paradoxical, but if you consider the large measure of agreement, almost unanimity, attained in this country during the war as the result of the German danger, and note the bitter currents of division that begin to appear as peace looms nearer, you will perforce agree with me. Tired as we are, and anxious as we all are to pursue our private lives, and to develop our talents in peace, we shall find, as we found before the war, that it is impossible to stand aside from the political and economic battles to come. They are all-embracing, and they impinge on the life of every individual. Like Milton, whether we are poets or less gifted people, we shall find ourselves writing political tracts and being forced into compromises which spoil the neatness of our theoretical positions. We may know what we want, but we may have to take all sorts of strange roads to get there. Walking in Ireland, a friend of mine asked a man he met in a country lane if he knew the way to Ballygoorly. "Sure," said the man, "I know the way to Ballygoorly, but if it were Ballygoorly I were going to, it wouldn't be from here I'd be starting." That is just how I feel. I know the way to the New Jerusalem and the International Federation of Socialist Republics in which mèn are free and equal, but just how to go from here is not obvious to me. We are in for a difficult life in which liberty remains the end to be achieved, and politics unfortunately remains the tortuous path which we have to tread.

THE EXAMPLE OF MILTON

By Mulk Raj Anand

I

THERE ARE SOME OF US IN INDIA WHO HAVE LOOKED TO EUROPE FOR inspiration in the integration of a new awareness. And that is not because we are half-baked modernists who prefer to wear borrowed plumes to hide our primitive nakedness, but rather because we are a people who have been traditionally inured to believe that the world is many-coloured, that there are a variety of ways of living, that one is free to live in East or West—so long as one lives thoroughly. Our own civilisation was predominantly a verticalist one, always bearing towards the clouds, reaching out to the Truth above all truths, burning like a phœnix to renew itself, its flames rising ever higher. Often when this rare bird alighted on to the earth again, with wings singed by its own fire, it found that it had forgotten how to live on the horizontal plane altogether. So out it hopped on its feeble frame and travelled across the oceans to exercise its limbs and to receive the impact of all the winds that blew, and it came back free and whole, as one can only be by returning to the place from which one has gone away, by having rediscovered oneself in the light of other suns and universes. We have been a hospitable people, the natural givers. So please do not grudge us the h'pennyworth of common sense we have bought off you English, nor the pennyworth of dreams that we still haggle over, nor the sixpennyworth of the *Areopagitica* that has accrued to us almost as the huckster's profit.

We are engaged in the task of creating a new synthesis of values, and we do not think that culture or civilisation are the monopoly of any one race, or nation, or people. So we take what we like from wherever we like, always of course acknowledging our debt, but sometimes, to the chagrin of Mr. Unwin, ignoring the copyright convention. And through all this give and take we are finding out that the world is one, that there is a continuity running from one end of the globe to the other like the blood in a man's body, and that wherever this pulse beats strongest there is humanity at its intensest.

II

I annexed Milton into my world of dreams at the age of twelve when I learnt to recite the first book of *Paradise Lost* by rote. That feat was not peculiar to me in India. Most of our ancient verse and prose is in the possession of the people through the mnemonic tradition by which people learn from father to son and son to son whole yards of poetry, often without ever reading it. I early discovered that the girl poet, Toru Dutt, knew more than half of *Paradise Lost* by heart, and that, particularly in Bengal of the late nineteenth century, Milton was as much a household name as Shakespeare and Kalidasa, or Wordsworth and Valmiki. The most important formal innovations in Bengali poetry, the introduction of blank verse, was achieved by Michael Madhu Sudan Dutt, directly under the influence of John Milton. And this device of running on the sense from line to line in a new kind of rhythm was followed by a great many writers of epic and dramatic verse in the other vernacular languages. How often one hears, in that land where people are not afraid to string their ordinary conversation with copious quotations of poetry, the proud recapitulation of the passages in Milton which have any reference to India! The most frequent quotation, of course, is:

"Eyeless in Gaza, at the mill with slaves . . . ."

Also, that bit of fauna, the description of the banyan tree under which Adam and Eve took shelter after their expulsion from Paradise, appeals both for its local reference and its tonal qualities:

> "They chose
> The figtree, not that kind for fruit renowned,
> But such as, at this day to Indians known
> In Malabar or Decan spreads her arms,
> Branching so broad and long, that in the ground
> The bended twigs take root, and daughters grow
> About the mother tree, a pillared shade
> High over-arched, with echoing walks between.
> There oft the Indian herdsman, shunning heat,
> Shelters in cool, and tends his pasturing herds
> At loop-holes, cut through thickest shade."

And Milton had a love for sonorous, majestic names which Indians share with him.   Adam's vision is very. much of our side of the world:

> "the destined-walls
> Of Cambalu, seat of Cathanian Can,
> And Samarcand by Oxus, Temir's throne,
> To Paquin of Sinanan Kings, and thence
> To Agra and Lahor of Great Mogul."

Some people may think it rather strange that a culture so set in its own peculiar mould as the Indian should be amenable to English poetry, particularly the work of a seventeenth-century English poet like Milton. For, even most of those who know that English is spoken and written in India still tend to think of it as being spoken and written by Mr. Punch's classic Babu.   Of course, we have Babus in India, badly taught products of the Macaulay scheme of education, evolved in 1835, and still going strong.   But the great English poets do not appeal to them.   The sanction of English poetry applies rather among a new generation which has consciously turned its back on the putrid British-Indian education system, and which has gone, in spite of the prohibitions of authority, to the very sources of European art and literature.

This growing generation is as yet a tiny minority.   But, conscious of its role as the builder of a new renaissance, it is sedulously creating a new sense of values, an amalgam of Asiatic humanism with the experimentalism of the West.   To an Indian of this generation, English poetry is not some college text of a Milton poem, with cram notes and questions and answers prepared by some stodgy professor, but a real book, a fable in a series of allegories which expresses the struggle of the human spirit for liberation from the temptations of weakness and corruption, and from the yoke of authority.   The lines which really ring a bell in the head of an Indian of this generation are such as these from Samson:

> "O, how comely it is and how reviving
> To the spirits of just men long oppressed,
> When God into the hands of their deliverer
> Puts invincible might . . ."

For the Indian Revolution is, like Milton's Samson in his strength, shaking its invincible locks!

III

What is this Indian Revolution I speak of?

Plainly, it is the emerging awareness among Indians of the right to be free, to talk, think, write and read freely, to go about without fear of arbitrary arrest by executive authority, the right to be equal before the law, the right to reject the divine rights, whether of Kings or of priests, above all, the right to eat and drink and enjoy the fresh air, without someone else always monopolising these to his advantage. Small aims and modest aspirations, they all seem, and you wouldn't think anybody would deny them to anybody else. And yet two hundred years after Milton fought for them in this country a struggle started in India to achieve them which has so far realised very little, a great deal less even than what you had already realised through the industrial revolution. Well may the Indian Samson in his strength shake his invincible locks!

Though the *Artha Shastra*, the political code of the Hindus, recommends continual grousing against authority as the only way to keep the State from oppressing society unduly, personal liberty was seldom the strong point of the caste-ridden, "feudal" Indian tradition. Religious toleration was a fairly constant factor in Indian civilisation, surprising as this seems to us who only know the Hindu-Muslim controversy—though to a large extent this really cloaks the clash of more mundane interests among Indians. For there were the little village republics, owning only a temporary allegiance to whoever happened to rule at the capital. But the whole tradition was like that preferred by the Greeks, a rather splendid, aesthetic, generous, aristocratic democracy. Since then the introduction of machine civilisation has started all those processes which destroyed the very basis of the old life, through the railway engine, the roads, the postal and telegraph system, the central bureaucracy and the penny Press. So that to-day we aspire, with you, to another kind of democracy, the one which had its birth here in Europe and whose destiny is being decided in our time.

IV

There follow from this transformation a number of philosophical attitudes in India. But the main tendency of the young out there is to ask questions even if they do not get any positive answers, and they prefer a kind of radical scepticism, if you would like to call their shrewd, hesitating, doubting attitude such. I am not sure what their attitude would be towards the main issue before us, namely, the place of Spiritual and Economic values in the future of mankind. But as I am speaking much more for myself than for anyone else, I would like to suggest that the words "Spiritual," "Economic" and "Value" need more exact definition.

Inured for thousands of years to philosophical controversy about the invisible and the intangible, we are chary of using the word "Spiritual" because too often it has so easily become a cover for sheer mendacity and superstition. On the other hand, I think that in the absence of another more appropriate word, it has to be used. I would like to signify by it breath, the life-breath of human existence, the quality of living, the flame. The word "economic" has been a little better defined, dealing as it does with *quantities*, even though any talk of quantities has very deep "Spiritual" implications. And "value" by which is understood anything which an individual contemplates with the deepest and most sincere conviction, may come in future to embrace a much larger universe of discourse than our present prejudices will allow.

So that the question whether the exaltation of "Spiritual" or "Economic" values will be better for the future of mankind seems to me to be a simplification of the world struggle, which is various in its implications and predominantly a human struggle, the rediscovery by human beings of the fundamentals—human dignity, bread, water, air and freedom. The categories "Spiritual" and "Economic" will not cover all these, and I am inclined to think that a great deal of our present misery is due to the categorising habit current in Europe. Analysis there must be for clarity, but rigid categories too often lead to the compartmentalisation of the human personality, and this attitude, whether deliberate or unconscious, leads to evasion. The world will not be saved by taking sides in controversies which are outdated and outmoded, but by an emphasis, in the present crisis, on the many-sided nature of man, and by an attempt at synthesis, by seeking, as far as possible, the perspective of the whole man with all his faculties alive, by recommending to every man the cultivation of a few more eyes, as it were, two at the back of the head, one on each side, one on the forehead above the natural eyes, and another in the heart as well. For to say that the outside is important is to ignore the inner eye. To look only inward is to stumble in the outer darkness. And any partial view invites disaster, as the tasks facing us in this broken and ruined world of ours are so enormous that only men, whole men, who think of the inner and outer as one, can envisage them. And such a view, dependent as it is on the sensibility of the artist, the linguist who speaks ten different languages, the revolutionary who is for ever renewing human experience in the face of the ever-increasing crudification, naturally makes for the only way in which the balance between good and evil may be kept up in this world, in the creation of more art, a higher and a greater one.

I do not want to minimise the difficulties of achieving this balance between good and evil, or rather of the need to tilt the scales for good against evil. We may need all the strength and agility we can muster to make any difference. But each one of us can only try to seek balance, to learn to be a tight-rope walker, as it were, before anything like equilibrium can be restored to this lopsided world. And then it has to be the joint effort of many men, distinct and individual, but together, people who have realised their personality and are able to act for a community not yet born. The means of achieving this change within the vast change of our time may be neither merely knowledge nor merely will, but both, in the form of a deep and intense realisation of the world, such as may make knowledge a kind of will, and such as may make men fully themselves, men, *individuals* as well as *examples*, human beings of a new world and a new era, such as may become the precursor of a new renaissance, greater than the one of which our present world was the product. . . .

In making the last few observations I insist that I have been speaking entirely for myself. But I have a feeling that many of the young in India share in this kind of humanism. And, may I venture to say, that perhaps the young in Europe also do, even though there may be certain differences of emphasis between us. Certainly to the young in India there is no bifurcation between moral values and political values: in my country morality is politics and politics morality. And perhaps the European young are beginning to feel the same way about it.

Anyhow, in this regard, the generation of Indians I am speaking about are together with the European young, for they, too, have tested their insight in the light of Kant and Hegel, Mazzini and Proudhon, Marx and Mill, even as their contemporaries in the West have done. We have no illusions that Europe is at the moment like a lavatory with no one to pull the chain. But in spite of the horrors it has let loose through its "material" greed and selfishness, the present European form of civilisation is the only one which the world possesses, for good or ill, and it is the only instrument which, in the hands of men with clear heads and stout hearts, may bring a little more happiness to those who have so far been mere pawns in the hands of a more acquisitive elite. The present generation of Indians, therefore, wants a moral and material revolution. It knows the penalties for the choice it has made; it knows that to move from the old order is to undertake a long journey through chaos to a dream world which may recede further and further with every advance; but it has made the choice; it is within the orbit of the democratic idea.

V

If John Milton were alive to-day, he would have approved this choice. "Superstition and tyranny," he wrote, "are the most prevailing usurpers of mankind." "Liberty," he said, "is the nurse of all great wits." And justice and equality were to him better than undue wealth, for he says in *Comus:*

> "If every just man that now pines with want
> Had but a moderate and beseeming share
> Of that which lewdly pampered luxury
> Now heaps upon some few with vast excess,
> Nature's full blessings would be well dispersed."

As for intellectual freedom—the fact that three hundred years after the publication of *Areopagitica* I, an Indian, come to celebrate this book is proof of the intensity of Milton's belief and of the universality of its significance.

Yes, Milton would have approved of the choice of the younger generation of India. For, defying the ordinances which ban books and newspapers at the least little excuse in their country, they call out with the English poet:

> "Dare ye for this adjure the civil sword
> To force our consciences?"

But who are these "forcers of consciences"? Please don't be perturbed. They are not in this room. They are outside the orbit of the democratic idea. They do not belong to the family of liberty for all their prating about "freedom and democracy." They are not the Englishmen who make England's name synonymous with the Habeas Corpus Act or with the rights of the individual. They are not admirers of Milton, Wordsworth, Coleridge, Byron and Shelley, and they would say that E. M. Forster is a cad because he wrote *A Passage to India*. They talk of the divinity of trusteeship but carry it, for safety, in their gun-cases and portmanteaux. They profess self-government and equality before the law, but when it comes to applying them, they find enough safeguards and reservations to keep the reality of power in their own hands. Their legal and constitutional ideas are so flexible that they can easily pick up any law of a hundred or two hundred years ago and use it to suppress a newspaper or a book which they don't like in case they have no mock parliament available to pass a law for them when they need it. The only tests they know are the empirical and practical ones: the man on the spot, in their estimation, always knows better than the M.P. who takes the grievances of his constituency and the subject peoples seriously. They see the sun so much that they think it shines on the just and the unjust alike. And they regard Imperialism as the highest attainment of the ideals of law and representative government. They prefer property to equality and their own interests to those of their neighbours or society. They are Englishmen—"the best people, you know!" And yet I must confess that I am biased and prefer those other Englishmen, the gentle, homely people who don't boast about their Empire, who believe in Democracy as a way of life, and who don't worship what William James called the "bitch-goddess Success." I am with the heirs of Milton who raise their voice every time they get to know that a minority opinion has been suppressed. And it is because I share this belief in free speech and opinion with these latter Englishmen that I have come here to-day.

When I first bought the sixpenny brochure of the *Areopagitica* in an old bookshop in Calcutta some years ago and read it, I seemed to have the illusion that some Indian savant had adopted the seventeenth-century manner to camouflage his attack on the present censorship in India. Since then I have re-read it in relation to the events of 1640, Marston Moor and all that, and I marvel at its magnificent prose even as I understand the local circumstances which caused it to be written.

If I venture, therefore, to claim the *Areopagitica* as a handbook to help us preserve our civil liberties in India, I am sure my presumption will be forgiven. I hope I am not taking it out of its context. But it is a book we need even more than you do. And I assure you that we will make good use of it. We might reprint a few maxims out of it and distribute them in New Delhi and Whitehall. "When complaints are freely heard, deeply considered, and speedily reformed, then is the utmost bound of civil liberty attained, that wise men look for"—that would be a good text for us to encourage our newspapers to print on the pages they nowadays leave blank as a protest against the Viceregal ordinances that ban certain forms of discussion. And that great passage about the value of a book, "almost kill a man as kill a good book; who kills a man kills a reasonable creature, God's image, but he who kills a good book, kills reason itself, kills the image of God, as it were, in the eye"—that we would ask our students to inscribe on their luggage labels so that the consciences of the Customs authorities at Bombay will be touched. For, perhaps you do not know that these worthies at the port of Bombay are in the habit of confiscating Tolstoy's *Anna Karenina* as well as Lenin's *What is to be Done?* because they are both written by Russians. And the following phrase of Milton's we will adopt as our motto for generations to come, both as an aspiration and a warning: "Truth is a streaming fountain; if her waters flow not in perpetual progression, they sicken into a muddy pool of conformity and tradition."

For, more and more during the last twenty-five years there has been blowing from the high towers on which authority is seated, a breath of prohibition against the despisers of the general shame, and against those who feel that it is impossible for them to obey any laws which do not involve a moral sanction. Hundreds of newspapers have been suppressed and the securities, they are required to deposit, seized by the Sarkar. For a time it was an offence for a paper to report the proceedings of the central legislature. And thousands of books are on the banned list. The position of the press became abject when newspapers had to obey the press officers of the Government of India and print only official hand-outs, even before the war. Some correspondents of English newspapers have recently protested against the severity of the censorship by refusing to send any more cables and have insisted on their recall home. An Indian correspondent of an English newspaper, who had specially gone out to India, returned because all his reports on the famine in Bengal were badly mutilated and some were not allowed to go out of the country at all.

The obvious result of this suppression has been that a number of papers have gone into liquidation or have voluntarily ceased to appear altogether. For in India there has been current an idea that it is the duty of all the victims of authority to invite upon their own devoted heads all the suffering that they are capable of undertaking.

But the inner implications of this suppression are that the soul of India is fast corroding, for frustration and unhappiness are the inevitable corollaries of suppression. And the effect on the creative minds of India of this frustration is immeasurable, for the fear of fear imposes a self-censorship on the minds of writers which saps their innermost convictions. Then, not only does the courage to create suffer eclipse, but all the promptings of the heart are twisted and perverted, and the writer often begins to lie because he is afraid of being discovered telling the truth and punished. Thus, the great ideal which, perhaps, more than any other inspires the writer, the love of Truth, is travestied. And there settles upon him an apathy, a listlessness which makes for barrenness and a paralysis of the desire to live.

Face to face with a tyranny that is almost Hitlerian and with the gigantic task of constructing something positive out of the transformation that is going on in our country, in the midst of a renaissance which is also a reformation, the writers of India are to-day gasping for breath and waiting for something to happen—something they know not what. The intellectual imagination, the incandescent passion for the discovery and expression of truth, the inexorable urge to explore the ultimate sources of human experience, the gift which interprets and renews life by rousing the emotions and creating works of art so that they may enlighten and stimulate the will, the genius of the artist, call it what you will, cannot flourish under a tyrannical State. The struggle of the artist against his own personal inhibitions is always difficult enough. But when to this are added the rules and ordinances of the roughnecks of Delhi and toughnecks of Whitehall, who spit at everything that comprises man's moral greatness, then creative effort has not a chance.

I am not unmindful of the fact that the demands of the artist's imagination have seldom found a congenial atmosphere in the past. The man whose vision can penetrate into the deepest and most unsuspected layers of reality and reveal the sordidness and pettiness of existence, as well as realise the subtlest perfumes in the garden, and the most evanescent moods of human beings and animals, the man who is more human than the rest, is bound to be suspect. Did they not give Socrates the hemlock to drink? And did they not imprison Galileo? . . . But surely there has been no time like the present so far as the writers of India are concerned! A deep, dark night engulfs the mental life of Hindustan. . . .

VII

At a time like this, therefore, the example of Milton is likely to be of inestimable value to the writers of India.

Already, as I have indicated by my observations on the increasing tendency among Indians to believe in a knowledge made will, they have been inclined to place a high value on *example* as such. They had long since come to realise that in a putrescent, unclean age like ours, the role of a writer was not merely that of a sanitary inspector, the provider of hygiene and disinfection. Equally they had realised that his role was not to depart from the poet's attitude and become merely a man of action, a party organiser. They knew that there are plenty of ideas lying around the world, as well as a great deal of violent action. They have, therefore, been emphasising in their behaviour what I may describe as the integration of idea and act in the form of the *example*. When a writer recognises that he is a man and a citizen, and takes a stand in defence of an idea, he is, in this sense, offering himself as an *example*. Almost all our intellectuals have aspired to this kind of Truthful action, not always successfully and at a sacrifice perhaps of some part of their nature, but they have been forced by the peculiar demands of India to place this ideal before themselves. In fact, if you ask me what is the peculiar contribution that the Indian intelligentsia can make to the rehabilitation of the world to-day, I would say that it is to show how a writer can be a man and make an *example* of himself and illustrate how the moral force of an individual can defy the organised might of tyrants.

Milton, too, ostensibly believed in the force of an *example*. For he, too, as a man and citizen took a stand at each critical point of the violent history of his time, and even lost his sight in the ceaseless struggle he waged for twenty-odd years. Like all writers, he naturally disliked the arena and resented the fact that he had to leave "the quiet and still air of delightful studies," but he, nevertheless, spoke out and acted on his beliefs. The poet and the man in him were one and, it is arguable that from *Comus* to *Samson* and *Paradise Lost* his work would have lost a great deal of its intensity without the rich experience of life that lay behind it.

The example of Milton is, therefore, a very important one for Indian writers. For Liberty for them is a question of life and death. And they see in his life-work a model for their own. They remember his warning:

> "Sometimes nations will decline so low
> From virtue, which is reason, that no wrong,
> But Justice and some fatal curse annexed,
> Deprives them of their outward liberty."

And in the present conflict, with its immense possibilities of doom, they are devoted to the task of sweeping the putrescent rubbish of philistinism and tyranny so that men can fill their lungs with fresh air.

Already in the work of one of the boldest and most brilliant poets of Northern India, Josh, one hears an almost Miltonic ring. In a stanza of the *Chorus of Humanity*, he sings:

> The long dark night is ending,
> Sails of colour and fragrance float in the air,
> The sky is fresh, the earth is covered with a veil of mist
> And through the soft gloom of the horizon,
> A gold red dawn is breaking . . ."

VIII

That a few spirits in Britain are so devoted to the conception of liberty that they can be willing to see all aspects of it, even those which remind them of the fact that freedom of speech and opinion are as yet the privilege only of a few lucky people here, fills me with hope. For the continuity of our interests furthers communication. And as communication is the life-blood not only of the existing relations but the possible thread which may unite the supra-national individuals of the future, it is possible that together, we can rise and ask that all oppressors be overthrown, that the gravediggers of humanity be abolished, that men be allowed to rise to their real stature and dignity as men.

But liberty is something each one of us has to believe in, from his or her own inmost heart. And how difficult it is for most people to believe in it? For, cowardice asks, is it safe to believe in liberty? Vanity asks, is it popular to believe in liberty? . . . And many there are who, therefore, shut their eyes to glaring violations of liberty and merely pay lip service to the ideal.

There is, always, however, the voice of conscience calling aloud in the dark, "liberty, liberty," and asking—"Is it or is it not better than slavery?"

May I remind you of the voice of your consciences?

AN AMERICAN'S TRIBUTE

By HERBERT AGAR

I

ON THIS 300TH ANNIVERSARY OF MILTON'S "SPEECH . . . FOR THE LIBERTY of unlicens'd printing," the world is still warring over the principles of *Areopagitica*. Our enemies of to-day deny these principles utterly, in their dealings with themselves as well as with us. And if the experience of the last war is any guide we may soon hear voices raised in our own countries in favour of suspending free expression, at least in part, abroad if not at home.

The backwash of a great war breeds intolerance and favours arbitrary acts of suppression. It is perhaps a good time for us authors, who live by the word, to review again the old arguments for the freedom of the word.

First, before seeking any modern applications, I wish to suggest that *Areopagitica* is of help in interpreting Milton's great epics. This is a point which seems often to be overlooked by students of Milton.

In arguing against a licensing Act which would subject all books to State censorship, Milton was naturally led to support what Justice Oliver Wendell Holmes calls "free trade in ideas—that the best test of truth is the power of the thought to get itself accepted in the competition of the market." According to this view, if all thoughts believed to be false are suppressed, truth will also languish necessarily.

"When God gave Adam reason," said Milton, "He gave him freedom to choose, for reason is but choosing; he had been else a mere artificial Adam . . . God therefore left him free, set before him a provoking object, ever almost in his eyes, herein consisted his merit, herein the right of his reward, the praise of his abstinence." And Milton adds that when we use the method of suppressing false ideas, "how much we thus expel of sin, so much we expel of virtue: for the matter of them both is the same; remove that, and ye remove them both alike."

And again he says: "good and evil we know in the field of this world grow up together almost inseparably; and the knowledge of good is so involved and interwoven with the knowledge of evil, and in so many cunning resemblances hardly to be discerned, that those confused seeds which were imposed on Psyche as an incessant labour to cull out, and sort asunder, were not more intermixt."

You will recall the famous passage where he says that truth has been divided by a "race of deceivers" into thousands of pieces. "From that time ever since," he adds, "the sad friends of truth, such as durst appear, imitating the careful search that Isis made for the mangled body of Osiris, went up and down gathering up limb by limb still as they could find them. We have not yet found them all, Lords and Commons, nor ever shall do, till her Master's second comming." Therefore, he urges, since truth can only be known in conjunction with falsehood, sin in conjunction with virtue, the mind of man should be left free so that the "sad friends of truth" may continue their incessant search.

<u>All this is a Miltonic application of the Platonic (and the Stoic) thesis that virtue is knowledge—that only by knowledge of the eternal moral law (which may often conflict with the temporary laws of a community) can man attain virtue,</u> and thus εὐδαιμονία.

I suggest that if we apply this theory that virtue is knowledge to the epics, much that seems confusing becomes clear—including Milton's reason for preferring *Paradise Regained* to any of his other poems.

I shall not labour the point in reference to *Paradise Lost*, which is so well known; but I would like to call attention to the passage in Book XII where Michael tells Adam that the result of the Fall has been to subject man's reason to his passions and desires, and where Michael explicitly states that "virtue is reason":

> " . . .; yet know withall,
> Since thy original lapse, true Libertie
> Is lost, which alwayes with right Reason dwells,
> Twinn'd, and from her hath no dividual being:
> Reason in man obscur'd, or not obeyed,
> Immediately inordinate desires
> And upstart Passions catch the Government
> From Reason, and to servitude reduce
> Man till then free.   Therefore since hee permits
> Within himself unworthie Powers to reign
> Over free Reason, God in Judgement just
> Subjects him from without to violent Lords;
> Who oft as undeservedly enthrall
> His outward freedom: Tyrannie must be,
> Though to the Tyrant thereby no excuse.
> Yet sometimes Nations will decline so low
> From vertue, which is reason, that no wrong,
> But Justice, and some fatal curse annext
> Deprives them of thir outward libertie,
> Thir inward lost: . . ."

This theme of the identity of reason and virtue, and of virtue and liberty, also occurs throughout Milton's *History*.

Now, if man sinned and lost Paradise because he did not make proper use of his reason, and if the result of the Fall was the complete subjugation of the reason to the passions and desires, we should expect Paradise to be regained by a reassertion of the supremacy of reason.   And that exactly is the theme of *Paradise Regained*.   In the beginning of the First Book, Satan, speaking to his followers, says:

> "This Universe we have possest, and rul'd . . .
> Since Adam and his facile consort Eve
> Lost Paradise deceiv'd by me . . ."   (P.R., i, 49-52.)

He then goes on to say that the long-promised redeemer of mankind has appeared on earth, and that he must be opposed, not with force, but with "well couch't fraud" (1, 97).   In other words, they must attempt to deceive him, to overcome his reason, as they had already done with Adam and Eve.

As Jesus is about to enter on his ordeal, the hosts of Heaven sing as follows:

> "Victory and Triumph to the Son of God
> Now entring his great duel, not of arms,
> But to vanquish by wisdom hellish wiles."   (P.R. i, 173-5.)

And a few lines further on, Jesus tells of his own youth and aspirations, saying that his chief ambition was:

> ". . . (to) teach the erring Soul
> Not wilfully misdoing, but unaware
> Misled."   (P.R. i, 224-6.)

Paradise Regained, in fact, is a long series of arguments brought about by Satan's attempt to appeal to one after another of the passions of Jesus: first to his hunger and thirst, then to his compassion, then to his cupidity, his ambition, his pride of intellect, his pride of power. In each case, Jesus reasons with Satan, and points out to him how these temptations appeal only to the appetites, but are easily rejected by the mind. The poem can best be understood if it is read as a series of Socratic dialogues, in which Jesus exposes the Sophist Satan. In spite of the mountains, or the storms, or the other stage settings, each of the scenes between Jesus and Satan resolves into an argument concerning the wisdom or folly of some particular attitude toward life.

The result of all these arguments, in the words of God the Father, is as follows:

> ". . . now thou hast aveng'd
> Supplanted Adam, and by vanquishing
> Temptation, has regain'd lost Paradise,
> And frustrated the conquest fraudulent . . ." (P.R. iv, 606-9.)

By defeating Satan in an argument, by re-establishing the supremacy of reason, Jesus has "regain'd lost Paradise." When Adam and Eve were deceived, they sinned and fell; when Jesus proved that he could not be deceived, that his wisdom was superior to evil, the original sin was atoned, and Paradise regained.

II

I have argued this point, not because it makes much difference why Milton preferred *Paradise Regained* to his other poems (I am afraid time has decided against him on this point), but because the ideas which caused Milton to prefer *Paradise Regained* are of permanent importance to all of us. I think it is worth noticing that in *Areopagitica* Milton was setting forth his central convictions on public and private morals. Man must have access to *all* knowledge because only through knowledge can he gain virtue and only through virtue can he gain liberty.

If we try to suppress bad books, we shall either fail or we shall succeed in hampering the search for truth. And in any case who is to keep guard over the censors? And how can we insure that they are wiser men than the authors they mutilate? And who is to know whether a passage in a wretched book may not set some great mind soaring?

Let the book appear, said Milton. If it is indecent or libellous, or if it otherwise contravenes the accepted usages, let it be proceeded against as would any other illegal act of a citizen. *But let the book appear.* The consequence of any form of censorship in advance may be fatal to civilisation.

Perhaps you think this long battle has been won in our Western world, and that when we have beaten back the tyrannies that assaulted us we shall have genuine free trade in thought. I hope so; but we had better not think it is too easy.

Most American citizens, I suppose, would agree automatically to the following sentence: "If there is any principle of the Constitution that more imperatively calls for attachment than any other it is the principle of free thought—not free thought for those who agree with us but freedom for the thought that we hate."

Yet the words appeared only a few years ago in a *dissenting* opinion by Mr. Justice Holmes. Most of the members of the Supreme Court of the United States did not seem to agree, at least in practice. They undoubtedly agreed in theory; but as usual the theory was hard to apply. And for twenty years before that time Justice Holmes had been fighting, in his dissenting opinions, for the spirit of the *Areopagitica*. Again and again the majority appeared to take the view that violently unpopular opinions could be suppressed on the ground that they were an incitement to trouble.

"Every idea is an incitement," answered the great Justice. "The only difference between the expression of an opinion and an incitement . . . is the speaker's enthusiasm for the result."

Shall we live up to this high doctrine when the war is over? There will be many temptations to suspend our allegiance to *Areopagitica*, at least so far as the enemy is concerned. There will be many temptations to believe we can have "free trade in thought" inside a closed system—like America's free trade in goods behind an immense tariff wall. There will be many temptations to forget that while we can control men's bodies and their use of machinery, with results that are either beneficial or, at worst, temporarily harmful, if we try to control their access to free thoughts, to knowledge without which there can be no true virtue, we may step down into the same ditch with our enemies.

Does this mean that hateful doctrines may be republished in the countries that almost murdered our world? I think it does. I do not think we can have free thought for those who agree with us without "freedom for the thought that we hate." And if we who consider ourselves to be right think hard enough and express ourselves clearly enough, I do not see why we need fear "the competition of the market." At the most I can imagine imposing negative controls on our enemies to make sure that they *do* keep the market open and competitive, to make sure that they do not publish *only* dangerous rubbish.

All this may seem far afield from Milton's pamphlet of 1644. But I find it a reassuring fact that we cannot consider a great author or do honour to a great book without being led to speculate on our own fate, on history and on the soul of man.

We, too, when at last the shooting shall have stopped, with the war won, shall be

> ". . . entering a great duel, not of arms,
> But to vanquish by wisdom hellish wiles."

Let us see to it that the "sad friends of truth" in every country have as much access to wisdom as possible—not the wisdom which we consider proper for them, but the wisdom which can only come from the knowledge of good and evil.

Let us forbid them the use of arms. Let us make such disposal of their persons and their property as we and our allies think appropriate. But let us not try to tell them what they may read, or even what they may print.

We should have to be as wise as God, or as ruthless as Satan, to carry through such a project. We are certainly not the former, and I suspect we are not the latter. Our attempt to play deity or demon would fail, and while failing it would diminish the cause we serve.

What I am saying need not apply to the early days of military occupation; but I think it should apply thereafter.

We of the West must stand for the civilisation of the West. There is nothing else we can stand for, except a mean and sterile opportunism. Our civilisation does not restrain us from punishing bad men, or from denying dangerous men the physical chance to do harm. But it does restrain us from tampering with the minds, and thus with the souls, of our fellow human beings.

It will be irksome if the Germans rush into print at the end of this war with a nauseous literature of self-pity and self-aggrandisement. I assume we shall have the physical power to prevent it—or, at least, to drive their worst books underground—by licensing printers and by providing paper and metal only for such books as we approve. I pray that we shall not use this power.

The redemption of the German spirit must come from the German mind. I think we shall hasten that redemption if we abide by the principles of *Areopagitica*. I think we should merely contribute to our own fall if we refused to apply those principles to any of our fellow men who were in our power.

This is not the traditional weakness of liberalism, which tends to put the weapons for its own destruction into the hands of its enemies. On the contrary, I am arguing for the old distinction between the things which are Caesar's and the things which are God's.

In this world of Caesar's, let us be as hard with the Germans as is needed for our future safety, and for that of all our allies. But in the world of the spirit, let us believe that truth can only prevail if we insist on the rule of free thought.

This, I suggest, is the meaning and the greatness of *Areopagitica*.

A MARXIST CONTRIBUTION

By F. D. KLINGENDER

IT IS NOT SURPRISING THAT THIS CONFERENCE, CALLED TO DISCUSS THE FUTURE role of spiritual and economic values, should have turned again and again to the experience of the Soviet Union. In his paper on *Soviet Writers and the War*, Mr. Ivor Montagu has already shown what the new life means in practice to one group of Soviet citizens. I should like to supplement his remarks by dealing as briefly and simply as I can with those general principles of Marxist thought in the light of which the relationship between spiritual and economic values has been completely transformed in the U.S.S.R.

Marx's view of the relation between economic and spiritual values is most clearly expressed in a passage in the third volume of *Capital*[1] where he points out that what he calls the "realm of freedom" only begins where material production proper ends. Whatever their stage of social development and whatever their economic system, men must spend a large proportion of their energies in merely producing the goods and services they need in order to survive. This is what Marx calls the "realm of necessity," and the only freedom that can exist in that realm is that men learn to plan their common labour rationally, instead of being controlled by their economic system as by a blind force. But such freedom can only be conditional, it means that a necessary job is done with the least expenditure of energy and under the most satisfactory conditions, but the job must be done if society is to survive, and therefore the true realm of freedom can only begin after society's necessary work is accomplished. The realm of freedom, according to Marx, is that in which human ability is developed for its own sake. It always rests on the realm of necessity as on its foundation. For the larger the proportion of human energy that is absorbed by the realm of necessity, the smaller will be the proportion that can be freely developed, and therefore the shortening of the working day is one of the first essentials for a full and rich realm of freedom.

If it is conceded that Marx's definition of freedom as disinterested activity is an essential ingredient of spiritual value, it follows that men partake of spiritual value in so far as they escape, or seek to escape, from what Defoe so memorably described as their "daily circulation of sorrow, living but to work, and working but to live, as if daily bread were the only end of a wearisome life, and a wearisome life the only occasion of daily bread."[2]

The whole of human history can be regarded as a struggle to achieve that liberation. But until recently the growth of our productive resources has never sufficiently outstripped the expansion of human wants to enable more than a small minority to escape from the drudgery for daily bread. And in the last two centuries when modern science and industry have created the material conditions which would enable mankind as a whole to partake of the realm of freedom, we have lost even that relative degree of freedom which more primitive economies possessed to some extent, of controlling the process of social production, instead of being controlled by it as by a blind law.

[1] English ed. iii, p. 954; Marx-Engels Institute ed. III, p. 873-4.
[2] *Robinson Crusoe*, ed. 1812, vol. II, pp. 8-9.

Nor is that all. The glimpse of freedom vouchsafed to small minorities in the past, and the spiritual values gained by them, were themselves contaminated by the price at which they were gained.

Production had first been raised above the primitive level of hunting and gathering by a division of functions between different communities and between different groups within the community. At a certain stage of this process mental labour was divorced from physical labour, each becoming the more or less exclusive preserve of a separate class of society. The spiritual values created by the priests and poets and thinkers of the past were thus gained at the cost of unrelieved drudgery by the vast majority, and the finest flowers of the human spirit necessarily bore the mark of their origin. Never has human thought more nearly attained the goal of freedom—the quest of truth for its own sake—than in the classical philosophy of ancient Greece. Yet Plato and Aristotle defended slavery and denied the very essence of human dignity to the majority of their fellow men. And Christianity, the consolation of the humble and oppressed, could only square its sense of justice with the realities of life by removing its scheme of rewards and punishments altogether from the world of experience.

The process of division which has placed spiritual activity into opposition to material labour, at the same time tainting spiritual value with economic interest, reached its culmination in the era of industrial capitalism. To the machine-hand even the spiritual enjoyment which the craftsman had derived from his work was denied, and he was forced to spend his working life under the regimented discipline of the factory. The very name of "hand" which replaced the older "journeyman" at this period sufficiently expresses the mutilation of human personality which the new relationship of capitalist employment implied.

Nor was it only the wage-earners whose lives were stunted by the extreme segmentation of social functions. Mental work, too, and the pursuit of the liberal arts, became more and more specialised, isolated from the wider fields of experience and devoid of human content. As for the capitalists themselves—one need only read Dickens' *Dombey and Son*, not to mention Balzac or the great Russian realists of the nineteenth century, to realise how utterly the new "captains of industry" were enslaved to their own wealth. The violence done to love, and to the relation between the sexes generally, in the interest of property is, of course, one of the oldest themes of literature, but it is only in the last half-century that a whole new profession has grown up to deal with what might be called the occupational neurosis of the idle rich. In short, if one examines the world's great literature one will find but few works which are not, fundamentally, concerned with the tragic conflict between material interest and human self-fulfilment. "We should be tempted to assert," wrote Hazlitt in 1810, "that men do not become what by nature they are meant to be, but what society makes them. The generous feelings, and higher propensities of the soul are, as it were, shrunk up, seared, violently wrenched, and amputated, to fit us for our intercourse with the world, something in the manner that beggars maim and mutilate their children, to make them fit for their future situation in life."[1]

So much for the evidence of literature and history: but the power of material interest to debase and enslave man's soul is nowhere more horrifyingly revealed than in the savagery to which fascism has reduced the German people by means of the insidious lie of racial supremacy.

The fate of Germany, and the world-wide struggle in which we are engaged to-day, are so much the more tragic, since the realm of freedom is already within our grasp. Thanks to modern science and to the spectacular growth of productive resources in the last two centuries, it is possible to-day to satisfy the minimum wants of mankind without reducing the life of the majority to a ceaseless grind of unremitting toil. But it is evident from the experience of the last twenty-five years that this is only possible if we achieve that *relative* degree of freedom which consists, as Marx pointed out, in the rational control of social production.

To eliminate the twin evils of economic crisis and war with their pitiful waste of human and material resources must therefore be our first step on the road to freedom. The Atlantic Charter and the Teheran Agreement, the aims of social security and full employment, are evidence that the united nations are determined to take that step.

On the foundation of the realm of necessity thus rationally controlled it will then be possible for us to build the true realm of freedom. The pursuit of spiritual values for their own sake is of the essence of the realm of freedom. History shows that spiritual values tend invariably to be tainted by economic interest as long as the economic interests of separate individuals, social classes and whole nations are mutually opposed. But it does not follow, as is often supposed, that material and spiritual values are from their very nature incompatible. In a really free community the voluntary co-operation of all in supplying their material needs creates a sense of brotherhood which is in itself one of the greatest spiritual values and the only sure foundation for a rich and harmonious spiritual life. To achieve the realm of freedom we must, in other words, reintegrate our economic and spiritual values.

Let us turn to our own country and ask ourselves what this aim of reintegration implies. For the great majority of our people it means a tremendous advance in education. Their innate sense of beauty atrophied by the living conditions which were forced on them by the industrial revolution, their homes and meeting-halls rendered cheerless by the baneful sway of chocolate paint, they can scarcely be expected to retrieve even an elementary visual sensibility unless they are assisted by the most painstaking efforts of artists and educationists. And similar conditions prevail in other fields of spiritual enjoyment. It is hopeless to expect this state of affairs to be remedied by a system of education which is committed, on the one

[1] *Memoirs of the Late Thomas Holcroft*, ed. 1816, vol ii, p. 194.

hand, to the mass production of specialists devoid of general culture, and on the other, to imbuing the sons of gentlemen with a due sense of the station which they are called upon to occupy. What is required is a new target for the whole course of education, from the nursery-school to the university and adult class, the target of helping to produce harmoniously developed human beings fitted equally for the various tasks of material production to which they will devote their working lives and for the pursuit of those spiritual values which will give meaning to their leisure hours.

But that is only one side of the picture. A change as great, if not greater, will be required in our own outlook as artists and intellectuals, if we are to remain, as we surely must aspire to be, worthy of our time. From our position as a privileged minority which has monopolised all spiritual labour and from the consequent impoverishment of the spiritual lives of our fellow men, many of us have drawn the conclusion that art and science and pure thought are from their very nature accessible only to the few elect. Those who take this view dread that their standards will be vulgarised and their integrity contaminated by contact with the common multitude. They forget that their precious exclusiveness is as much a product of a sectionalised robot civilisation, as the spiritual impoverishment of the masses, and that both will appear equally sterile and incomplete, when the new life unfolds itself. To the artist and the searcher after truth the new life will be a world never before explored, a world in which the generous feelings and higher propensities of the soul are no longer seared and mutilated and human nature reveals itself for the first time in the free and harmonious development of individual ability.

Meanwhile, however, those who hold the keys to the spiritual heritage of mankind must do their best to help awaken the innate but dormant sensibilities of their fellow men. Without sacrificing their integrity they must build a bridge from the experience of ordinary people to that finer appreciation to which they aspire. And our common heritage provides ample material for building such a bridge.

The reintegration of economic and spiritual values, in short, implies the breakdown of the ancient barrier between physical and mental labour and of the sectional isolation which that barrier has created in all spheres of life. That is what Marx meant when he wrote with pointed emphasis: "The exclusive concentration of artistic talent in certain individuals, and its consequent suppression in the broad masses of the people, is an effect of the division of labour. . . . With a communist organisation of society, the artist is not confined by the local and national seclusion which ensues solely from the division of labour, nor is the individual confined to one specific art, so that he becomes exclusively a painter, a sculptor, etc. . . . In a communist society there are no painters, but at most men who, among other things, also paint."[1]

[1] *German Ideology*, quoted in Lipschitz: *The Philosophy of Art of Karl Marx*, English translation by Critics Group, New York, 1938.

The community which will ultimately emerge from our present struggles will be a world-wide commonwealth in which human beings will seek self-fulfilment by contributing, according to their ability, to the necessary work of production and sharing, according to their inclinations, in a rich spiritual life.

THE FUTURE FUNCTION OF THE INTELLIGENTSIA

By JOHN KATZ

I KNEW SOME DAYS AGO THAT AT THIS SESSION OF THE CONFERENCE I WAS to stand on a common platform with two other speakers, but it seemed to me very improbable that we should find ourselves speaking on a common subject.

I knew, of course, that we were in duty bound to show an interest in the future of the spiritual and economic values of mankind; in other words, to show an interest in the future of man and of civilisation. Certainly an ample theme! But this very amplitude, this generous amplitude, of our common theme seemed, at first sight, to make it unlikely that our several contributions would arrange themselves in a linear perspective, or, to change the metaphor, would yield a highest common factor. I believe, however, that the highest common factor exists. I find it in the hypothesis that, in some sense, all of us are members of the intelligentsia. What that sense is I hope to make clear.

The term "intelligentsia" is a recent borrowing from the Russian; the term "vodka" is another. But the Russian intelligentsia is at least as old as Alexander I and the Holy Alliance. For a century the Tzardom felt the bite of its savage criticism. It was the work of this intelligentsia which prepared the way for Lenin.

Nor must we imagine that the intelligentsia is an exclusively Russian institution. I hope to show that in all highly civilised societies, at a certain critical point in their history, there is a tendency for an intelligentsia to develop. Amongst the Greeks, Socrates and the Sophists do the work of an intelligentsia; among the Chinese, we have correspondingly the work of Confucius and his followers. We have always disliked the term "intelligentsia." An Englishman dislikes being described as intelligent for the same reason that an Englishwoman objects to being described as virtuous. They feel that a doubt is being insinuated as to whether the intelligence or the virtue is first class.

"Intelligentsia" is a collective term. A member of the intelligentsia would, I suppose, be termed "an intellectual." Now if I were to describe myself as an "intellectual," the mass of ordinarily intelligent people would resent the assumption that there are two sorts of intelligence: a very lofty and superior sort which, by an act of divine intuition, inspects reality and reads off the truth about it; and a common and garden variety which handles the brute facts, experiments with them, and by trial and error finds out how to manage them. This dichotomy between theoretical intellect and practical intelligence is of the same order as the dichotomy between spiritual values and economic values, and is, I think, similarly indefensible.

The claim that intellect is loftier than intelligence was long ago advanced by the Greeks. Philosophers, pure mathematicians, and theologians were credited with intellect. Engineers, applied mathematicians, and shop-keepers were credited only with intelligence. Intellect thinks; and thought is a pure function of the spirit. Intelligence works; when we work, we move the body or the tools which are the artificial extensions of the body. Intellect is a gentleman of leisure. Intelligence is just a working man.

Taken distributively instead of collectively, the intelligentsia is a group of intellectuals. And I am suggesting that the intellectual can easily fail to understand his peculiar function, and the hostile critics of the intellectual can as easily fail to understand him, because of an opposition between theoretical intellect and practical intelligence which harks back to the time of Plato.

Plutarch tells a story about Archimedes which illustrates this opposition rather piquantly. At the siege of Syracuse by the Romans, Archimedes assisted the defence materially by applying his mathematical genius to the construction of military machines. As Archimedes was a Greek and Syracuse a Greek city, and the King of Syracuse a friend and relative of Archimedes, it would seem to us that the behaviour of Archimedes called for no special explanation. But that is not Plutarch's view. He tells us elaborately that Archimedes "repudiated as sordid and ignoble the whole trade of engineering and every sort of art that lends itself to mere use and profit and that he placed his whole affection and ambition in those pure speculations in which there can be no reference to the vulgar needs of life. These machines he had contrived not as a matter of any importance but as mere amusements in geometry." If Archimedes had taken military machines seriously, or, indeed, any kind of experimental mechanics, he would, so Plutarch tells us, have been siding with those advocates of applied mathematics who had incurred the indignation of Plato. It was Plato's view that if pure mathematics degenerated into impure mechanics, "it would be shamefully turning its back upon the unembodied objects of pure intelligence, recurring to sensation and asking help from matter."

I have no doubt that if Plutarch had studied Marx, he would have seen how natural it was in a slave-holding society for mechanics to be assigned to the base mechanicals, while the cold and austere joys of pure mathematics were reserved for gentlemen of leisure. Plutarch might also have seen that the sharp division between persons engaged in spiritual, and persons engaged in economic, pursuits was to prove a handicap in the Classical World's struggle for existence against the unsophisticated barbarians of the North.

Plutarch has every right to be considered an intellectual in the modern sense of the term: for he made it his business as well as his pleasure to influence the process by which a disintegrating Greek civilisation was transformed into a new Graeco-Roman civilisation. But Plutarch is also a forerunner of the medieval clerk and chronicler, who saw himself as a spiritual person elevated above the battle of struggling and quarrelling men. The seductive pleasure of detachment has ever been the temptation of the intellectual. If he gives way, history passes him by.

For the intellectual to-day is no unworldly clerk contemplating history as made by men of the world. The temper in which the twentieth-century intellectual goes to work has to be as practical as that of the trained and educated engineer. Indeed, the intelligentsia is—or ought to be—a loosely associated body of consulting social engineers.

For the texture of civilisation is continually changing, and the structure of the societies that operate civilisation changes simultaneously. Can these changes be controlled? Can control be sufficiently intelligent and farseeing as to make it possible for your consulting social engineers to say: We envisage a number of alternative futures for society, and it seems to us not impossible that by the creation of such and such institutions and the encouragement of such and such attitudes to life—such *Weltanschauungen* or world-views—one of these alternative futures will be realised.

As long as a civilisation is a going concern of more or less fixed routines and of more or less unconsciously working habits, the intelligentsia remains unborn. It is when the routines and the habits no longer work, it is in the hour of crisis that the intelligentsia begins to stir in the womb of society.

It was the breakdown of the Greek city-state, just as it was the breakdown of the Chinese feudal principality, which agitated the minds of a Plato and a Confucius. They were called upon to plan the outline of a new society. They responded; but they responded very differently.

Confucius worked out a new ethic and a new world-view which made it easy later on for the feudal principalities of China to be united in an empire; and this empire has persisted throughout the changes of two thousand years. But Plato had all the aristocratic conservative's hatred of change. There had been many changes in the structure of Athenian society since the successful conclusion of the war with Persia. Plato rejected them or regarded them with suspicion.

Plato despised the business men of Athens trading in olive oil and slaves, with interests in shipping, silver mines, and usury. Plato would have liked Athens to return to a subsistence-economy modelled on barbarian Sparta. He forgot that the business men and craftsmen of Athens had made possible the by no means negligible share of the social surplus which Plato and his pupils consumed in the Academy. And Plato lived to be eighty.

Plato has his modern imitators. These people advocate peasant proprietorship and the scrapping of machine industry in favour of the arts and crafts. They are romantic escapists, denouncing the present system and yet living on it.

It may seem to you that I am denigrating Plato; that, anyhow, I am making an invidious comparison between Plato, the romantic reactionary, and Confucius, the practical revolutionary. But I am not really denigrating Plato. Plato closes, while Confucius opens, a great epoch of civilisation. Most of what is first class in Chinese civilisation is later than Confucius; most of what is first class in Greek civilisation had already flowered by the time Plato had founded the Academy. To Plato, Time and Change were not messengers of hope, but rather demons of death and decay. Hence Plato's yearning for an Eternal World where there are no problems, no uncertainties, no hazards, no vulgar encounters with matter and money.

Where one epoch ends, another begins. A dying civilisation carries a successor in its womb. It is because of this birth out of death that the services of the intellectual are required. The intellectual is midwife to civilisation.

You know that when a birth is so difficult that mother and child cannot both live, an acute problem is set to the moralists. Are they to favour killing the child and saving the mother or killing the mother and saving the child? The intellectual, because of his office as midwife to civilisation, is impaled on the horns of a comparable dilemma. Which is better—or, if you like, which is worse—matricide or infanticide? Bear in mind that the intellectual is himself a child of the civilisation that is dying, and that the crisis of the dying civilisation is the birth pangs of the new. Is he to remain attached to his *alma mater*—if you like, to his old school tie—or is he to join the revolutionaries who want to put her in the cart. Clearly the intellectual is in danger of being caught in a Freudian conflict between impulses to mother-fixation and impulses to matricide.

If we review the history of the intelligentsia from the age of the Greek Sophists to the age of the Russian Marxists, we cannot help noticing that mother-fixation has had a much longer run than matricide. Plato, Aristotle, St. Augustine, St. Thomas Aquinas are all of them inclined to mother-fixation. Matricide was not very popular much before 1600 A.D. When I speak of matricide committed by intellectuals in connection with civilisation, I am thinking of such people as Voltaire and Diderot, Marx and Lenin. And you will note that these four intellectuals are important because of two great world revolutions, the French and the Russian. Speaking of revolutions and of the part that intellectuals have played in them, we are reminded of John Milton and John Locke in connection with the English revolutions of the seventeenth century, and of Benjamin Franklin and Thomas Jefferson in connection with the American Revolution. Are we to classify them with the matricides or the mother-fixationists? Perhaps with neither. These four intellectuals were admirable exponents of liberal conservatism and conservative liberalism in the classical tradition of British compromise.

I hope I have succeeded in showing that the intelligentsia has been functioning for a considerable part of recorded history, that it has exercised and is exercising an indispensable cultural function, and that those present at this conference have a legitimate claim to be members of it.

In the short time left to me I propose to say something about the task before the intelligentsia to-day. In the first place, what we have now is a world-wide and a world-conscious intelligentsia. In Plato's time the intelligentsia was exclusively Greek; non-Greeks were dismissed as barbarians of no account. In Voltaire's time it was European. To-day it is world-wide. Chinese, Indian and Turkish intellectuals can no longer be excluded from the world intelligentsia. When, in the future, a world congress of intellectuals meets, it will be a congress of world-conscious men—conscious of the unity of the earth, of mankind, and of civilisation; conscious that all the peoples of history, Egyptians, Sumerians, Arabs, Chinese, as well as Greeks and Romans and Teutons, have contributed to the pool of significant human experience.

The world congress will be impatient with the plea so often advanced in reactionary circles that civilisation is essentially European; that European civilisation is essentially Catholic; and that Catholic civilisation is essentially an affair of gentlemen, clerks, and labourers.

But because the world intelligentsia will be international, I see no reason why it must be cosmopolitan. Cosmopolitanism is a form of individualist escape from the responsibilities of group living. All the warm things of life are group-bred. I hope, therefore, that when an Englishman puts his case before the congress, he will speak neither Esperanto, nor Basic English, but just the best English he can command.

Secondly, the intellectual must emancipate himself from that fear of the masses which is the paralysing obsession of so many good Liberals—in this country and elsewhere. He must accept the fact that, for the first time in world history, nations forty million strong, hundred million strong, yes, two hundred million strong, are hundred per cent. literate. Because the intellectual can read and write and is, therefore, in the medieval sense a clerk, he will not claim for himself any special privileges, least of all the privilege of clergy. The intellectual will to-day accept the fact that the radio and the film provide new means of spiritual communication, new means for the pooling of experience. To-day it is physically possible for one man to address the whole human race, and for one and the same film-subject to be seen by every member of it. What openings there are here for the consulting social engineer! Yes, and what tremendous dangers! I agree that the dangers are there; but so are the possibilities.

Thirdly, the intellectual must not demand a guaranteed minimum of £800 a year—I am giving Bernard Shaw's figure—or, indeed, any privileged fraction of the community's income. The job he has to do is that of a consulting social engineer. But whatever may have been the case in the past, the job in the future is not necessarily going to be done by intellectuals drawn from the bourgeois class. In the coming world society such a class may no longer exist. Shaw and Wells are inclined to eternalize the bourgeois class to which they happen to belong. It is not impossible that the profession of consulting social engineer will be open to the masses. After all, the masses may want to be consulted about the future shape of civilisation; and unless they are consulted, your world society will be anything but a democracy. Perhaps, in the future, the intellectual will tend more and more to coincide with the common man of whom Vice-President Wallace has prophesied—much to the disgust and indignation of many privileged persons.

Let me now summarise my view of the future function of the intelligentsia. What is perennial about the intelligentsia is the nature of its job. Somebody has to ease the pains of parturition at the rebirth of civilisation. The intellectual, then, must be midwife to civilisation. Somebody has to make alternative plans for future states of civilisation. The intellectual, then, must be a consulting social engineer. Somebody has to have enough insight into human nature and its collective possibilities to guide us through the perils of change. The intellectual, then, must be a philosophical statesman. Midwife, engineer, statesman—all these symbolically are constituents of his function. What the intellectual must not be, and is ever tempted to become, is an introverted mystic detached from the experimental life of man.

One last word. Engineers can co-operate understandingly because there exists a body of scientific principles in which they all believe. Intellectuals, I have said, are consulting social engineers. And social engineers will be unable to co-operate intelligently in the work of creating the Great World Community unless they, too, have a body of common beliefs. Remember that in the world-situation of to-day it must be a body of beliefs to which the intelligentsia of all countries and all races can subscribe. Humanism alone can supply the foundation for such a common faith. Humanism believes that the best life for man is life lived in community—in world community. Such a life will not be perfect, but it will be great. There will be new problems, dangers, trials. But there will also be a new sense of partnership—of honourable partnership in civilisation. Only when the masses feel that the civilisation sustained by their labours is truly theirs, will a new age of freedom flourish on the earth.

THE *AREOPAGITICA* OF MILTON AFTER 300 YEARS

By Harold J. Laski

I

NOT A DOZEN PAMPHLETS OF THE FORTY-ODD THOUSAND WHICH WERE printed during the Civil Wars of the seventeenth century have become as fully a part of the British tradition as the great essay of which we celebrate the tercentenary to-day. Yet it is well known that, despite the reputation of its writer, it raised no discussion of any kind. There is an occasional hint that it had been read in the pamphlets of famous contemporaries, by Lilburne, perhaps, and, I think, by James Harrington. But it is not until the age of the enlightenment, some half-century after his death, that the *Areopagitica* became a living element in the minds and hearts of the time.

That is not because the substance of its argument was new when Milton wrote it. For at least a hundred years before it appeared the passion for liberty of thought was both widespread and profound. The great humanists of the Renaissance, the more generous of the early Reformers, had all of them seen that the right to print freely was the central concomitant of a free mind and a free conscience. The demand for religious toleration goes to the very roots of sixteenth-century ideas. It may be that the Governments of the day looked with profound suspicion on that right to speak freely which every minority is almost bound to demand. Men like Sebastian Castellion spoke of religious persecution in terms which Bayle would not have repudiated a century and a half later. That is true of the great Acontius; it is true of the great spiritual reformers like Hans Dench and his successors. It is true, also, of their English disciples, like John Everard and that Giles Randall who appeared before the Star Chamber in 1637 for preaching against ship-money which was, he declared, "a way of taking burdens off rich men's shoulders and laying them on the necks of poor men." From their origins, too, the Anabaptists had sought for freedom of conscience; and among the first treatises we have of their English successors, Busher and Murton and Richardson, to take examples only from the little congregation which returned with Helwys from Amsterdam after the death of their leader, John Smyth, in 1612, the plea for free thought in religious matters occupies a place of primary importance.

There is nothing, therefore, in Milton that had not already been said with persuasive eloquence when he wrote his tract. What is, I suggest, significant in its pages is not merely the noble rhetoric with which they are adorned. What is significant is the range he gives to the idea of freedom. In the revolutionary age in which he wrote there were protagonists of every sort of freedom, religious, poetical, economic, social. It was for political freedom that John Eliot died; it was for social and economic freedom that

Lilburne, Walwyn, and Winstanley fought with a courage that has assured them a reawakened interest in our own day. Yet it is remarkable that none of them saw, as Milton saw, the relevance of a free press to their purpose; and it is perhaps even more remarkable that the most bitter critics of free thought, men to whom, as to Prynne and Edwards and Pagith, Milton's ideas on church government and marriage made him an enemy to be attacked with passion, the *Areopagitica* can pass without censure or attack. And this is the more impressive because no one can compare the tracts Milton had written on ecclesiastical matters without seeing that there is in the *Areopagitica* a breadth of spirit, a power to look at social issues without using the glasses of sectarian theology, which is new in him and very rare in this passionate time; outside of Overton and Walwyn, Winstanley, and, in a very different way, that stout reactionary, Thomas Hobbes, I doubt whether there is any thinker in these twenty years who bears comparison with Milton.

What explains this sudden extension of his range? How does it happen that Milton who, *Comus* and *Lycidas* apart, had so far been an angry foe of the English Church, and had written his eager plea for a new education, should, as it were overnight, become the protagonist of a secular humanism the principles of which we have not yet ventured to apply after three centuries of further experience? Milton, let us remember, has no sort of doubt about the immense power of printed books. He admits the harm they can do, though he is emphatic that their potential good outweighs the harm. He recognises fully that "a fool will be a fool with the best book." But he insists that none is fit for the task of censorship; it is, indeed, but one form of murder: "as good almost kill a man as kill a good book." And we must press on from religious change to reform both economic and political; if we fail in the task "we have looked so long upon the blaze that Zwinglius and Calvin hath beaconed up to us, that we are stark blind." He calls for reformation in all spheres of life, and it is to be effected by the cut and thrust of limitless debate. It is beneath the dignity of a man who cares, as he cares, for righteousness and truth, to be harassed and hampered by the need for the *imprimatur* of some censor. And if it be said that by this power of prohibition, evil may be suppressed, Milton replies with a zestful eagerness that almost leaps from the printed page that "evil manners are as perfectly learnt without books a thousand other ways." It may be music, or eating or drinking, or the lover's whisper, or the way we dress or the companions we choose. There are a thousand ways to evil. Why should one way alone, the path of the printed word, be chosen as the one road barred to man? Is it not wisdom to let men freely examine without the "tonnaging and pounding" of truth? And is it not from that free examination that there is born the knowledge out of which the nation may most nobly shape its destiny?

No one can read these impassioned pages without arriving at some definite conclusions. There is in them, obviously, the Milton who has inherited the great tradition of classical humanism which swept over

Europe in the sixteenth century. The *Areopagitica* is to the other prose writings of Milton somewhat as is the *Utopia* to the theological pamphlets of Sir Thomas More. It is written in the mood of the dreamer who sees the hope of great accomplishment before his eyes. Just as there must have been days when Colet and More and Erasmus saw in the new knowledge the promise of a new birth, so to Milton, in the ecstatic fervour of an England that, to his enchanted vision, out of the victory of Cromwell and his Ironsides, there grew hope of a new birth, too. "The shop of war hath not . . . more anvils and hammers working, to fashion out the plates and instruments of armed justice in defence of beleaguered truth, than there be pens and heads . . . sitting by their studious lamps, musing, searching, revolving new notions and ideas wherewith to present, as with their homage and fealty, the approaching reformation: others as fast reading, trying all things, assenting to the force of reason and convincement. . . . The people . . . disputing, reasoning, reading, inventing, discoursing . . . things not before discoursed or written of."

Is it not clear that two inferences may legitimately be drawn? Milton, to himself, is, like Heine two hundred years later, a "soldier in the liberation war of humanity." As Cromwell's men go forward to their victories with sword and gun, the writer uses his pen as a weapon in the same battle. Their enemies are the same, and their victory will be a triumph over a common foe. And the Milton who writes these ardent pages sees in the people of England a nation fit to choose between the clash of opinions, able, out of its own inherent wisdom, to attain the truth it needs. The Milton of this pamphlet is, as it were, aflame with an optimistic faith in popular wisdom. He has nothing but contempt for those who would seek to insist that "truth and understanding are . . . such wares as to be monopolised and traded in by tickets and statutes and standards." He had not himself submitted to the licence of the censor any of his previous tracts on the government of the Church or on divorce. With Cromwell's triumph at Marston Moor, he had seen episcopal tyranny overthrown; and he could not doubt that the immense discussion, whether in cities like London, or over a hundred camp-fires, when pamphlets like his own, published by the hundred without licence, had contributed to the result. If, he seems to have asked himself, discussion could achieve so great an end in affairs of the Church, when censorships no longer dared to inhibit men' ideas, what could it not accomplish similarly in affairs of State?

For, as he himself seems to indicate, the liberty of unlicensed printing was his right as a citizen. He had written of the Church and its ruling; he had written of divorce in the tragic light of his marital unhappiness; and it is clear that when he thought about the implications of marriage, he saw that the problem of children was involved, and, thence, their education. And it is not, I think, fanciful to connect this ardour for freedom with his vehement dissent from the methods in vogue at Cambridge when he was an undergraduate there, his loathing of medieval scholasticism, and his warm enthusiasm for the new studies Bacon was advocating. Certainly there are phrases in the *Third Prolusion* which the author of the *Areopagitica* was content virtually to repeat; and the claims made for the man of learning in the *Seventh Prolusion* suggest that, as early as his student days, Milton sought to be numbered among those who shape the mind of his generation. It is, I think, legitimate to argue that the pamphlets of these intense years were, for him, in some sort the fulfilment of that ambition. They are the work of an "intellectual" who regards the battle of ideas as not less related to the making of the future than the battle of the soldiers in the field. And the *Seventh Prolusion* is important in this context because it shows that the ideas of the great tract had been maturing in his mind for close on twenty years. Alike as an undergraduate, and as a poet of European renown, it is interesting to note in Milton the passionate enthusiasm of that Renaissance belief that learning unlocks all doors both to virtue and to rightful power, combined with the sense that the Long Parliament has begun a new and fruitful epoch in the history of the world.

I do not think the *Areopagitica* can be understood unless we read it in the special context of Milton's psychology. I am confident that Sir Herbert Grierson is right when he insists that Milton's "views on almost every question to be discussed were determined by the accidents of his own career. For an experience to affect Milton it had to be *personal*." This is not for one moment to doubt the reality of his ideals. It is to say only that all his ideals were the objective translation, in prose, or in poetry, of needs he felt passionately out of some incident which affected him deeply. When the Long Parliament came he felt, no doubt with all the intensity of his being, that "the foundation was laying for the deliverance of man from the yoke of slavery and superstition." But when his marriage ended in disaster and he sat down to write on the *Doctrine and Discipline of Divorce*, it is, no doubt, true, as he tells us in the *Defensio Secunda*, that he "perceived that there were three species of liberty which are essential to the happiness of social life—religious, domestic, and civil." Of the third he felt the same confident optimism we find in Blake and Paine and Wordsworth at the dawn of the French Revolution. But when the new Presbyter begins to emerge as Milton's critic, when he is but the "old priest writ large," he feels the call to speak his mind upon the aims of civil freedom, which, at the outset, he had thought the State-power might secure. Thus, in my own view, the *Areopagitica* is the sublimation of a Milton who resents the criticism of his marriage-theories; and, as always, because he identifies his private self with the public need, his plea for an unlimited freedom is, above all, an insistence that no barrier may be set to the expression of his views. It is, I do not doubt, a noble sublimation; but it is inexplicable unless we emphasise the special place it occupies in the development of his life.

The historical significance of the *Areopagitica* is, of course, that whatever the origin of its theories, it is the first fundamental plea for extending the idea of religious liberation to every sphere of secular life. That extension, I suggest, is the outcome of his rejection, built of his personal experience, of marriage as a sacrament, and his consequential view that it is a civil contract. From this there follows the inherent necessity of considering the implications of marriage in a secular way—the relations of husband and wife, the education of their children, the property-context in which marriage is set. But if we generalise these problems, it is inevitable that there should be claimed a right freely to discuss all social relations. If we bear in mind the mental climate of the period, the growth of science, the impact of geographical discovery, the emergence of the Cartesian philosophy, the rise of the middle class, Milton's pamphlet has connections which give it a significance far wider than he knew. He himself, when he published it, still thought that a new world was in the making which should "put an end to all earthly tyrannies," and proclaims God's "universal and mild Monarchy through Heaven and Earth." At this moment he has full faith in Cromwell and his army, and even feels that the common man is worthy of his trust and fit for freedom.

But that mood does not last for long. Despite the ardent eulogy of Cromwell in 1652, and the famous tribute, two years later, to the man "who has either extinguished or learned to subdue the whole host of vain hopes, fears and passions which infest the soul," it is increasingly obvious that he finds little comfort in the Protectorate; when, indeed, it ended, he spoke of it as a "short but scandalous night of interruption." The "Readie and Easy Way," indeed, which he published only two months before the Restoration ruined all his dreams, shows that the glowing hopes of 1644 were already dead in his heart. He had given greatly to the Commonwealth; not least, he had moved from the position of a sectary in religious matters to the position of someone whose religious views are perhaps more akin to Arianism than to any other outlook, but who also, at the same time, has come to think of political problems in essentially secular terms. He has come to think of the ideal commonwealth not as a kingdom laid up in Heaven, but as a body of concrete proposals it is the business of statesmen to fulfil in this world of here and now. The enthusiast who wrote the *Areopagitica* is slain by the conflict of sectaries and politicians. The Milton of the years from 1659 lacks any glow of that optimism which, fifteen years before, had made the adventure of ideas the supreme task in which the citizen could engage. I am not, indeed, sure whether it is not true to say that the Milton who once seemed not unlike a seventeenth-century Shelley had not become, out of an experience ever more bitter in each year, more alien to the founder of that Jesuit sect which nothing could induce him to tolerate. He had lost his faith in men; and the reader of his later works before the Restoration will not find it easy to reconcile their temper with the ardent faith of the poet-prophet who, in 1644, thought that "the power of determining what ought to be published and what to be suppressed, might no longer be entrusted to a few illiterate and illiberal individuals, who refused their sanction to any work which contained views or sentiments at all above the level of the vulgar superstition." For he had come to the conviction that the "vulgar superstition" was more likely to fasten itself upon that multitude in whose power to develop he had, in 1644, possessed so deep a conviction. They no longer "revolve new notions and ideas wherewith to present the approaching reformation." If, indeed, it is to approach, he has come to the conclusion that it can be secured only by imposing it upon them.

II

It is easy to portray Milton as the typical revolutionary whom experience transforms into someone akin to a reactionary. It is even easy to argue that the *Areopagitica* is, in fact, an eloquent defence of intellectual anarchism. But I am convinced that it is a mistaken judgment to seek to impale him upon the horns of either of these dilemmas. For, in the first place, the significance of Milton's pamphlet does not lie in any doctrine proposed as an end, but in a method by which an end, whatever it be, may be attained. What he urges upon his contemporaries is that it is urgent to take account of experience, that what men learn by reason they should seek to get accepted by persuasion. With all its limitations, it is a plea that power should be the subject and not the master of rational argument, that authority should be the result of discussion and not the definition of its limits. Granted his background and his position in the government of the Commonwealth, that plea had an importance one ought not to underestimate. For though it is more than probable that Milton would have made the limits of free discussion far narrower than many of his contemporaries, and though the direct influence of his argument was felt less in his lifetime than in the period after 1688, he was related to an atmosphere of discussion it is not possible to overlook. It may well be that the men who made this atmosphere would have been regarded by him as partially or wholly evil. He would not have shared their views, and when they were attacked or ignored by the Protector and his council, it is at least likely that he felt no sense of grievance.

Yet the remarkable fact is that the men who ignored his work and whom he in his turn ignored were in a large degree insisting upon an attitude that, in his halcyon days, he had accepted with enthusiasm. We, too, little realise that the Civil War is a phenomenon of great complexity, and that while, on one side, Cromwell and his supporters were the makers of a revolution, from another angle, the incidence of their effort was counter-revolutionary in character. If all those who supported Parliament knew what they were against, they were far from agreed what it was that they were for. Once episcopacy had been overthrown and the sovereignty of the State transferred from King to Parliament, there was a section of opinion which saw no ground for further change. But the Milton of 1644 could not accept this view. For him, as for the Left Wing of the Puritans, there was a prospect of new truth which might be the outcome of free discussion, which would not be attained if free discussion were to be stifled by censorship. When he wrote the *Areopagitica* he could have subscribed with ardour to the famous words which John Robinson spoke to the Pilgrims seeking a new world. "I am verily persuaded," said Robinson, "the Lord hath more truth yet to break forth out of His holy word. . . . I beseech you to remember it is an article of your Church covenant that you be ready to receive whatever truth shall be made known to you from the written word of God. . . . It is not possible that the Christian world should come so lately out of such thick anti-Christian darkness and that perfection of knowledge should break forth at once." "To be still searching what we know not by what we know," Milton wrote, "still closing up truth to truth as we find it . . . this is the golden rule in theology as well as in arithmetic."

This "golden rule" is a legacy from that Renaissance spirit of free inquiry which was born of the discovery of new continents and new truths. There is in it, no doubt, in these first years of the Civil War an element that Milton would later have rejected as Utopian. The march of events is so swift and so epoch-making that the poet turned publicist is fully convinced that the nation is destined from the fruit of free inquiry to have a new birth. And here his thought is linked to dreams which reached far beyond any boundaries he was later to reach. It has links with the confident optimism of the radiant John Goodwin, to whom, it is worth noting, the political writings of Milton were well and favourably known. The resemblance of its eager hope to what John Saltmarsh would publish, two years later, in his *Smoke in the Temple* (1646) is remarkable. It is, too, difficult to disassociate its doctrines from William Walwyn's *Consultation of Physicians* (1646), which is especially notable because it is only one link in the chain of that remarkable thinker's pamphlets in which he seeks to extend the platform of free discussion to the foundations of the national being. And it is obvious from the *Clarke Papers* that the Army had become a school of free speech in which, as a Captain John Ingram told Fairfax, discussion in council was useless unless those present could speak their minds "without check, controull, molestation or fear of ruine and destruction." At this point, unmistakably, the *Areopagitica* connects Milton with the great proponents of leveller theories; for it was Richard Overton who wrote in his *Defiance Against All Arbitrary Usurpations* (1646) that "this persecuted means of unlicensed printing hath done more good to the people than all the bloodie wars; the one tending to rid us quite of all slavery; but the other only to rid us of one, and involve us in another."

The link is clear, though we must not make it clearer than it was. Few of the levellers, liberty of religion apart, understood, as Milton did, the range that freedom required. Lilburne himself may plead passionately for the right to attack tyranny and treachery, but he is equally ready to complain with bitterness, that permission is granted to print libellous attacks upon himself. Apart, indeed, from the famous Petition of 18th January, 1649, of which the authors say that unlicensed printing has done as much for the army's victory as the censorship had done against it, there is no official radical document which asks, on Milton's terms, for full and free discussion.

Of all the men who saw the new tyranny which the rule of the Army was to involve, William Walwyn alone so wrote as to suggest that he understood the place of persuasion in a democracy as Milton understood it. The reader of the *Compassionate Samaratane* (1645), for example, would not have found it difficult to argue that he was in touch with a disciple of Milton; phrases like "they shunne the barrell that doubt their strength" have a Miltonic ring about them. But even Walwyn, by 1646, has come to believe in the duty of Parliament to check the attacks upon the independents; and when, come three years later, he is again pleading for a free Press, it is difficult to know whether this represents his permanent conviction, or is simply the outcome of his realisation that his little band of radicals was doomed to pitiless defeat.

The truth, in fact, is that the *Areopagitica* is, in the totality of its argument, unique in its period, and perhaps unequalled in the range of freedom it demands until the *Liberty* of John Stuart Mill, more than two centuries later. It was, of course, written by one whose original Calvinism was permeated by a humanist outlook which binds him, through the central tradition of the great Elizabethan age, to the world of the European Renaissance, and, through its influence, to a culture that is at least as much Greek as Puritan in its inner essence. When we look among the men of Milton's age for kindred views, we must remember how few could hope to enjoy the advantages that had been opened to him. The son of a wealthy father, enjoying at once the privilege of long years of leisure and the experience of foreign travel, driven on by the passionate ambition to create something "which the world would not willingly let die," preparing himself for the twenty years before the *Areopagitica* appeared, to traverse a vast field of secular learning, he approached the issues of the Civil War from an angle, and with advantages, that few men on the Puritan side could hope to rival. How could a bankrupt tradesmen like Winstanley, or an apprentice turned soldier, like Lilburne, a tradesman like Walwyn, or an independent clergyman like Goodwin, compare with him in a category of thought where, like the eagle, he soared into heights where none of them could hope to follow him. Hobbes, no doubt, surpassed him in depth of political insight, as Harrington surpassed him in the power to measure the significance of economic change. But, among men of his own way of thought, Milton was as lonely as he was pre-eminent. He had never, of course, to do battle for his ideas, like Lilburne and his supporters; and an experiment like that of Gerard Winstanley would either never have occurred to him or seemed to him of trivial import.

What he proposed in the *Areopagitica* was a method of determining social relationships which, even yet, the world has not been able to accept. He desired to replace the use of power by the influence of persuasion. He urged men to put their trust in reason as the single solvent of their difficulties. There is a sense, indeed, in which Milton's tract is, above all, a majestic hymn to the power of truth to prevail over falsehood in the battle of ideas. He insists, almost, that, given the free play of the market, truth is bound to prevail. And this leads him to what is virtually the function of a defence of philosophic anarchism in the realm of ideologies, partly on the ground that a "cloistered virtue" is a worthless thing if it has not emerged victorious over temptation, and partly because, in a "free and open encounter," it is the verdict of history, as he affirms, that no one has ever known "Truth put to the worse" even "though all the winds of doctrine were let loose to play upon the earth."

It would be insolent to praise the gorgeous tapestry of rhetoric that Milton wove in defence of his plea. Whole phrases of his tract have become a part of the classic heritage of free men. It is not, I think, excessive to say that there are not a dozen documents in the history of mankind that breathe a nobler ardour for liberty. Few men have written more splendidly in defence of the free mind; none has even rivalled that splendour in defence of the right to keep the mind in chains.

And yet we are bound to remember that Milton did not retain the vivid and optimistic faith set forth in these pages. The contrast between the *Areopagitica* and the *Ready and Easy Way* is the contrast between the student who has dreamed great dreams, and the cynical official who has seen from within the habits of the men, even of the great men, who dispose of political power. Not that the tract fell lifeless by the wayside. Fifty years after its publication the Licensing Act was not renewed; and whenever the power to control the printed word has been sought by any Government in this country, it is, I think, true to say that the request has been jealously scrutinised as its administration has been closely examined. After all, in the fifth year of the greatest war in the history of the human race, one daily paper and one weekly journal have been, each for a period only, suspended; and the comment of the journalist has remained unfettered in a degree unknown in Milton's time. There has been no outrage in this war comparable to the trial of John Lilburne, or, to take a later period of crisis, to the Treason Trials of 1794. I do not think it is illegitimate to attribute some, at least, of the credit for that result to the *Areopagitica* of John Milton.

I would add this final word. The classic thesis that Milton maintained is not, I suspect, held by many in the way in which he held it. For most of us know how rare it is for Truth to have a "free and open encounter" with falsehood in an unequal society. Most of us know how heavily the scales are weighted in behalf of vested interest, religious, political, social, economic, racial, national, it matters not. Most of us know that it is a far easier thing to set out on the journey towards truth than to arrive at its end. We are learning that the so-called objectivity of Reason does not extend very much beyond the multiplication table, and that even there its relativity tends to emerge if the result is likely to serve some emotional end. We are learning, too, how urgent it is to give our citizens a large-scale map of the universe if they are to have any hope of finding their way through its labyrinthine complexities; and we are also learning that, when the map is asked for, there arises in every hedge and thicket on the road interests to protest against the guidance it makes possible, with the same shrill indignation as Thomas Edwards in his *Gangraena* or Ephraim Pagitt in his *Heresiographia*. It was Anti-nomianism or Formalism in the period of the Commonwealth; it has only altered its names in our own day. The Inquisitor is always at hand. What alters is less the end he serves than the mask which covers his face.

And that is why, as it seems to me, the passion for the free expression of ideas which Milton uttered with so noble a majesty is not less important for our generation than it was for his own. It is still true that whoever kills a book, as it were, kills a man. It is still true that "a good book is the precious life-blood of a master-spirit embalmed and treasured up on purpose to a life beyond life." It is still true that a community which seeks to suppress ideas soon begins to lose that vital sense of self-respect which permits its members the chance of imagination and creativeness. And it is from these qualities, as they are exercised in freedom, that men come to an enduring love of their country and to the expression of a pride in its service. It is in this fashion that a society is able to raise the level of its civilisation. It develops the mood in which science prospers and the temper in which great literature and art are born. That is what Milton saw, with the insight of genius, three hundred years ago; and that is why, as Mr. Justice Holmes said in that great dissent in which the spirit of the *Areopagitica* seems once more to come to life, "we should be eternally viailant against attempts to check the expression of opinions that we loathe and believe to be frought with death." For, as Charles James Fox insisted in the House of Commons in 1795, it is the free peoples of the world who become the effective masters of their own destiny.

SPIRITUAL VALUES : AN ANCIENT HERITAGE AND A MODERN GUIDE

By H. S. L. POLAK

IN MY EARLY DAYS, PEOPLE WERE FOND OF QUOTING KIPLING'S LINE, "Oh, East is East, and West is West, and never the twain shall meet." It was characteristic of the time to emphasise human differences, to speak glibly of racial superiority, to ignore cultural debts, to insist upon economic credits. Those who did so—and they are not all dead yet—forgot Kipling's further passage:

> "But there is neither East nor West,
>   Border, nor Breed, nor Birth,
>   When two strong men stand face to face,
>   Though they come from the ends of the earth."

Already, we have begun to speak a different language and to think differently from these older folk. To-day, the "ends of the earth" have drawn immeasurably closer. Black, brown, white, and yellow men fight side by side, far from their homes, on common battlefields, in the same great cause, making common sacrifices, and demonstrating the same courage and skill. The peoples of Africa are suddenly thrust into the maelstrom of modern life. With India and China, representing nearly half of mankind, helping the other United Nations to gain a strangle-hold upon and to destroy utterly the diabolical alliance of Hitlerite Germany and Hirohito's Japan and all that it represents, we can no longer speak truthfully—if, indeed, we ever could—of the *Yellow* Peril. What Nazi, again, has ever distinguished between the European and the Asiatic citizens of Soviet Russia, when it came to loot, destruction, massacre, or torture? And who among ourselves can venture to do so, since the transfer of her industry and her skill to her Asiatic territories and with the training and absorption of her people of all origins in the common task of defeating the desperate enemy in the West?

What, then, are these spiritual values that we are considering? The East has contributed to the West of its spiritual wisdom from very early days, long antedating the emergence into Europe of Christianity. In his Introduction to the *Sacred Books of the East*, Professor Max Muller emphasised that, hidden in them all, was "something that could lift up the human heart to a higher world, something that could make man feel the omnipresence of a Higher Power, something that could make him shrink from evil and incline to good."

That the soul of man is immortal, that its future is the future of a thing whose growth and splendour have no limit, was taught in ancient Egypt. Another fundamental Eastern teaching, from Egypt to the Pacific, is that each man is his own law-giver, the dispenser of glory or gloom to himself, the decreer of his life, his reward, his punishment.

But what are we to learn from these teachings? That, though matter and form change, fade, and disappear, the Spirit is enduring, and that as It is all pervading, that which It pervades has a common origin and a common destiny. Translated into terms of human relationship, all this means nothing less than a real brotherhood of man with a common purpose, namely, self-realisation in the fullest sense. It means, too, that man's life, which is infinitely varied, is not limited to a single incarnation, and that it is framed within the realm of law, a law of retribution and reward, a law of cause and consequence, but also a law which recognises the power of the human will to modify, to change, and eventually to conquer pre-destination, save in the sense of that ultimate self-realisation which is man's common concern and destiny. Finally, it means that every man has his individual place in the pattern of life, and that, without him at his highest development, the pattern would be incomplete and imperfect.

Nor is our debt to the East in terms of physical science and the practical affairs of everyday life any less ancient. Professor G. Eliot Smith reminded us, just before the war, that in the simple acts of writing and taking note of time, we owe to the East, over a period of some fifty centuries, the clock, the calendar, the paper on which we write, the language with which we express our thoughts, and the symbols of our script. And, as the Indian membership of the Royal Society indicates, this contribution of the East is being renewed and carried into our own time.

If, then, by the fortunes of history and special experience, the West has been able to make some return to the East with good administration, based upon a regard for law and order and a recognition of individual worth and right; if the West can now offer to the East training and technicians in modern industrial and agricultural skills and techniques; if the Western political doctrines of democracy can to-day be offered to the East by way of illustration, emulation, modification, or adaptation; if the humanism of the West, as exemplified in its social and educational services, can be offered to the East for its own rejuvenation; the East will be reaping the reward of past gifts and the West is privileged to pay its debts in a currency of a universal value.

What further lesson, then, have we yet to learn fully, imaginatively, creatively, whether we are of the East or the West? It is the right answer to one of the very oldest questions put—and wrongly answered by the questioner—in the Old Testament: "Am I my brother's keeper?" But the further question, "Who is my neighbour?" had, nevertheless, been amply answered in the declaration made in the very first chapter of the Bible: "God made man in His own image"—every man, black, white, brown, or yellow, irrespective of religious or intellectual difference, rich and poor alike. We have heard it repeated and repeated, until it has come to be little more than a figure of speech. It was Dr. Paul Deussen who recalled to us the ancient Vedic teaching, "Thou art That," and reminded us that in these three words we had both metaphysics and morals. "You shall love your neighbour as yourselves," he said, "because you are your neighbour, and mere illusion makes you believe that your neighbour is something different from yourselves." And now all the world is our neighbour.

Like the poor, the truth we have had always with us. But we seem to have preferred to keep men poor—both in body and in spirit—rather than to know and to act upon the truth. And yet, illusion must be destroyed and truth must, in the end, prevail if ours is to survive as a great and a fruitful civilisation. Is not the growing recognition of this the greatest spiritual value that we have to contribute to the new age? And will it be possible otherwise to achieve enduring economic values? Hitlerism, Fascism, and Nipponism alike held out great promise of a better social order, free from want and fear—for the conquerors. But for the conquered was reserved mental, moral and, doubtless too, physical enslavement such as the world has never known in all its deliberate and scientific completeness.

It is exactly that human disaster which we are to-day all pledged to prevent and to abolish. We have to learn consciously to be creative instead of destructive, in unity with variety. There is a world of wisdom

in the advice that Major Barbara's father gives his well-intentioned daughter
—it is not the thing in itself, which is inert, that matters, but the use which
we make of it and the purpose for which it is intended.   And even when
the purpose is destructive, as in the course of nature it must be at times,
it must, nevertheless, have a re-creative purpose behind it.   Is this not the
essential difference between the flying-bomb and the air-assault upon
enemy munitions-plants and strategic railway centres?

The ends of the earth are truly drawn closer together—but to what end?
An aeroplane can reach the other side of the world in a very few hours.
What is it going to carry in the days to come?   Death and destruction, or
the ample satisfaction of human needs, the early solution of human crises?
Until lately we might have heard Hitler bawling obscenities through the
microphone from one end of the earth to the other at any time that he
might choose to defile the realm of sound.   Surely, to-morrow the radio
will give to the peoples of the world messages of real hope, of genuine
good will, in which they may truly believe and which may once and for
all banish fear, because man has grown to adult understanding of his true
purpose and the right exercise of his vast powers.   To-morrow, at the very
time of its occurrence, we shall see on the screen anywhere in the world
the happenings of the hour.   What are we planning to show—a scene of
fear, horror, desolation, the threat of evil, or that which shall give to the
soul of man occasion for rejoicing and reciprocal good will?

Is it possible to create the permanent conditions of economic welfare
without a great human understanding?   The best-laid plans of mice and
men will "gang agley" once more unless they are inspired by a knowledge
and a certain assurance that we are, in very truth, all members one of another
—a lesson that we have at last, after grim and unimagined suffering, begun
to learn.

These ancient teachings of human interdependence, and that as we sow
so must we also reap, are among the spiritual and economic values that
we could have enjoyed from time immemorial.   The time has now surely
come to seize this wisdom and make it our own and to nurture the human
family in its spirit.   We must realise in fact, instead of merely in words,
that the only condition upon which war, whether military, economic, or
social, can be abolished is by grasping this very truth—-that the world *is* a
unit, that mankind *is* one and indivisible.

Meanwhile, as in our civil affairs, for the welfare of the law-abiding
citizen, so we must realise that the policing of life, not under an international
Gestapo but under a world-wide rule of law, and responsible to a world-
authority, is equally essential to the welfare of the human family, until each
adult member of it shall have established its independent sense of responsibility and can be entrusted with the key of the door.   It may be a long and
difficult job to cover adequately the transition period leading to the humanly
imaginable millennium, but undertaken in the right spirit and with a fixed
resolution, it is one that is well worthy of our great inheritance of spiritual
freedom and initiative.

SOCIETY AND SPIRITUAL VALUES

By Rev. Martin D'Arcy, S.J., M.A.

WHENEVER MEN MEET TOGETHER AND WHEREVER A SOCIETY IS FORMED, spiritual values are present as motives for action. They have never been abolished and they can never be totally excluded. There must always be some honesty, some regard for others, some pity, some love of truth, and at least a spasmodic fight against the brutal instincts and the abject impulses. Materialism, therefore, as a philosophy of life is unworkable. Its natural effect is to cloud over the source of what is spiritual and darken the landscape. It can, however, be of use as a reminder of the folly of thinking of man as pure spirit. In looking, then, to the future good of a society we have to guard against the narrowing of the range of these spiritual values and the exploitation of them for bad ends. How then do these two evils come about and how can they be checked? The simplest answer is to fall back on the need of right thinking, the possession of the truth about man and his relation to the Universe. This answer would be platitudinous did it not emphasise the value and responsibility of right thinking. Before any sinister and pestilential movement starts in a country or continent there is usually irresponsible thinking in high and influential places and amongst those who are thought to be wise. They are the Neros or Zeros who fiddle before the city burns; they are those to whom are applicable the words "la trahison des clercs."

Irresponsible thinking sows the seeds of disintegration, and the results are, as a rule, twofold. I say results, but it is not easy to say what is cause and what is effect. Spiritual values may be narrowing their range because a society is passing through a period of exhaustion and encouraging frivolous thinkers, and the frivolous thinkers may be hastening the decline by their undue influence or the void they leave. There is probably reciprocal causality at work. Exhaustion is certainly a fact with which we have to reckon, and when there is a void it is too often filled by seven devils. Moreover, there is at all times, in times of plenty as well as emptiness and exhaustion, a tendency to follow the easier and broader way, to prefer an exciting "shocker" to Hamlet, the lurid film to a music festival, the football stadium to the Greek theatre. Man, however, hates a void and dreads spiritual as well as physical unemployment, and so he can become an easy prey to the doctrinaire, the demagogue and the fanatic. And it is at this moment that the range of the spiritual values can be not only narrowed but perverted and exploited. The doctrinaire dissolves the long-standing habit of belief, but the fanatic recreates it under some magic, and sometimes hellish, formula. The fanatic always has a remedy for society; he catches the mood of the time and his appeal is so couched that men are dazzled by the immediate good he dangles before them and ignore the inhumanity of it and the symptoms of death which it contains.

Fas est et ab hoste doceri. There can be no doubt that the leaders of certain contemporary movements have enthralled or bewitched millions of young men and women. Bad doctors, though they may be, they have been very sensitive to the pulse of modern society. They have removed apathy and exhaustion by appealing to something, which had the appearance of a spiritual value and touched the heart, if not the mind. They seem to have proved, if it needed proving, that society is sick and that it needs a new diet. Now to some the most distressing sign of the present time is the subhuman, almost reflex action, wherewith modern society returns to its vomit. There is so little hope, so little of which they are proud in the writings of our younger contemporaries. They are turned in upon themselves and find no comfort within or without. And meantime those who like to talk about the future, or have responsibilities for that future, love protesting against what is contrary to their interests, but for remedies they do nothing but shuffle the old dirty cards which have proved so unlucky in the past. There is discontent but no radiant will; readiness to see the mote in others' eyes and unwillingness to be candid about the beams in their own so-called systems of thinking and habits of criticism. Democracy which could be invested with such immense spiritual values is used as a cover for personal prejudice, envious thoughts, class vendettas and vulgar living. The better minds, as a result, having no clear alternative before them, no better diet to take, are, without knowing completely why, sick at heart, while those who should know better return to their vomit.

I have said that democracy could be invested with immense spiritual values. Our task, as it seems, is to take a cue from our enemy and so to frame those values that they suit the mood of the present generation and set it on fire. We have to produce what Sorel called the "revolutionary myth," something which men want here and now and calls out the best in them; and at the same time something which has the long wisdom of the West to guarantee it as true and not mythical. I myself believe that the Christian values, if properly and relevantly set out, as truths "ever ancient and ever fresh," can alone perform this function. By long habit of mind we have come to treat persons as persons, to build our justice and our generosity on that truth, to demand of education and of State legislation that it should protect and promote personal life and not smother it; we wish to increase personal responsibility and freedom and to give a firm philosophical foundation to the notion of equality, which is otherwise indefensible or mystical But on to this original pattern so much has been sewn, so many ugly and ornate and fanciful motifs added, that the embroidery has hidden the original design and given a general effect of confusion. In developing this theme I must confine myself to one illustration, which may be of practical interest. We rightly estimate freedom, but too often we only pay it lip service or attend to one of its forms. We pay it only lip service when we call for it in the market-place and deny the existence of the soul and freedom of will in our study or lecture room. We attend to only one of its forms when we cry out for liberty of the Press, freedom of thought, liberty of contract and of the independence of nations, and neglect that other form of freedom which consists in a growing emancipation from the servitude of our own habits, mental and moral. To Socrates and Plato and their Christian successors this latter freedom is the more important and is necessary as a counsellor to the first kind of freedom. We do not start free within to do what we like; we are thwarted by what is unprincipled in us, by habit of body, by instincts and passions, savage impulses and deep-set hates. The greatest privilege and responsibility of freedom is to make a Venice out of the watery swamp of our human nature, to overcome the worst, and by our own effort make what is at first inferior in us and rebellious into a perfect work of art. I do not believe myself that we can do this without an unworldly aim and without divine assistance; but it should be clear to all that freedom has some ulterior object beyond itself and that external liberties are almost waste of time if we are not free enough within and fit, by mastery of ourselves, to make proper use of those liberties.

A democracy can work only if in diminishing extreme compulsion we stress interior sanctions, but as it is, so vast has society become and so complicated its activities that the easiest method of dealing with it is to regiment it. As the individual ceases to count he is compensated by having more and more done for him; but what is done for him has to be done as for a unit of society and not as for a person. The result is that the word "person" is now used as a kind of scarecrow to keep away obvious tyrants and oppressors; but the individual person is so lost in society and so taken up with that society that he forgets what personal freedom means. He has no interior life, no personal ideal as contrasted with ambition, no belief in self-control or private happiness. He ceases to take a loving pride in the skill of his hands or the fair use of his talents; he is no longer sensible of the value of his word, the winnowing necessary before he make or pass judgment. He treats his soul and body as if they were a public park instead of a temple of the Holy Spirit. Naturally as he is no longer a person to himself he uses others as if they were not persons, and he seeks for power and position without any sense of responsibility or love for his fellow men. Wisely, if too vaguely, Whitehead defined religion as man's use of his solitariness.

For these reasons the place of spiritual values in our future society depends largely on the understanding we have of freedom and the respect we pay to it. Freedom is a painful gift; it is a kind of crucible in which our personality is developed. It is so painful, in fact, that like many invalids we try every other remedy except the right one, which is self-mastery. There are always people who will invent new techniques to make mankind happy; there will always be shibboleths and quack nostrums. Their only effect will be to make easy new explosive revolutions or to cuddle persons into a final inertia, with lucid intervals of agonising despair. The trouble of being a person is that no external means and no other human being can take one's place and turn one into a happy personality. That is between us and God.

THE END